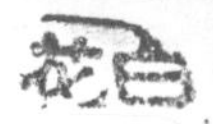

Traditional T'ai Arts in Contemporary Perspective

Studies in Contemporary Thailand

1. *Thai Society in Comparative Perspective*
   Erik Cohen

2. *The Rise and Fall of the Thai Absolute Monarchy*
   Chaiyan Rajchagool

3. *Making Revolution, Insurgency of the Communist Party of Thailand in Structural Perspective*
   Tom Marks

4. *Thai Tourism: Hill Tribes, Islands and Open-Ended Prostitution*
   Erik Cohen

5. *Whose Place is This? Malay Rubber Producers and Thai Government Officials in Yala*
   Andrew Cornish

6. *Central Authority and Local Democratization in Thailand. A Case Study from Chachoengsao Province*
   Michael H. Nelson

Studies in Contemporary Thailand No. 7
Series Editor: Erik Cohen

Traditional T'ai Arts in Contemporary Perspective

Editors

Michael C. Howard
Wattana Wattanapun
Alec Gordon

White Lotus Press

White Lotus Co. Ltd.
G.P.O. Box 1141
Bangkok 10501
Thailand

Telephone: (662) 332-4915 and (662) 741-6288-9
Fax: (662) 741-6287 and (662) 741-6607
E-mail: ande@loxinfo.co.th

Printed in Thailand

ISBN 974-8434-28-1 pbk White Lotus Co. Ltd., Bangkok

Front cover picture: Drawing by Thawan Duchanee.
Back cover picture: Muay Thai boxing action.

Contents

1. Introduction
Michael C. Howard 1

2. Identity and Traditional and Tradition-based T'ai Textiles in Contemporary Thai Society
Michael C. Howard 13

3. Change as a Method of Identification and Dating of T'ai Textiles
Patricia Cheesman Naenna 47

4. T'ai Lü Textiles: Cultural Reproduction
Songsak Prangwattanakun and Patricia Cheesman Naenna 57

5. The Effects of Socio-cultural Change on the Textiles of the T'ai Mao from Muang Mou Luang, Burma
Raynou Athamasar 139

6. From Buddha Images to Mickey Mouse Figures: The Transformation of Ban Thawai Carvings
Erik Cohen 149

7. Women in Thai Society as Depicted in Mural Paintings
Alec Gordon 175

8. The Use of Traditional T'ai Images in
Contemporary Thai Painting
Wattana Wattanapun 193

9. Traditional T'ai Dance in Vietnam
Under *Doi Moi*
Michael C. Howard and Be Kim Nhung 201

10. The Martial Art of *Muay Thai* in Thai Society
Michael Mackenzie 213

Bibliography 239

Contributors 245

1

Introduction

Michael C. Howard

The collection of chapters included in the present volume examine contemporary developments in T'ai arts as well as offering contemporary views of T'ai arts from the past.[1] The focus is on the arts of T'ai peoples in Thailand, but attention is also paid to T'ais in the neighboring countries of Laos, Burma, China, and Vietnam as well. Such a geographical spread reflects a growing interest in the comparative study of T'ai-speaking peoples living in different political and social settings in an effort to better understand common themes in T'ai culture as well as how it has evolved and manifested itself throughout the region.

In addition to having a geographically diverse coverage, the chapters examine a variety of forms of artistic expression, including weaving, carving, painting, dancing, and boxing. The inclusion of such an array of topics elicits definitional questions, especially in regard to distinctions that are commonly drawn between arts and crafts. It is not my intent here to engage in a definitional debate about what is and what is not art, but rather simply to employ a broad and widely accepted definition linking artistic expression with the production or performance of something that is judged to have a special aesthetic quality to it either by members of a particular society or cross-culturally. Accordingly, crafts have the potential to be works of art, but not all crafts are viewed as such. In this regard, the intent of the producer is not always a guideline, although it often is since within most cultures standards exist that set the exceptional bowl, basket, or dress apart from the everyday.

Perhaps nowhere is the difficulty in establishing a hard and fast rule about what is art and what is not more apparent than in the case of martial arts. It is undoubtedly easier to gain consensus regarding the artistic merit of almost any type of dance than it is to gain artistic respectability for even the most ritualized form of combat. Thus, the presence of a chapter on Thai boxing as a form of martial art may raise a few eyebrows. My own view is that, especially within the context of T'ai culture, such a martial art is a very important form of artistic expression and one that is, in fact, closely associated with dance in T'ai culture. This is not to say that all boxing is art any more than that all dance is art, but that both types of performance have the potential to be elevated to a form of artistic expression and that in T'ai culture some forms of martial combat have achieved this designation.

There are several themes that are especially important in contemporary analyses of T'ai artistic expression. One overall theme is the evolution of the practice and perception of traditional T'ai arts in the face of rapid change and unprecedented global influences. The T'ai have always drawn on outside influences in their arts, but have modified such influences in such a way as to maintain a distinctly T'ai character. Moreover, T'ai arts have never been static and have always shown an interesting blend of innovation and conservatism. However, the extent of external influences and pressures to change today are unprecedented and lead to questions about the ability of the T'ai people in the modern globalized world to continue to assimilate things from outside and to incorporate them into the creation of distinctly T'ai forms of artistic expression.

Many past art forms and traditional motifs are local versions that differ only slightly from those found elsewhere. The *nak* or *naga* motif found on T'ai textiles and adorning many temples is a common motif throughout much of South, East, and Southeast Asia. The same is true, of course, of Buddha images. Nevertheless, T'ai nagas and Buddha images generally are readily distinguishable from those produced elsewhere. Likewise, the work of many contemporary Thai painters is to some extent of an indistinguishable generic quality (paintings of flowers or mountains that could have been painted by artists almost anywhere), but a good deal of what is produced is distinctively Thai in terms of imagery, techniques, and the use of materials.

The above discussion leads us to another theme concerning questions of identity—national identity, ethnic identity, as well as class and personal aspects of identity. Artistic expression exists within a cultural context that intrinsically relates it to questions of identity. In this regard, art often functions to symbolize identity and, thus, can become embroiled in political initiatives to forge national or ethnic identities. The reverse is also true. Forms of artistic expression can be suppressed out of a desire to eliminate certain forms of identity that are viewed as standing in the way of goals of, say, nation-building. Many of the chapters in the present volume deal with the relationship between artistic expression and identity in relation, for example, to nation-building in Thailand, China's Cultural Revolution, and reforms in Vietnam.

In addition to questions of identity, art is also influenced by economic factors. Such factors include the process of economic development, relative inequality, and commercialization. Certainly the rapid economic development of Thailand in recent years has had a profound influence of the arts within Thailand. There are many facets of this, ranging from the emergence of new art markets among the newly rich to the development of a tourist market for certain types of handicrafts and forms of art. Similar processes are beginning in Vietnam, especially in regard to the appearance of a nascent tourist market for ethnic arts and crafts. Economic changes have also influenced the place of the artist in modern society. Many traditional activities, such as weaving, have either been undermined by modern market forces or transformed through new patterns of commercialization.

Economic changes and the process of commercialization in particular have had an impact on the religious nature of much of traditional T'ai arts. Traditionally virtually all arts of the T'ai were imbued with religious aspects, ranging from textile motifs to the rituals performed prior to a *muay Thai* match. Much of artistic production and performance also centered around religious institutions—Buddha sculptures, temple murals, temple dances, textiles produced for religious ceremonies or as gifts to monks, and so forth. Religion remains an important influence on much of contemporary T'ai arts. This is true both in terms of art that continues to be directly related to religious institutions or practices as well as art that is secular in nature, but influenced by religious themes. At the same time, it is evident that artistic expression among the T'ai is increasingly secular in nature. This is most evident in painting, but can also be seen in dance, weaving, sculpture, and carving. Alongside Buddha images and elephant sculptures intended for spirit houses, a wide array of purely secular figures are being produced by T'ai carvers and sculptors. In addition, many religious images today are as likely to be used for entirely secular purposes to decorate homes as they are to be used for religious purposes in temples of home shrines.

Finally, there are questions concerning the degree of individualism found in traditional T'ai artistic expression. The relative lack of individual expression found in the best known form of traditional artistic expression in Thailand, bronze Buddha images, has tended to downplay the role of the individual artist and to differentiate it from the individualism of much of contemporary T'ai art. While to some extent this is true, there has always been an aspect of individualism even in traditional folk arts—and even if not widely recognized. Within communities individuals would often be recognized by their neighbors for their skills as artists or artisans. Moreover, just like traditional artists who were representative of a certain cultural milieu, the world of modern artists too reflects the influence of a distinct cultural setting that can lead to a degree of commonalty in what is produced. The works of many contemporary Thai painters are derivative—all too often following the lead of market forces for particular types of painting.

The collection starts with a group of four chapters concerned with textiles in Thailand and in relation to T'ai-speaking peoples in Laos, Vietnam, and Burma. The focus of these chapters is on the contemporary role of traditional and traditionally-oriented T'ai textiles. Of special concern is the relationship of such textiles to questions of T'ai identity. Handwoven textiles have long been highly valued in T'ai societies and have been among the most important artistic creations of many T'ai-speaking peoples.

In recent years there has been a great interest in Thailand in particular in better understanding the textile heritage of the T'ai as well as in incorporating older textiles and modern versions of them into contemporary fashion. This theme is explored in the chapter by Michael Howard. This chapter begins with a discussion of issues relating to questions of textiles and identity using examples from northern Vietnam. The author notes the need to recognize ambiguity and change in textile patterns even in traditional societies. The chapter then reviews the impact of Westernization and globalization on Thai fashion from the time of Chulalongkorn until the post-war period, including changes both in courtly fashion as well as in the dress of common people. Next, the author examines traditional textiles and traditionalist fashion in contemporary Thai society. This portion of the chapter looks at the role of royal patronage under the auspices of Queen Sirikit and especially her promotion of silk Mudmee from the northeast, as well as textiles produced for largely urban markets by the T'ai Lü, Lao Puan, and hill tribes. In the latter part of the chapter, the author argues that the current traditionalist revival in Thai fashion is not so much a reflection of some longing for the past in the face of rapid change as a desire on the part of contemporary Thais to define their identity within the context of global culture.

The next chapter, by Patricia Cheesman Naenna, focuses on the identification and dating of T'ai textiles in Laos as their structures and functions have changed since the last century. The author draws a distinction between a traditional era in which there were many sacred elements associated with textiles and when the role of each textile was very carefully defined and the post-war commercial era in which uses have changed or become blurred and in which textiles have lost most of their sacred aura. By means of cases studies, the author discusses five types of textile. First, she discusses the *pha khan soeng,* which prior to the adoption of Buddhism was used in healing ceremonies and later came to function as a shoulder cloth. The next cloth discussed is the *pha phae kep,* which originally was presented to a man to be worn as a shoulder cloth prior to his marriage and recently has come to be widely used as a woman's shoulder cloth. Then she describes the changes that have taken place in the styles and uses of two types of skirt, the *sin mi mai* and the *sin tin yai.* Finally, the author discusses *pha pok long,* which have functioned as coffin covers, heirlooms, and ordination cloths.

In Chapter 4 Patricia Cheesman Naenna and Sonsak Prangwattanakun examine the evolution of T'ai Lü textiles. They start by noting the very important role of textiles in T'ai Lü society in the past and then review some of the modern forces that served to undermine the production and use of these textiles in different countries. The bulk of their chapter focuses on the resurgence of weaving among the T'ai Lü in Thailand in recent years, in part in response to external promotional efforts and market demands. They point out that there are three distinct markets for contemporary T'ai Lü textiles. The first is a high class market for textiles woven by the best weavers using the finest materials. The second is the middle class market. Especially noteworthy here are civil servants who often wear traditionally oriented costumes on Fridays. Finally, there is the lower class market. This is the largest market and the cloth produced for it is of relatively poor quality and is generally made of synthetic fabrics. The authors also discuss recent changes in the production, structure, and design of cloths. Commercialization has led most weavers to employ technological innovations that allow for more rapid production of cloth, including changes in the weaving implements and the use of commercial dyes. A particularly noteworthy structural change that has resulted in commercial production for the largely urban market is that the skirts made now are much larger than they were in the past.

The final chapter on textiles is by Raynou Athamasar. Her chapter focuses on the impact of sociocultural changes on the textiles of the T'ai Mao (who are also known as Chinese Shan or Northern Shan) along the border of Burma and China. The chapter begins with a brief review of the background of the T'ai Mao and then describes their traditional dress (as well as the dress of the T'ai Nüa). The author discusses how external forces have led to the decline of weaving and the use of traditional costumes among the T'ai Mao in both countries. This is particularly noteworthy in China, where during the Cultural Revolution efforts were made to eradicate all traces of T'ai Mao culture, including their textiles. Even in Burma acculturative forces have resulted in the widespread adoption of Burmese-style clothing. Even T'ai Mao wearing such clothing, however, often continue to wear a distinctive red sash around their waist as a marker of ethnic identity. In more remote areas more traditional forms of dress have survived and weaving still takes place. The author also reports one weaving center which provides T'ai Mao clothing for other areas.

Chapter 6, by Erik Cohen, is concerned with carving. This chapter focuses on the northern Thai carving village of Ban Thawai, located near Chiang Mai. Contrary to common belief, Ban Thawai is not a traditional carving village. As Cohen points out, the origins of carving in Ban Thawai date back only to the late 1960s, when villagers were employed by a Chiang Mai antiques dealer to restore carvings imported from Burma. Later the villagers began carving replicas of Burmese Buddha images and from this grew what is today a substantial industry with links to regional, national, and international markets. Cohen argues that such commercialization of traditional crafts leads to disassociation of the component parts of craft production and consumption. He divides these component parts into: materials; knowledge, skills, and technologies; designs and decorations;

workforce; production process; and distribution and consumption. In regard to materials, for example, not only did the raw material change from teak to raintree as teak became increasingly difficult and more expensive to obtain, but sources of the wood became increasingly distant from the village itself. Today raintree wood is obtained from a variety of sources as far away as Thailand's northeast.

In his examination of designs and decorations, Cohen divides the images carved into five categories. The first type he refers to as classicist. It is a tradition that draws on the classical aspects of the cultural traditions of Burma, Cambodia, China, and India. The second group he calls traditionalist. These are Burmese-style Buddhas and related images. The third category is comprised of neo-traditional carvings. These are images of elephants, tigers, and the like that are derived from the popular culture of northern Thailand and China. The fifth group of carvings he refers to as local-innovative. This category includes items inspired by themes from northern Thailand such as carvings of figures of hill tribe people. Finally, there are Mickey Mouse images and other such figures drawn from a variety of sources around the world that belong to what Cohen refers to as the extraneous-innovative category. Cohen notes that the range of images carved in Ban Thawai has become increasingly varied over time as carvers have responded to an ever more heterogeneous market.

The next two chapters are concerned with painting. Chapter 7 by Alec Gordon offers an innovative interpretation of Thai temple murals dating from the mid-1600s to around 1900. While most writers on such murals have focused on their religious aspects, Gordon focuses on the numerous scenes featuring the *pharb kark* or the dregs—that is, the common people. Beginning in the 1600s, accompanying architectural innovations created more space on temple walls for mural paintings, Thai temple art came to include real-life scenes. Through examination of a few examples, the author explores what these portrayals can tell us about Thai society at the time and especially about the role of women. He provides examples of murals portraying women performing what are commonly thought of as male tasks (such as female *mahouts*) and of courtship and sexuality. Scenes depicting sexual activities are commonly encountered in murals during the period being discussed, but both Thai and foreign writers generally ignore their presence. Finally, the author remarks on the virtual absence of scenes of rice cultivation in the murals despite this being such an important aspect of Thai life. He notes that a partial explanation may be that most mural scenes are set in towns or in the jungle, but feels that this is not sufficient to understand why this should be so.

Chapter 8 by Wattana Wattanapun is on the use of traditional images, materials, and techniques in contemporary Thai paintings. Wattana himself is an important Thai artist and this chapter reflects his views concerning the development and current status of art in Thailand. Wattana's chapter examines change and persistence in Thai artistic style and the role of both external and internal influences. In his discussion of the past, Wattana points out that while Thai art was influenced by a variety of external influences, especially from China and India, Thai art developed its own style that also reflected internal influences and which in no way was inferior to works from China or India. In the past Thai artists preferred to use simple materials, such as clay and wood for sculpture and earth pigment (tempura) for painting. Wattana argues that Thai artists still respond to internal influences in their selection of materials, techniques, motifs, and themes. He illustrates this point with the work of two contemporary Thai painters: Angkarn Kalayanapong and Thawan Duchanee. (His own work illustrates the point as well.) Next Wattana offers some critical remarks on external influences on contemporary Thai art emanating from the country's art schools. He notes that while such art (e.g., installation art) has been very popular with students, it has not been received well by the Thai population at large, which he believes feels alienated from it. Wattana argues that the problem with this art is that it is not well enough grounded in Thai culture and comments that such forms of happening or installation art appear inferior, for example, to a traditional funeral ceremony: "Most Thais see greater artistic merit in the burning of the prasat than burning a few rags in a contemporary work of happening art."

The final two chapters are concerned with two art forms that are interrelated in T'ai culture: dance and boxing. Chapter 9, by Michael Howard and Be Kim Nhung, discusses dance by the T'ai minority in Vietnam, with an emphasis on the impact of the so-called *doi moi* reforms that have led to a reduction of state support for the arts and greater emphasis on market forces and to the incursion of global cultural influences. The chapter begins with an overview of traditional T'ai dance in Vietnam. It then discusses public support for dance under the communist government from the early post-war period to the doi moi reforms. For the T'ai, such public support took on a variety of forms, including funding for the well known Son La dance group. With the implementation of the doi moi reforms public financial support for dance was drastically reduced. For those accustomed to such support the transition to greater reliance on market forces has proven difficult. Traditional dance has also been undermined by the impact of global culture in Vietnam and the onslaught of discos, karaoke, and the like. Nevertheless, there have been positive developments. Tourism offers one potential new source of money to support dance. In addition, there has been something of a cultural revival among the T'ai of Vietnam in recent years and, although public interest in traditional dance has waned in some T'ai communities in others it remains quite strong.

The final chapter is by Michael Mackenzie and examines Thai boxing or *muay Thai.* Muay Thai is the national sport of Thailand and is highly popular both in Thailand and abroad, but, as Mackenzie notes, muay Thai is more than a spectator sport. It is a form of performance art that is deeply imbued with spiritual elements and that draws on many important traditional elements of Thai culture. The chapter reviews the history of muay Thai from its origins as part of the weapons art of *krabi krabong* and highlights its close association with Thailand's martial past and its kingship. It then discusses various aspects of the philosophy surrounding muay Thai, the ceremonies that are an important part of it, training, the use of charms or *kruang ruang,* the important role of music in the matches, and the fight itself. The final part of the chapter deals with contemporary muay Thai and the tension that exists between its traditional form, with its important spiritual components, and the more secular aspects of muay Thai as a spectator sport associated with gambling and social inequality.

As can be seen, while the chapters provide accounts of a wide range of artistic expression among T'ai-speaking peoples throughout Southeast Asia, these accounts draw attention to the dynamic way in which the past influences contemporary T'ai art as the T'ai people adapt to a rapidly changing world and define themselves within the modern global context.

Note

1. Earlier versions of all of the chapters, with the exception of the one by Michael Mackenzie which was written specifically for this volume, were originally prepared for a symposium on T'ai arts held at the 6th International Thai Studies Conference, in Chiang Mai, October 1996, and organized by the editors.

All of the photos accompanying the various chapters are by the author(s) of the particular chapters unless noted otherwise.

2

Identity and Traditional and Tradition-based T'ai Textiles in Contemporary Thai Society

Michael C. Howard

People's style of dress is a reflection of many aspects of their lives and is seen by social scientists as making important statements about the wearer's society and the place of the wearer within a particular social setting. This chapter is concerned with the relationship of dress to ethnic, regional, and class identity in modern Thai society. In particular, it focuses on a recent fashion trend employing traditional and tradition-based textiles and this trend's association with questions of national, regional, and ethnic identity.

In this analysis of identity and contemporary Thai fashion it is important to keep in mind a few general points about the fashion trends and textiles involved. First, while today's fashions in Thailand are changing at a much more rapid pace than in the past, fashions also changed in the past, albeit usually at a much slower pace. This was true in rural areas just as it was in more urbanized settings, although the dynamics of change tended to be different. I make this point in part to emphasize that there is a link between the past and the present in the fashion world of Thailand rather than a sharp distinction between a closed, unchanging world of tradition and an open, rapidly changing modern world. In terms of questions concerned with identity and fashion, this has always been a dynamic relationship with many nuances and ambiguities.

Turning to more specific points relating to fashion and textiles, there are several different aspects of dress that should be kept in mind when analyzing changes in fashion and relationships between fashion and identity. Thus, a distinction needs to be made between everyday wear and special occasion clothing. Such a distinction existed in the past just as it does today. Each of these types of dress is likely to change in different ways and may relate to identity in different ways. Gender is another crucial factor to consider when looking at clothing in relation to fashion and identity. Not only do men and women wear different clothing, but generally in mainland Southeast Asia women's clothing has been the more distinctive ethnic marker while men's clothing traditionally tended to be rather uniform (some sort of loincloth or dark blue or black baggy cotton trousers and shirt). Finally, it is also important to recognize the role of social stratification in fashion in terms of distinctions in dress among those of different classes in society as well as the influence of the fashions of one class on those of another. Again, this was a factor in the past just as it is today.

Textiles and T'ai Ethnic Identity in the Past

Dress is often used and perceived as a marker of ethnic identity and writings on and collections of folk or traditional textiles commonly identify them according to ethnic group. In many situations this is a valid approach, but such identification is rarely without its ambiguities. Thus, not only do members of a particular ethnic group sometimes dress differently, but styles of dress commonly identified as markers of their ethnic identity may be worn by members of other groups. Nowhere is this more in evidence than in the case of the various peoples in mainland Southeast Asia and the neighboring regions of India and China identified as ethnic T'ai. The problems in this regard concern distinguishing T'ai dress from that of other ethnic groups and identifying differences in dress among groups within the general ethnic category of T'ai.

By way of example I will use the T'ai of Vietnam or Thái as they are known in Vietnam. The Vietnamese recognize fifty-four ethnic groups and the Thái are one of these. Within this category of Thái are the various sub-groups of T'ai such as the T'ai Khao (White T'ai), T'ai Dam (Black T'ai), T'ai Dón (southern T'ai Khao), T'ai Muoi, T'ai Thanh, and Phu T'ai (Putai). But not all T'ai-speaking groups are placed within this official category. Thus, there are separate official categories of Lào (Lào Noi) and Lu (T'ai Lü). These various T'ai groups live in northwestern Vietnam near the Lao border. Within the areas where they live are also members of other ethnic groups, including various Hmông, Dao (or Yao), and Mon-Khmer speakers comprised mainly of several smaller groups generally categorized as Kho-mú.

While it is easy to distinguish members of any of the T'ai groups from Hmông or Dao on the basis of dress, with other groups this is not so easy. Thus, the Kho-mú groups in northern Vietnam by and large adopted the clothing patterns of neighboring T'ai-speakers and it is difficult, if not impossible to distinguish them on the basis of dress. (*Plate 2.1*) In one instance, for example, the only distinguishing characteristic is the way in which the Kho-mú women make the clasps on their blouses, otherwise their dress is identical to that of neighboring T'ais. Additional examples of this problem of T'ai dress being adopted by non-T'ai peoples in whole or part are illustrated in recent works on ethnic minorities in Thailand. There are several examples, for instance, in Chu Thái Son and Dào Hùng's, *Vietnam: A Multicultural Mosaic,* such as photos of an O-Du woman wearing a Black T'ai headcloth and blouse that is similar to that of the Black T'ai, a blanket identified as La Hu that is of a type woven by the T'ai, and Công women wearing a style of dress usually identified as T'ai.[1] The O-Du are a Mon-Khmer group whose dress is influenced by the T'ai and Viêt while the La Hu and Công are Tibeto-Burman speakers whose own textile traditions differ considerably from those of the T'ai. I have also seen White Hmông women wearing Black T'ai head scarves, although folding them in a different manner. (*Plate 2.2*)

Thus, some non-T'ai groups can be seen to have adopted portions of what can be readily identified as T'ai elements in their dress while others have adopted T'ai dress almost entirely. The latter seems to be primarily the case among those Mon-Khmer groups with little or no weaving tradition of their own who have adopted many T'ai elements in the culture, while retaining a distinctive ethnic identity. Undoubtedly, such a process occurred frequently in the past as the T'ai spread across northern Southeast Asia and assumed dominance over other local groups.

What about distinctions in regard to dress among sub-groups of T'ai in Vietnam? The two largest groups of T'ai in Vietnam are the T'ai Dam and T'ai Khao and the T'ai Khao can be subdivided into two distinct groups: the northern T'ai Khao of Lai Châu Province and the southern T'ai Khao of Thanh Hóa Province and Hóa Binh Province who are known as T'ai Dón. Out of the one million plus people in the Thái ethnic category, well over half are T'ai Dam and about twenty percent are T'ai Khao. The dress of most of the T'ai Khao of Lai Châu and neighboring provinces and the T'ai Dam today is essentially identical, women wearing long plain black skirts and plain colored blouses, with the exception of the woman's head scarf, the former traditionally wearing a white one and the latter a black one. (*Plates 2.3, 2.5*) It is also a style of dress that has had no significant influence on fashion in Thailand.

This T'ai Dam and T'ai Khao style of women's dress is different from that worn by some of the other, smaller groups of T'ai. Lào women, for example, wear a dark skirt with a hem piece decorated in multicolored bands of supplementary weft weave and Lu women wear a short decorated vest and a skirt often heavily decorated with supplementary weft patterns (the men wear decorated trousers). Decorated skirts are also worn by some T'ai Dón women. These various supplementary weft patterned skirts are of the type usually associated with the various T'ai groups in Laos and probably represent a style of dress that was once more widespread among the T'ai in Vietnam. Contemporary T'ai Khao or T'ai Dón women's dress in Hòa Bình and Thanh Hóa provinces is often similar to that of the neighboring Muòng. The skirts are identical, with plain black bodies and two or three decorative hem pieces, while the blouses differ slightly in design. In western Thanh Hóa province T'ai Dón women wear a variety of decorated skirts with supplementary weft and ikat patterns similar to those worn by T'ai living across the border in Laos.

As in the case of T'ai textiles from Laos, while some types of pattern can be identified with a particular T'ai sub-group among these smaller groups in Vietnam, such identification is not always possible and there appears to be considerable interchange among the sub-groups. This point is of relevance for Thailand where a variety of traditional and tradition-oriented textiles of T'ai origin from within Thailand as well as from neighboring countries have become popular in recent years.

The T'ai Dón of Ban Lác, Mai Châu, Hòa Bình province, are especially interesting in regard to such interchange. In the mid-1990s these T'ai have shown considerable entrepreneurial spirit and emerged as an important source for traditional and tradition-oriented T'ai textiles for markets in Chiang Mai, Laos, and elsewhere. (*Plate 2.4*) In 1996, for example, they began producing blouses from pieces of handwoven cloth exclusively for the tourist market. Ban Lác is close to the Lao province of Houa Phan, where many Ban Lác textiles are said to originate when sold in Chiang Mai for marketing purposes. The textiles worn, made, and sold in Ban Lác are quite heterogeneous in origin and influence and T'ai Dón dress here follows the southern Muòng-like style rather than that of the T'ai Khao living to the north. (*Plate 2.6*) Skirts are found here with supplementary weft, warp ikat, and weft ikat patterning that represent most of the T'ai sub-groups found in Laos and adjacent areas in Vietnam. [2]

It is often assumed that interchange of clothing styles is a relatively recent development and that at some time in the past much more specific correlation between sub-group and design was possible, but this may not be the case and it is doubtful that the situation was ever universally rigid in terms of sub-group boundaries or textile pattern use. In this regard, further research on the history of women's fashion among the T'ai of northwestern Vietnam should prove particularly useful.

Current interest in traditional textiles associated with groups within Thailand concentrates on élite textiles of Indian origin (or at least closely copying such textiles), silk textiles produced by the Khmer of the northeast, mainly cotton textiles produced by certain T'ai-speaking groups primarily in northern and northeastern Thailand, and textiles of several of the hill tribe groups such as the Hmông, Yao, and Akha in northern Thailand. In this chapter I am concerned primarily with the textiles of those whose heritage is associated with one of the T'ai languages and the Khmer and their relationship to contemporary Thai identity. I will not deal, except in passing, with the various hill tribes or with other Mon-Khmer-speaking groups.

Traditional textiles from within Thailand can be distinguished on the basis of status and ethnicity or region. There existed marked distinctions between the clothing of élites and commoners in Thailand in the past. The clothing of the élite was often made of silk or imported cotton and was most strongly influenced by relatively ornate Indian fashions, while that of commoners was usually of local cotton and much simpler. The more ornately designed clothes sometimes were found among commoners for use on special occasions and as valuable heirlooms, but, for the most part, more complex textiles were made by slaves of aristocrats or members of their families or by members of a few distinct communities with an affiliation to the aristocracy. Among the élite there were further status and regional differences. Regional differences were mitigated to some extent through trade in luxury cloth, but differences were still noticeable.

Current traditionally oriented fashion draws especially upon the more complex textiles produced for women's clothing by T'ai-speaking minorities or Khmer. The background of such cloth often can be identified by the intended status of the wearer as well as by locality, with varying degrees of specificity, and the ethnic affiliation of the patterns. In terms of ethnic affiliation the relevant textiles are generally those produced by the following ethnic groups: the Khmer of northeastern Thailand, the Northeastern or Isan T'ai, the Northern or Lan Na T'ai (also known as the T'ai Yuan), the Phu T'ai of the northeast, the Song or Lao Song Dam of central Thailand, and the Phuan or Lao Phuan of central and northern Thailand.

Patricia Naenna provides a concise survey of the weaving styles of the various ethnic groups found in northeastern Thailand.[3] The upper portion of the region is inhabited by T'ai Lao and Lao Phuan who migrated to the region from the north of Laos. They mainly weave cotton and employ weft ikat and supplementary weft techniques. Further south are T'ai Lao and Phutai who are originally from southern Laos. These T'ai Lao have a tradition of weaving in silk employing weft ikat and supplementary weft techniques that is distinct from the more northerly T'ai Lao. The Phutai also have a distinct tradition of supplementary warp and weft ikat weaving in silk. Furthest to the south there are also T'ai Lao from southern Laos and Khmer-speakers who weave silk using weft ikat techniques in patterns that are different from those of the T'ai Lao and bear the mark of strong Indian influence. There are also several other T'ai (Nyor, Yui, Kaleung, and Sak) and Mon-Khmer minorities (Kui, Brew, and So) scattered in the northeast. Today these groups, if they weave, produce textiles similar to their respective T'ai Lao or Khmer neighbors and have no distinctive textiles of their own.[4] Within the T'ai Lao and Khmer groups there are some distinctive regional or community styles..

The largest ethnic group in northern Thailand is the T'ai Yuan who are found throughout most of the northern part of northern Thailand. There are also other, smaller T'ai-speaking groups including the T'ai Lü who came from Sipsongpanna and live in Nan, Phayao, and Chiang Rai provinces and various Lao groups including the Lao Phuan of Sukhothai province, Lao living in Uttaradit province, and the Lao Khrang who are scattered throughout several of the more southernly provinces in the north. All of these groups have produced distinctive special occasion skirts for women. The T'ai Yuan and Lao Phuan are especially known for their *teen chok* (discontinuous supplementary weft) hem pieces and the T'ai Lü for their decorated skirt bodies employing a variety of weaving techniques. The Lao Khrang make distinctive women's skirts with silk bodies with weft ikat patterns and cotton or silk hem pieces with supplementary weft patterns. In recent years the weaving styles of these T'ai-speaking groups have been mixed to some extent, but in the past they were distinct. Also living in the north are the non-T'ai hill tribes. The Karen, Hmông, Yao, Lahu, Akha, and Lisu have distinctive traditions of dress, while Lawa dress is similar to that of the Karen.

Within central Thailand there are a variety of distinctive textiles woven by T'ai minority groups who were resettled in the region from Laos and northern Thailand during the latter part of the eighteenth century and the first part of the nineteenth century. These groups include T'ai Yuan, Lao Phuan, Lao Khrang, and T'ai Dam and the closely related Lao Song Dam. Following their resettlement in central Thailand, several communities of these minority groups maintained distinctive weaving traditions and some continued to wear distinctive dress that set them apart from the neighboring T'ai majority well into the postwar period. The T'ai Yuan, Lao Phuan, and Lao Khrang were discussed above in relation to northern Thailand and all have distinctive textile traditions. The T'ai Yuan live in Ratchaburi and Nakhon Pathom provinces in central Thailand. There are Lao Phuan in central Thailand in Lop Buri province. The Lao Khrang settled in Uthai Thani, Chai Bat, and Suphan Buri provinces in central Thailand. The Lao Song Dam live in Phetchaburi, Ratchburi, Suphan Buri, and Nakhon Pathom provinces and produce dark indigo-colored cotton cloth (some skirts have silk warp threads).

The people of southern Thailand often speak a distinct form of T'ai known as Pak T'ai and have a long history of influence not only from neighboring Muslim areas, but also from beyond as a result of communities on the region's coast serving a trading centers. There are a number of distinctive textile traditions in southern Thailand. One of these is *pha yok* brocade woven mainly from Nakhon Si Thammarat province since the Ayutthaya period for members of the court. This cloth is woven with silk and metallic threads. Another distinctive textile tradition is represented by the cotton cloth found on Ko Yor, Songkhla province. The weavers of Ban Na Mun Sri, Trang province, also have an identifiable textile tradition. Ban Na Mun Sri is known especially for its shoulder cloths which are worn by grooms during wedding ceremonies (and by older people during various Buddhist ceremonies). There are also textile styles associated with the region's Muslim population. These include brocades woven of silk and metallic thread from the Muslim population of Phum Riang, Surat Thani province. Throughout the region styles of dress are influenced by neighboring Malays and Indonesians.

Thai Fashion in the Face of Westernization and Globalization

Western influence on Thai dress dates from the reign of King Mongkut in the mid-nineteenth century, although it did not really become significant until the time of King Chulalongkorn. Davis refers to the courtly dress of this period as "an odd mixture of Siamese and European fashion."[5] Such a mixture remained in evidence until 1935, with fashion changing slightly in keeping with European tastes. Davis notes that during these years "blouses and skirt lengths kept pace with those in Europe" and "traditional pasins were adopted to fit in with more modern tops."[6] In a survey of Thai military uniforms, Sanunya Suriyarattanakorn, comments that during the Ayutthaya period military uniforms were influenced by fashions from Persia, India, and China, and that they underwent Westernization during the reigns of kings Mongkut and Chulalongkorn.[7]

Reflecting the nature of social stratification within Siam, however, such Western influence on clothing styles was seen primarily among the dress of a small number of the Thai élites and better off urban dwellers, while the vast majority of Siamese continued to wear non-Western types of clothing. This is not to say that external influences were unimportant among the poorer classes. Chinese immigration at this time, for example, was related to the widespread adoption of Chinese-style indigo-dyed baggy trousers known as *tieo sado* and collarless shirts known as *mohom* by men in rural areas, especially in the north. Western influence among the urban poor and rural population was significant in a somewhat different way. Following the signing of the Bowring Treaty it mainly took the form of introducing imported aniline dyes and commercial threads and fabrics used for making clothing. In many parts of Siam, Wyatt points out that "village handicrafts diminished or died out completely as people bought imported goods, like cloth and tools, instead of making them themselves." [8]

The twelve "cultural mandates" issued under the Phibun government between 1939 and 1942 sought to promote a sense of national identity in a manner that incorporated many Western influences. Such Western influence was especially notable in the requirement to dress in modern fashion that was decidedly Western. This included men wearing trousers, shirts, coats, and a tie, and women wearing skirts and blouses. While these requirements mainly applied to the urban élite, they did serve to reinforce the notion that to wear Western-style dress was modern and viewed positively among the population at large, while to wear more traditional types of dress was seen as old fashioned and only for those who could not afford to wear more Westernized clothing made of commercial cloth. Women's tubeskirts or *pha sin,* for example, came to be seen as suitable clothing for servants and poor people or for leisure wear around the home.

While Phibun's dress regulations were no longer in force after the Second World War, the dress patterns and cultural values about dress that they articulated continued to be a strong force in Thailand in the post-war era. In rural areas, government employees and institutions played an important role in spreading Western-style fashions and positive values associated with such clothing. In a conversation with Thai artist Wattana Wattanapun, who grew up during this period in a rural setting outside of Bangkok, he noted that when he was a boy in school he felt embarrassed to wear handmade clothing to school, even if it was made of silk. Such clothing was seen as inferior to the white shirts and dark pants made of commercial cloth. In addition, he recalls that his father and fellow teachers were the first men to wear T-shirts and khaki trousers in the community and he remembers female members of his family becoming excited whenever new imported cloth became available in local shops.

Rapid economic growth in Thailand in recent decades has served to further the decline of weaving by hand, which has survived mostly in the poorest areas of the country, especially in the northeast and north. Western-style dress also has come to dominate in all regions of the country and among all sectors of society. Among the country's T'ai majority, by the 1970s, traditional-looking dress was to be found almost exclusively among the rural poor and, even then, increasingly being worn only by older people. For most Thai men and women, more traditional pants, shirts, or tube-skirts were at best something to be worn informally at home. (*Plate 2.7*) In recent years even this practice has diminished as such clothing has been replaced by Western-style athletic clothing like warm-up suits or jogging shorts and by T-shirts. The near universality of Western-style clothing is, of course, most noticeable among younger Thais who evidence a tremendous appetite for the latest Western-inspired fashions.

Traditionalism in Contemporary Thai Fashion

Although it is apparent to any observer that Western-style dress is now almost universally worn in Thailand, it is equally apparent today that there is a growing interest in wearing more traditional types of dress as well. This tendency has become especially noticeable in the 1990s among élite and middle class Thai women. The following is from an article about Somruthai Prasattongosoth, whose family owns Bangkok Airways, and the description could apply to many well-off contemporary Thai women: "at work or in social gatherings, she usually wears a suit because it portrays the image of working woman, whereas on special occasions she will be in traditional Thai style costumes, wearing phasin made in Northern, or Northeastern Thai, Laos, or Cambodia."[9] Moreover, while many contemporary Thai women's interest in traditional textiles is limited to wearing dresses made of handwoven cloth inspired by traditional patterns, Khun Somruthai collects and often wears skirts made of older textiles: "I like buying old textiles. In fact, I prefer old textiles to industrial Thai silk because it is easier to take care of. I also believe that old textiles will become popular again" and, she comments in regard to this old cloth, "my family loves everything reflecting Thai characteristics."[10]

The popularity of such traditionally oriented dress is quite recent in Thailand, but the roots of this development go back over several years. The roots are twofold. First is the promotion by Queen Sirikit and other Thai élite figures of northeastern silk for clothing relating mainly to an internal Thai market and linked to community development. This initiative dates from the early 1950s, but did not become a significant endeavor until the 1970s. Second is the promotion of northern hill tribe textile handicrafts by a variety of individuals and institutions, including members of Thai royalty, Thai government departments, and foreign aid agencies. These efforts began in the 1960s, but, again, did not become significant until the 1970s.[11]

Queen Sirikit has played an important role, if not the most important one, in promoting tradition-oriented Thai dress for many years. Her interest has focused on weft ikat or *mudmee* silk from the northeast. Queen Sirikit's interest in mudmee silk was apparent as far back as the days of her status as a "royal fiancée," when she was often photographed wearing mudmee phasin. She was also often seen wearing such clothing during the wedding and coronation in 1950 and during a tour to the northeast in 1953.[12] These activities, of course, paralleled the birth of the modern Thai silk industry, often associated with Jim Thompson's meeting with the editor of *Vogue* in New York in 1947 and the subsequent use of Thai silk in the 1951 musical *The King and I.* [13]

Subsequently, the Queen initiated a study of the history of Thai dress with the intent of creating a national dress that was more in keeping with Thai traditions than the fashions promoted by Phibun. The outcome of this study was the adoption of five national costumes for Thai women, based on the dress of earlier periods, that were introduced to the public in January 1963. These were mainly made of silk and employed weft ikat (mudmee) and the use of gold brocade. The five costumes included an informal daytime dress, a formal daytime dress, a formal evening gown, and two costumes for special occasions. Later, two more formal special occasion styles were added and men too were provided with something to wear, the *phrarajathan* shirt, usually of silk in long or short sleeve style, and often employing the mudmee technique. Such clothing was clearly not intended for the masses, but did serve to give the royal seal of approval to clothing that combined Thai and Western influences, while employing cloth that could clearly be identified as Thai and as coming from rural weavers. It also helped to promote the weaving style of a particular impoverished portion of the country and thereby indirectly linked élite fashions with rural development and nation-building.

This association with rural development became more pronounced in the 1970s. Queen Sirikit became interested in promoting traditional mudmee weaving in the northeast in 1970 when she was on a visit to the region bringing assistance to flood-ravaged villagers. The Queen remarked that sericulture and silk weaving were ideal cottage industries to promote in the northeast to help women earn supplementary incomes for their families. In 1972 the Mudmee Silk Project was launched under the Queen's patronage to promote silk mudmee weaving in the northeast with the aim of improving the quality of the product and by encouraging more women to become weavers. At the time mudmee phasin were viewed by most Thais, including those in the northeast, as clothing for poor rural people only. The Queen's activities helped considerably to give silk mudmee wider acceptance in Thai society.

Such activities were further expanded following the establishment of the Supplementary Occupation and Related Techniques (SUPPORT) Foundation in 1976. SUPPORT served to enlist a larger number of élite Thais in the promotion of mudmee silk production as well as the production of other handicrafts. The number of weavers involved with the Mudmee Silk Project has grown from a handful at the beginnings to over 7,000. SUPPORT has also been involved in a variety of exhibitions and educational activities intended to promote silk mudmee. Perhaps the most important of these was an exhibition in Bangkok organized in August 1990 to celebrate the Queen's birthday and twenty years of her efforts to promote silk mudmee.[14] The exhibition included selected new pieces from the northeast and pieces from the Queen's personal collection.

Initially, this new mudmee clothing was worn only by a relatively small number of élite Thai and foreign women. Slowly during the 1980s, however, it gained in popularity among women belonging to the country's growing upper and middle classes and today it is widely worn throughout the country. Mudmee silk clothing has been less popular with Thai men, perhaps in part because of the ambiguous status of silk mudmee shirts somewhere between formal and informal wear. As formal wear they have not been able to compete with formal Western-style men's clothing and as informal wear they have not done well in competition with Western-style leisure fashions. Men's mudmee shirts have certainly not achieved the status of batik shirts in Indonesia, for example.

A particularly interesting and important spin-off from the above development is the emergence of modern fashion employing cotton pha sin that feature a variety of traditional supplementary weft patterns or contemporary patterns inspired by these older ones that are associated with certain T'ai-speaking minorities found in Thailand. Especially important in this regard are *pha teen chok.* The term teen chok refers to a type of discontinuous supplementary weft weave used primarily in producing hem pieces for tube-skirts. As indicated earlier, teen chok traditionally is associated with the Lao Phuan and T'ai Yuan. A somewhat more recent development has been the emergence of fashion based on pha sin using patterns inspired by traditional T'ai Lü textiles in addition to teen chok woven by other groups.

Weaving pha teen chok traditionally was an important part of Lao Phuan life and signified an important rite of passage for young women, indicating that they were mature enough to marry. After the Second World War, there was a sharp decline in making teen chok. Lao Phuan women in particular became ashamed to wear such traditional clothing in public since this marked them as being of Laotian origin. When a few foreigners and Thais began collecting teen chok in the 1960s and 1970s, many of the older clothes, which were no longer worn and had lost most of their important cultural connotations, were sold.

A gradual revival in making teen chok began in the 1970s, mainly in the Sukhothai province village of Had Sieo.[15] Initially, small amounts of handwoven cloth were produced for sale as souvenirs or on order for individuals and businesses in the vicinity wanting bags and other items, often bearing the name of the person or store ordering them. In the 1980s, what had begun as a small revival in hand weaving turned into a virtual boom as a result of the growing demand among middle class and élite Thais for clothing made of traditional-looking handwoven cloth. Younger women in Had Sieo began learning teen chok weaving from older women as a result of the appearance of this new market. By the late 1980s, in the face of steadily rising demand for Had Sieo teen chok, new weaving techniques were introduced that allowed more rapid production. This innovation also led to changes in teen chok patterns since some older patterns could not be made by the new techniques and these techniques also allowed women to produce some new patterns. This modern teen chok came to be used for more than decorating women's dresses. For example, it has been applied to men's clothing and on pillow covers.

While the modern teen chok revival is identified in most people's minds with Had Sieo and Si Satchanalai, the teen chok boom has had an influence throughout the traditional teen chok producing communities and beyond, including the production of machine-made cloth with teen chok-like patterns. The development of this modern teen chok industry in many instances has been promoted by the SUPPORT Foundation. SUPPORT has provided financial, technical, and marketing support for a number of projects concerned primarily with promoting teen chok and teen chok-like weaving as a means of community development, while the Queen and others have promoted it as an item of fashion.

Production of the new teen chok and other traditionally-inspired cloth has become especially important for T'ai Lü and T'ai Yuan weavers in the north. Several T'ai Lü villages in Nan province, for instance, now produce large quantities of traditional-looking textiles for sale to markets in Chiang Mai, Bangkok, and overseas. This was not always the case. Despite the effort of development workers, by the mid-1980s only a few communities still produced textiles and the number of weavers continued to decline until the late 1980s.

In recent years, however, the trend has been reversed. Development workers Decha and Nusara Tiangket settled among the T'ai Yuan of Mae Chaem and helped to promote the local production of handwoven cloth.[16] (*Plates 2.8, 2.9*) Under their auspices, weaving cooperative groups were formed and weaving in these villages changed from a household to a community activity. The number of T'ai Lü women in Nan province weaving for the new external national market has grown steadily in recent years. (*Plate 2.11*) This development in Nan has also resulted in the emergence of a small number of relatively affluent local entrepreneurs serving as intermediaries. Such entrepreneurs today find themselves in a fast-changing and competitive business. The more successful ones avidly read fashion magazines to ensure that the cloth they are selling is in step with the latest traditionally-inspired designs or in an effort to produce innovative designs that will attract the attention of urban fashion designers and boutique owners.

Modern teen chok, and teen chok-inspired textile production has also developed in central Thailand. The T'ai Yuan of Ratchaburi provide an example of this as the SUPPORT Foundation and Ratchaburi Jok Art Center have promoted modern forms of production and mass marketing of teen chok and teen chok-inspired cloth.[17]

Modern tradition-oriented fashion also makes use of textiles associated with the non-T'ai hill tribes of northern Thailand. While all of these hill tribes have distinctive traditional styles of dress, not all hill tribes have had much influence on modern Thai fashion. Those who have had the most influence are the Hmông, Yao, and Akha, while the influence of the Karen, Lawa, Lahu, and Lisu has been negligible. I will not go into detail in discussing these textiles and their commercialization since this has been widely discussed by others elsewhere. Essentially, in the 1960s and 1970s hill tribe textiles attracted the attention of those concerned with problems associated with the hill tribes. Such attention was motivated in part by a desire to reduce opium production in the highlands and concern over the problems faced by hill tribe refugees from neighboring countries. Textile handicraft production was seen as a way to promote community development among the hill tribes.

At the outset, hill tribe textile handicraft production and sales were oriented almost exclusively to the foreign tourist market. Small quantities of textiles were sold in their original form, while more were sold transformed into clothing more suitable for Western tastes or as pieces added to Western-style clothing. This is a process that Cohen has referred to as "boutiquisation."[18] The foreign tourist market remains the most important one for such clothing, but gradually a market for these textiles has also grown among Thais, taking the form of what a 1989 article in *Accent Thai* refers to as "Hilltribe Chic."[19]

A variety of Royal projects have been involved in promoting hill tribe textiles, but these have had relatively little direct influence on the emergence of hill tribe chic fashion and such fashion has generally appealed to a different group of Thai women than those attracted to mudmee or teen chok pha sin. This hill tribe fashion is largely the product of the work of boutique designers in Chiang Mai and Bangkok who catered initially to foreigners, but who have gained increasing recognition among Thais as well. This clothing appeals more to younger middle class women who are interested in clothing that is less formal than the mudmee and teen chok pha sin and that is perhaps a bit more daring.

Textiles for the hill tribe fashion market come primarily from the Hmông, Yao, and Akha. During the 1990s, producers of hill tribe fashions have turned increasingly to members of these groups living outside Thailand in Myanmar, Laos, China, and Vietnam for cloth. Chiang Mai, in particular, has come to serve as an important regional market for the used and new hill tribe cloth that supplies this market.

A book published in 1996, featuring the creations of sixteen leading fashion designers in Bangkok, *Deluxe Fashion Thaisilk Collection,* provides a useful overview of the current trends in tradition-oriented fashion.[20] The book opens with a picture of the Queen and includes 388 women's costumes and one man's costume.[21] The vast majority of costumes employ traditionally-inspired textiles and most can be said to have a distinctly Thai look to them in terms of either overall design or use of fabric. The categories of ikat, supplementary weft, and hill tribe in the table below relate to the three fashion origins discussed above. In reference to the type of clothing distinguished in the table, attention is paid to whether the item is an original older traditional piece of cloth or a contemporary traditional piece of cloth or whether it is more fitting to view it as inspired by such piece. Only one traditional blouse or top is worn by a model, but tradition is clearly a factor in selecting tops for a large number of the costumes since many of the models are wearing neo-traditional blouses inspired by central Thai courtly dress. It should also be noted that older traditional textiles and modern versions of them are used in chapter openers and often for decorations in the photos.

Type of clothing	*ikat*	*Type of textile* *suppl. weft*	*hill tribe*
skirt-original	7	6	2
skirt-inspired	105	84	1
top-original	0	1	0
top-inspired	24.5	77.5	1
shoulder cloth-original	0	7	0
shoulder cloth-inspired	1	6	0
waist cloth-original	1	0	0
waist cloth-inspired	0	0	0

Table 2.1: A Survey of Recent Fashion Trends from *Deluxe Fashion Thaisilk Collection*

While silk mudmee skirts and dresses dominate the fashions in this collection, supplementary weft skirts and tops are also much in evidence. Significantly, most of the supplementary weft patterns are of T'ai Lü origin or inspired by T'ai Lü patterns. Lao Phuan and T'ai Yuan teen chok are not nearly so important as inspiration for these designers. Of the traditional textiles actually used, perhaps the most interesting one is a man's loincloth from the Mon-Khmer speakers of southern Laos used as a shoulder cloth by one of the models.[22] Lastly, it should be noted how little use is made of hill tribe textiles in this collection. With the exception of the loincloth, all of the other traditionally-inspired costumes rely on fabrics and designs associated with T'ai-speaking people or the Khmer.

Before concluding this section I would like briefly to discuss contemporary traditionally-oriented fashion for men. By and large, men have been left out of this fashion trend. If one looks through recent fashion magazines, most devote considerable attention to women's fashion in this regard, while one rarely sees such men's fashion featured. This is quite apparent in the book discussed above, with its sole male model. Moreover, when I have shown Thai men clothing of this sort and asked them if they would wear such things, the reaction has almost always been negative. The same men, of course, often respond favorably to the idea of women wearing traditionally-inspired clothing.

There is one style of traditionally-inspired dress for men that has become popular. This is the mohom-style shirt and associated baggy trousers that have come to be worn by some populist politicans such as Chamlong Srimuang.[23] A 1991 article in *Chiangmai Travel Holiday* magazine discusses the mohom-style shirt thus:

> Distinctive, practical and bargain priced, the North's "national dress" is proving a fashion hit with sophisticated visitors...the *Mohom* has been unanimously regarded as the national costume for Northerners...They are produced in several provinces in the North, but most notable in Prae and Lampang. Still, they are available throughout the country. Casual-looking and even fashionable, *Mohoms* usually denote the simplicity and easy-going nature of the wearers. They are very popular not only among Thais, but also among foreigners...[24]

While many mohom shirts continue to be made in the traditional manner, more fashionable ones have also began to appear in shops in Chiang Mai and Bangkok and it has become increasingly acceptable to appear at even formal gatherings sporting an upmarket version of a mohom shirt.

Traditional Textiles That Have Missed the Boat

The above section has focused on communities, groups, and regions that have seen the current tradition-oriented fashion trends lead to a revival and even boom in hand weaving. At the same time it is important to recognize that there have also been examples of failure, where weaving traditions have not been revived or have been revived to a limited extent, but have failed to take off. In each of the situations where this is the case the reasons can be quite different, but by far the most important reasons in most situations have to do with the comparative economics of the weaving industry in relation to other areas of the Thai economy. Quite simply, the profits or wages for weavers are often too low in relation to those available from other sources to attract weavers in many settings, even with the sharply increasing demand for handwoven cloth. Another factor is the inability of some types of traditional cloth to gain popularity. Not all traditional cloth has become popular and those with a tradition of producing such cloth have had to choose between giving up trying to sell it in the current market, accepting a marginal role in this market, or learning to make a type of cloth that is more popular. Here I will briefly look at two examples where weaving has not done very well despite outside efforts to promote it: the Lao Song Dam of central Thailand and the weavers of Ko Yor in southern Thailand.

The Lao Song Dam living west of Bangkok have a tradition of producing a variety of relatively plain, largely black textiles. These textiles are rarely completely plain and often contain small, very fine designs. In addition, the black and some of the other colors until recently were often made from natural dyes. Such clothing was commonly worn in the early post-war period and as its popularity declined for everyday wear it continued to be used on special occasions. During early 1990s, however, many younger Lao Song Dam have ceased to wear such traditional clothing even on special occasions.

Missionaries from the Church of Christ in Thailand initiated a project in 1966 to promote handicrafts among the Lao Song Dam in Nakon Pathom province.[25] Over the years this project grew to include a number of villages. Handicrafts, including handwoven cloth, were sold in Bangkok by the church, especially prior to the Christmas season, and efforts were made to encourage tour buses from Bangkok to visit Lao Song Dam villages. The number of tourists visiting the villages never became very large and later declined. Handicraft sales in Bangkok have continued, but have shown no sign of growing along with the current market for other traditional-looking goods. Moreover, not only are traditional textiles now rarely worn by the Lao Song Dam themselves, but few younger women are interested in weaving and the textiles have not become an important component of the commercial handicraft repertoire of the Lao Song Dam.

Economic and cultural factors are relevant in the declining popularity of weaving and wearing traditional clothing among younger Lao Song Dam women. The style of the traditional clothing is undoubtedly an important factor in its failure to catch on in the contemporary fashion world. The black tube-skirt offers little that sets it apart from a range of other black skirts available and long black jackets of the Lao Song Dam as well as those of others groups such as the Yao and Lahu have not been popular with modern Thais.

The weavers of Ko Yor in Songkhla province have a tradition of producing a small range of high quality textiles mainly of cotton that are either plain or feature relatively simple geometric designs. Prior to the Second World War this cloth was woven for domestic use and weaving declined after the war. It was revived in 1972 on a commercial basis and over the years various government and private initiatives have sought to keep it going.[26] Such efforts and a small, but constant market for the cloth have proven insufficient to keep this weaving tradition alive. On a 1996 visit to Ko Yor I witnessed one of the few remaining weavers on the island making her last textile. (*Plate 2.10*) She stated that no young women were interested in weaving since they could earn much more money working in the nearby seafood processing industry. She also remarked that the prices she could charge were restrained by competition from cheap commercial cotton cloth so that she could not earn enough to make it worth her while to continue. Again, the presence of more attractive sources of income has meant that young women are not attracted to weaving. Also, the Ko Yor cloth has insufficient distinguishing features to make it attractive to the current fashion market. Men wanting a checked cloth to wear around their waist with their mohom shirt are more likely to buy cloth from the northeast or elsewhere.

Traditionally-oriented fabrics for current women's fashion have come primarily from peoples in north and northeastern Thailand who have a tradition of making textiles with extensive distinctive patterns. It is not enough that a style of textile hark back to some tradition within Thailand, it must also contain imagery that is readily visible and that attracts attention. Interestingly, this is not the case with men's fashion. The use of such imagery with men's clothing has not worked well. In fact, just the opposite has occurred. It is precisely the more simple plain or checked cloth that has gained popularity among men.

Current Fashion and Identity

How do current fashion trends relate to national, regional, and ethnic identities in Thailand? First of all, in terms of everyday dress and a good deal of special occasion dress as well, very few T'ai or Khmer- speaking peoples in Thailand today wear anything that marks them as belonging to a specific ethnic group. Most wear clothing that is derived from Western fashion or, in the case of poorer women, tube skirts made of commercial cloth that indicates no specific ethnic identity. Within the realm of such styles of dress, clothing serves as an indicator of identity mainly in terms of gender and often class and age. Not only does this type of dress not indicate ethnic identity in any specific way, such as being a T'ai Lü or Lao Song Dam, but it usually does not specifically indicate that the wearer is Thai either.

It is against this background that the growing popularity of traditionally-oriented fashion can be set. The traditionalist revival in Thai dress should be placed in the context of the same process of Westernization and globalization that has led to a decline in the use of traditional clothing as modern Thais have adopted fashions seen as modern and worldly, while at the same time some have also adopted dress for use on occasion that helps to define their Thainess within this globalized context. Thus, the growing interest in and wearing of more traditional types of dress from the region in recent years is, I think, one manifestation of a desire that has developed especially among better-off urban Thais during the past few years to retain something of their heritage and cling on to some things that are distinctly Thai in the face of very rapid change. Somruthai Prasattongosoth's remark quoted above that her family is keenly interested in things with noticeable Thai characteristics is a reflection of just such sentiments. Rather than reflecting insecurity amidst such change or a desire to return to the past (i.e., nostalgia), however, I believe that for many Thais such an interest in what is perceived to be more traditional aspects of Thai life is a reflection of their growing sense of security as they seek to define more consciously a modern Thai society that is not simply a creation of the whims of global cultural and economic forces.

The above describes what is going on in general at the national level, but there are also important local and regional developments relating to the incorporation of the symbols of local populations into a broader national culture as well as regional revivals.

Let us turn first to the process of incorporation. Many of the motifs and some of the styles of dress that comprise the repertoire of current traditionalist fashion formerly were symbols of more localized group identities. Take, for example, the teen chok patterns of the Lao Phuan of Had Sieo. At one point the women of Had Sieo stopped wearing pha teen chok since it was "a shameful sign of being 'Laotian'."[27] As new teen chok began to be produced in Had Sieo the old motifs were used as well as new ones based on them and such motifs were used not only on textiles, but also in a variety of media used to promote Si Satchanilai National Park and other locales in the region. This type of textile thus changed from being a signifier of a particular ethnic community to representing the entire district of Si Satchanalai.[28]

Used on clothing, Had Sieo teen chok has assumed a dual identity. While most Thais, and some non-Thais, recognize such cloth as coming from at least the area around Had Sieo, few today associate the pattern with the Lao Phuan. Thus, it is associated with a particular region, but not an ethnic group. In addition to this regional identity, when used in contemporary fashion, it is also intended to convey Thainess and, therefore, it is also associated with a national identity. A similar point can be made in regard to most of the motifs now used: on the one hand they are associated with a specific region and not an ethnic group and on the other hand they have become symbols of a Thai national identity. To some extent hill tribe motifs still convey the identity of a particular ethnic group to some people, but, again, many people blend the motifs together and identify them with the hill tribes of the north in general.

The process of incorporation in the northeast has another interesting dimension. While such a nation-building role can be seen in the process of incorporation of other motifs and types of textiles as well, it has probably been of most significance in regard to the northeast. The identification of northeastern mudmee fashion with the Thai monarchy and members of the élite helps to take a regional type of cloth from an area that at the time when it was initially being promoted was politically very sensitive and link it to national identity. In addition to such political considerations, the association of Khmer ikat silk and the Thai monarchy is an old one that is only one dimension of the important cultural links that existed in the past between the Thai monarchy and Hinduized Khmer culture.

Let us now turn to regional revivals. For the most part, these have taken the form of individuals in a particular locale taking an interest in the textile heritage of a relatively small region such as Si Satchanilai or Ratchaburi. But in recent years there has also been a revival associated with northern Thailand, or Lan Na, that has both regional and national dimensions. Not only have Lan Na textiles attracted historical interest (*Plate 2.12*), but modern versions of them have come to be worn in a variety of contemporary settings as symbols of a distinct northern Thai culture. Government initiatives to promote northern culture were especially pronounced under the governorship of Dr. Pairat Techarin. In 1988, during his term in office, a letter was circulated among government workers and non-government organization employees asking for them to wear traditional clothing one day a week to assist in this endeavor. While many women responded to this request by wearing traditionally-inspired clothing and jewelry, men have been less responsive.

Chiang Mai University and members of its faculty have played a central role in the revival of northern culture, including Lan Na textiles. Especially important in regard to textiles has been the work of Professor Vidhi Panichphan, of the university's fine arts faculty.[29] Among his more noteworthy early activities concerning textiles was a pioneering fashion show held in the mid-1980s featuring costumes based on research conducted in villages and of temple murals.

The growth of interest in distinctive northern dress has also assumed more popular dimensions in the 1990s. This is evident in movies and television programming featuring Lan Na-style dress as well as in local performances for tourist audiences. One other manifestation of this development is the appearance of a number of photography studios in Chiang Mai in which people are dressed up in northern-style costumes for traditional-looking portraits. (*Plate 2.13, 2.14*) In addition to the regional aspect of these developments, there is a national dimension as well. When something traditional is being portrayed through dress in television programs, for instance, it has become popular to use northern dress. (*Plate 2.15*) Thus, such dress has, in some instances, also assumed a national meaning associated with Thai traditions in general.

There is one other aspect of traditional dress and identity that bears mention. This is a regional dimension that transcends the borders of Thailand. Thais in recent years have shown considerable interest in T'ai peoples elsewhere in Southeast Asia. To some extent this is a 'roots' quest, as modern, urban Thais seek to better understand their origins and traditions.

In this regard, textiles of T'ai peoples in neighboring countries have not only served the needs of Thai fashion by providing imports to supplement local supplies, but also assumed importance as a prominent part of the heritage of T'ai peoples.

T'ai Textile Collections and Identity

Collections of textiles reflect past and present fashion trends and can make important statements about identity and how it is perceived. Collecting of T'ai textiles is carried out by public institutions and private individuals. Such collecting can be related to questions of identity in terms of the motivation for making the collection as well as the manner in which the collection is organized and displayed.

There are a number of textile collections in Thailand on display in public and private museums, including the National Museum in Bangkok and most provincial national museums.[30] While the collection of the National Museum in Bangkok focuses on the textiles worn by Thai royalty, those in the provincial museums focus on the traditional textiles found in the particular province. Private museum collections include those of the Siam Society in Bangkok and a handful of collections found around the country such as the Hat Siew Teen Chok Museum in Si Satchanalai established by Sathorn Soratprasopsant, who has also played an active role in marketing locally produced hand-woven cloth.[31] **(2.16)** The Siam Society collection contains textiles of the northern hill tribes as well as teen chok and the other private museum collections focus on textiles from their immediate vicinity.

Interestingly, what is missing is a truly national collection of textiles that combines textiles from Thailand's regions and ethnic minorities with those of Thai royalty. The National Museum in Bangkok, which can be seen as presenting an image of the Thai national identity through material culture, has relied almost completely on textiles of Thai royalty in this regard. Thus, it has sought to rely only on the image of the monarchy in the case of textiles for the purpose of presenting an image of national identity and not also sought to present national identity through a collection of the range of textiles found throughout the country— unlike many other national museums around the world.

As for the provincial museums, in focusing on local collections and usually not presenting a wider range of textiles from around the nation, they have concerned themselves with local matters and, in a sense, served to highlight peculiarities of local identities rather than seeking to provide museum visitors with a broader image of Thai identity by presenting textiles from elsewhere in the country and/or making an effort to place local textiles within a national context.

Thus, while Thai museums do serve as repositories of specific types of textiles and present material images of certain segments of Thai society, for the most part, they have not played much of a role in presenting a national identity through textiles.

Also missing from existing museum collections are many textiles that reflect more recent changes in textile fashion. The presentation of hill tribe textiles tends to be particularly static while collections of other textiles from within Thailand pay attention to changes in fashion primarily in the past. This is certainly true of textiles used by royalty, which are divided into periods according to reigns and major periods in Thai history and, in the case of textiles from the late nineteenth and early twentieth centuries, often according to changing fashions within reigns. Museums in Thailand are less interested in fashions during the post-war period. This is a pity since museums could play an important role in interpreting developments in textile fashion over the past fifty years in relation to local and national identity.

Interest in more contemporary textiles has been left mainly to private collectors. The most prominent 'private' collector is Queen Sirikit. As noted above, she has assembled an important collection of Thai silks. Her collection seeks to cover not only older fashions, but also more recent developments. In this sense, she has played an important role in promoting the acquisition of recent and contemporary woven silk material not only to wear but also for purposes of collecting and, thus, for purposes of preservation, display, and documentation. Besides the Queen, until recently, collecting such silks was limited essentially to some of the regional museums and these collections tended to be relatively limited in scope. Since the mid-1980s, however, collecting textiles has become increasingly popular or fashionable among members of the Thai élite as well as members of the middle class.

In addition to the activities of the Queen, such institutions as the Siam Society have also played a role in promoting an appreciation of handwoven textiles and encouraged an interest in collecting textiles. Significant in regard to the Siam Society is its intercultural role as a meeting place for foreigners and Thais to exchange ideas. Foreigners as well as Thais associated with or addressing the Siam Society have certainly been influential in encouraging Thai interest in textiles. Naiyanee Srikanthimarak is an example of one such collector.[32] She was influenced by another collector, Nisa Shenakul, who gave lectures on textiles to the Siam Society in the late 1970s. Khun Naiyanee worked for many years for the Goethe Institute and began traveling to the northeast and collecting silk textiles mainly from Surin around 1980. By 1985 she had collected some 500 pieces both old and new.

There are many textile collectors in Thailand who have focused on textiles from a particular region, often where they live or work. But few collectors remain so limited in scope and most come to collect textiles associated with Thailand as a country or with the T'ai peoples in general. The latter theme has appeared with greater frequency in collections and exhibitions in recent years and is best exemplified in the "Textiles and the T'ai Experience in Southeast Asia" exhibition that was held in Bangkok in 1992 before moving on North America.[33] The exhibition did not include textiles that were representative of all of the major T'ai groups in Southeast Asia, but in focusing on T'ai rather than Thai textiles it did draw attention to what is emerging as a major theme in Thai textile collecting and one that is closely linked to questions of identity. Thus, the theme of the exhibition was rephrased in one Thai publication as "Woven Cloth and the T'ai Race…the Yarn that Binds Us Together."[34] The latter is a clearer statement of contemporary Thai interest in such an exhibition that emphasizes the current Thai fascination with their roots and their identity within a larger Asian context.

Conclusion

As in the past, contemporary Thai clothing fashions reflect the nature of modern Thai society as people adapt to a globalized and fast-paced world. The Westernization of Thai fashion has indicated an eagerness to be a part of the larger contemporary world, while recent traditionalist fashion, at the same time, indicates the desire on the part of many Thais to ensure that they retain something that is distinctly Thai. The particular direction that such traditionalist fashion has taken reflects the hierarchical nature of Thai society and the important role of the monarchy in particular, but there are also traditionalist fashion trends that reflect egalitarian tendencies within Thai society. The latter is most clearly seen with mohom fashion as well as in some aspects of hill tribe chic.

Current traditionalist fashion also reflects changes in ethnic and regional identity in modern Thai society. While many hill tribe peoples in northern Thailand retain versions of their traditional dress, the most minority T'ai and Khmer no longer wear distinctive costumes, except in a few cases on special occasions. Nevertheless, it is these groups who are now providing the motifs and materials for current traditionalist fashions that are associated with a broader Thai identity. Although the general tendency is towards such incorporation, in the case of northern Thailand there has also been a largely Chiang Mai-based revival of regional dress along with a revival of interest generally in Lan Na culture. Such regionalism, however, can also be placed within a national context as Lan Na too features in the overall search for a better understanding of the roots of T'ainess beyond the confines of the central Thai courts.

Notes

1. Chu Thái Son and Dào Hùng, *Vietnam: A Multicultural Mosaic* (Hanoi: Vietnam Foreign Languages Publishing House, 1991), photos 222, 251, and 253.
2. Son and Hùng, *Vietnam*, photo 182.
3. Patricia Naenna, "Isan textiles," *Thai Textiles: Threads of a Cultural Heritage* (Bangkok: The National Identity Board, Office of the Prime Minister, 1994), pp. 77-95.
4. Naenna, "Isan textiles," p. 78.
5. Bonnie Davis, "Thai dress through the ages," in *Living in Thailand,* vol. 20, no. 9, 1991, p. 16; also see Chira Chongkol, "Textiles and costumes in Thailand," in *Arts of Asia,* vol. 12, no. 6, 1982, pp. 121-131.
6. Davis, "Thai dress through the ages," p. 16.
7. Sanunya Suriyarattanakorn, "Evolution of Thai uniform," in *Muang Boran,* vol. 18, no. 1, 1992, pp. 120-126.
8. David Wyatt, *Thailand: A Short History* (Bangkok: Trasvin Publications, 1984), p. 215.
9. "New generation who favours traditional textiles," in *Silk Magazine,* vol. 1, no. 1, 1991, p. 42.
10. "New generation who favours traditional textiles," p. 42.
11. Apparently, the first known attempt to collect and ship hill tribe crafts was when an American Peace Corps volunteer shipped some Akha and Yao goods to Bangkok in 1964; Ruth B. Sharp, "Tribal arts and crafts in northern Thailand," in Lucien Hanks, *et al., A Report on the Tribal Peoples in Chiangrai Province North of the Mae Kok River* (Bangkok: The Siam Society, Bennington-Cornell Anthropological Survey of Hill Tribes in Thailand, 1964), Appendix I, p. 16.
12. Vilawan Viranuwat (ed.), *Catalogue of the Queen's Mudmee Collection* (Bangkok: SUPPORT, 1991).
13. William Warren, *Legendary American: The Remarkable Career and Strange Disappearance of Jim Thompson* (Boston: Houghton Mifflin, 1970).
14. Viranuwat, *Catalogue of the Queen's Mudmee Collection;* and see "Queen gets back to the work she loves," in *Bangkok Post,* 27 July 1990, pp. 27-28; "The finest mudmee on display," in *Bangkok Post,* 4 August 1990, p. 21; "Her Majesty reveals mudmee collection: Prized collection highlights skills of rural Thais," in

Bangkok Post, 6 August 1990, pp. 8-9; and "Mudmee shines at party of the year," in *Bangkok Post,* 7 August 1990, pp. 27-28.

15. Uab Sanasen, "Notes on a weaving village," in *Muang Boran,* vol. 6, no. 1, 1979, pp. 5-7, 13-14.; Clare S. Rosenfeld and Mary Connelly Mabry, "Discovering the art of teenjok," in *Sawaddi,* September/October, 1982, pp. 23-25 (Bangkok: American Women's Club of Thailand); Suthon Sukphisit, "A showcase of antique teen chok," in *Bangkok Post,* 27 December 1988, p. 31; Suddan Wisudthiluck, *Changes in the Production of Traditional Cloth: Ban Haad Sieo, Amphoe Srisatchanaalai, Changwat Sukhothai* (M.A. thesis, Thammasat University, 1991); Suddan Wisudthiluck, "Changes in fabric design and meaning at Ban Had Siew," in *Muang Boran,* vol. 18, nos. 3/4, 1992, pp. 63-74.

16. See Sanitsuda Ekachai, "The last thread of culture: Weaving in and out of debt," in *Bangkok Post,* 14 May, 1992, pp. 25 and 42. Also see "'Mae Chaem' teen jok and hand-woven textile: A Lanna heritage that should be conserved and passed on to younger generation," in *Silk Magazine,* vol. 1, no. 9, 1993, pp. 80-85.

17. See Joyce Rainart, "Village that came back to life," in *Bangkok Post,* 21 July 1985, p. 13; Krit Lualamai, "Jok Khoo Bua: Survival of an art form," in *Hotel Information News,* vol. 1, no. 8, 1989, pp. 48-52; Somtawin Kongsawatkiat, "Grandma Son and Grandpa Mod Kamlangharn: Holding on to the dying skills," in *Saen Sanuk,* vol. 9, no. 5, 1989, pp. 4-7; and Orathai Phondi, "The Tai Yuan jok fabric designs of Ratchaburi," in *Silk Magazine,* vol. 2, no. 13, 1993, pp. 91-97.

18. Erik Cohen, "From tribal costume to pop fashion: The 'boutiquisation' of the textiles of the hilltribes of northern Thailand," in *Studies in Popular Culture,* vol. 11, no. 2, 1988, pp. 49-59.

19. "Hilltribe chic in Chiang Mai," in *Accent Thai,* vol. 2, no. 1, 1988, pp. 38-41; also see, "Ethnics in style", in *Bangkok Post,* 7 January 1987, p. 31, on an ethnic fashion show at the Prayer Textile Gallery in Bangkok.

20. Lek Amponpet, *Deluxe Fashion Thaisilk Collection* (Bangkok: BK Interprints, 1996).

21. Amponpet, *Deluxe Fashion Thaisilk Collection,* p. 241.

22. Amponpet, *Deluxe Fashion Thaisilk Collection,* p. 153.

23. The "Chamlong shirt" is mentioned, for example, in "Thailand's weaving revival," in *Sawasdee,* vol. 18, no. 12, 1989, pp. 29-32.

24. "Royal blue denims," in *Chiangmai Travel Holiday,* 16 August 1991, p. 24; also see "Mohon fabric: A symbol of the north," in *Saen Sanuk,* vol. 9, no. 5, 1989, pp. 24-25.

25. See, "Exquisite handicrafts by Lao Song hilltribe people on sale," in *Bangkok Post,* 20 September 1988, p. 31; "Helping craftsmen help themselves," in *Bangkok Post,* 1 November 1990, p. 30; Bert F. Sams, *Tradition and Modernity in a Lao Song Dam Village of Central Thailand* (Ph.D. dissertation, University of California, Los Angeles, 1987).
26. Chuda Jitpoituck, "Hand-made cloth in Koh Yor," in *Journal of the National Research Council of Thailand,* vol. 16, no. 2, 1984, pp. 1-18.
27. Wisudthiluck, "Changes in fabric design and meaning at Ban Had Siew," p. 74.
28. Wisudthiluck, "Changes in fabric design and meaning at Ban Had Siew," p. 74.
29. Vithda Srivichai, "Vidhi Panichphan: A conservator of Lanna heritage," in *Silk Magazine*, vol. 1, no. 8, 1993, pp. 36-40. Members of the Fine Arts Department at Chiang Mai University also sought to collect, display, and lecture on older northern Thai textiles starting in the late 1980s; see Songsak Prangwatthanakun and Patricia Cheesman, *Lan Na Textiles: Yuan, Lue, Lao* (Chiang Mai: Center for the Promotion of Arts and Crafts, 1987), and Songsak Prangwatthanakun and Patricia Naenna, *Chiang Mai's Textile Heritage* (Chiang Mai: Studio Naenna, 1990).
30. See Michael C. Howard, *Textiles of Southeast Asia: An Annotated & Illustrated Bibliography* (Bangkok: White Lotus, 1994), p. 16.
31. See Suthon Sukphisit, "A showcase of antique teen chok," in *Bangkok Post,* 27 December 1988, p. 31.
32. She is profiled in Roxana Brown, "Collecting—Surin silks," in *Living in Thailand,* August 1985, pp. 62-65.
33. Mattiebelle Gittinger and H. Leedom Lefferts, Jr., *Textiles and the Tai Experience in Southeast Asia* (Washington, DC: The Textile Museum, 1992).
34. "Exhibition on 'Woven Cloth and the T'ai Race…the Yarn that Binds Us Together'," in *Hotel & Culture,* vol. 5, no. 38, 1992, pp. 14-21.

3

Change as a Method of Identification and Dating of T'ai Textiles

Patricia Cheesman Naenna

Textiles in traditional T'ai societies were woven for specific purposes and identified according to the role they played in that society whether for personal, household, or religious use. There were a few multi-purpose cloths, such as the long red silk rolls of the T'ai Daeng with supplementary weft designs which could be made into bags, used as mosquito netting decoration, or hung at a ceremony to decorate a house. Apart from these, each textile had a specific structure and pattern arrangement which was followed strictly. Even though communication was minimal between areas, the T'ai groups had an extraordinary record of adhering to the traditional patterns over centuries and over vast areas, indicating a common original source and strong traditional values. For example, the Lao Khrang in Thailand who were moved from Huaphanh province in Laos by the Thais after the Chau Anou uprising in 1828 have textiles used for blankets and curtains that are very similar to the original textiles made in Laos except for slight differences in structure. Today there are only a few people who can tell the difference.

In the past it never would have been possible to consider using a certain cloth for a purpose other than that it was woven for. Women carried on this tradition and passed it on to their daughters together with the techniques for making the cloths. In contrast, today a design that was once reserved for a sacred cloth can be used for an everyday tablecloth and designs formerly used only for women's skirts are used to make man's upper garments—taboos restricting such uses no longer exist. In the commercial era (which I consider to be post-Second World War in Thailand and post-Vietnam war in Laos), the old values have changed, with obvious effects on the types of textiles woven, their wearers, and their purposes. No boundaries have been drawn to dictate what can or cannot be changed. Even sacred symbols have fallen victim to commercialization without protection or care.

There is no doubt that textile weaving can be an excellent source of income for women in T'ai societies, but all too often their work is not sufficiently rewarded. For the most part, much to the delight of middlemen and to the detriment of cultural heritage, hand woven products are placed in the lower end of the price range spectrum in today's market. Ancient designs are being adapted to the tastes of Western and urban Thai buyers and traditional structures are rearranged to fit modern fashions. These obvious changes in design and aesthetics can be picked out in many examples of traditional textiles that are produced for the modern market from fashion items to furnishings and accessories. In order to put a better perspective on these changes and to assist in the identification of T'ai textiles, this chapter focuses on certain ancient textile forms that have been adapted to the Buddhist style, in some cases quite recently. For those changes that occurred before the commercial era, it is interesting to conceive of the methods of communication and transference of design ideas in areas where transport and travel was very much restricted, especially for women.

Pha Khan Soeng

In my book, *Lao Textiles: Ancient Symbols, Living Art,*[1] I identified two certaintypes of antique long shawls made by the T'ai Daeng as being *pha biang*. One of these was red and with a silk base and the other dark blue with a cotton base. Unfortunately, this classification has been repeated by other authors and it is only as a result of research since my initial publication that it has come to light that this classification only refers to relatively recent cloths of similar design.

The T'ai classification method for their own textiles is primarily by use, and in this case pha biang indicates a cloth used for a woman's shoulder cloth. The use of a shoulder cloth for women was not known among the non-Buddhist T'ai societies of Thailand and Laos. The shoulder cloth for women is mainly used for going to temple on Buddhist holidays and life crisis or ceremonial occasions such as weddings, funerals, and house-warming parties. In the Buddhist areas these ceremonies are attended by Buddhist monks who lead the ceremonies. In non-Buddhist T'ai societies these ceremonies are led by shamans and shoulder cloths are not worn by women attending them. It is for this reason that I have associated the use of the shoulder cloth for women with Buddhism. However, this does not rule out its use by non-Buddhist T'ai women in recent years as a result of fashion influences, especially with modern communication such as television, and in this regard shoulder cloths may be seen as a contemporary trend. It is interesting to note that the use of shoulder cloths disappeared during the 1975-1985 period in Vientiane, Laos, at the same time that interest in the Buddhist religion was minimized by the revolutionary government. Since 1985 there has been a reappearance of interest in Buddhism and growing popularity of shoulder cloths among women. The use of a shoulder cloth can also be seen as an Indian influence, with the combination of the *pha sin* and pha biang (*pha sabai* in Thai) looking more like a sari.

The cloths for discussion here were woven by the T'ai Daeng, T'ai Dam, T'ai Khao, and T'ai Phuan of Huaphanh and Xiengkhuang provinces in Laos prior to the revolution in 1975 and were used as sacred cloths for healing ceremonies. The red silk cloths were used in sacred ceremonies involving healing through a spirit medium or shaman such as the annual *pang phi mon* ceremony and are called *pha khan soeng.* (*Plate 3.1*) The dark blue cotton cloths were used as altar cloths, magic cloths, and healing cloths for use by shamans in ceremonies such as the *tum ming tum naen* and are called *pha phi mon.*

Neither of these cloths was used traditionally as pha biang and the only known use of the pha khan soeng to wrap around the body is by spirit mediums who used two cloths tied across their chests over their blouses when entering a trance. There are quite a few references to this method of wearing these cloths in Lao legends and ancient manuscripts. Most of the existing examples of traditional pha khan soeng date from between the early twentieth century and the Second World War.

Since 1985, both the pha khan soeng and pha phi mon designs have been popular, particularly in Vientiane, on cloths used as pha biang by Buddhist Lao or as shoulder wraps or shawls by Westerners. (*Plates 3.2, 3.4*) In the case of shawls, they have been redesigned to a wider width with symbols throughout or with a balance of the same pattern at each end, unlike the traditional pieces that have different designs at each end such as the diamond design at one end, a plain section in the center, and banding of patterns at the other end. The new cloths should not be called pha khan soeng, but it would be correct to call them pha biang, *pha khum lai,* or *pha hom.*

There are, in addition, a large number of new pha khan soeng being produced for the commercial market by villagers in Huaphanh and Xiengkhuang who have not yet learned to change the structure. (*Plate 3.3*) Unfortunately, they are using poor raw materials and synthetic dyes for the sake of speed. These pieces are much truer to the original form than other new pieces, but they lack the dedication of the original pha khan soeng which were considered objects of power and were woven with great care and ceremony. Pha Khan soeng that date prior to the twentieth century are extremely rare and exceptionally well made with natural dyes and tightly twisted threads.

The antiques market being as profitable as it is, a number of fake antique pha khan soeng appeared in the mid-1990s. These are either faded in the sun, treated with smoke, or woven with muted colors to copy the ancient designs and structures. In most cases it is easy to pick these out either by the quality of the warp thread, which today is commercially produced, or by the fluff on the new threads. Stylistic differences are also a key factor in identifying old pieces.

Pha Phae Kep

Another interesting cloth which has been transformed into a woman's shoulder cloth due to Buddhist influence is the *pha phae kep,* which is now called pha sabai in Thai, pha biang in Lao, and *pha bing* in Phutai. (*Plates 3.5, 3.6*) This simple cloth, with continuous supplementary banding throughout, is made in silk or cotton, usually with a red base. These cloths originally were much shorter than the pha sabai. The pha phae kep was originally a man's cloth called pha phae kep from Xiengkhuang. They were woven as a love gift by young women prior to marriage.

The tradition of wearing a short shoulder cloth over one shoulder for men was still known among the shamanistic T'ai Phuan in Xiengkhuang prior to the Vietnam war period, but today is virtually unknown. The design is now seen among the Phuan and Phutai in Isan and southern Laos on women's shoulder cloths that are long enough to wrap around the body and pass over one shoulder. Since the time of the nineteenth-century Han Chinese raids in Xiengkhuang and probably before this, many T'ai Phuan and Phutai migrated from Xiengkhuang to provinces in the southern part of Laos and Isan in northeastern Thailand. During the Vietnam war, the province was evacuated. Some people fled to Vietnam for safety, while others were airlifted to Luang Prabang and Vientiane provinces.

The pha phae kep structure was first adapted for use as a pha biang by the Vientiane Lao and Phuan during the French colonial period. The cloths were made with silver and gold yarns following the patterns of the pha phae kep and incorporating other power symbols from T'ai textiles of northeastern Laos such as the *Siho* (long-nosed lion) and *nak*. In most cases the fabric width was reduced to twenty centimeters to avoid the necessity of folding the cloth lengthwise since the metallic threads were unsuitable for this.

Traditionally, the Phuan and Phutai had shoulder wraps or blankets called *pha hom lai khit* which were made in two sections, each approximately forty centimeters wide with continuous supplementary weft patterns, but these were different from the patterns on the pha phae kep. The two types of cloth were also different in structure. The pha hom lai khit has one plain and one decorative end. The pha phae kep and the pha sabai both have fringes and balanced end designs made in one single piece, averaging thirty to fifty centimeters wide.

There is a great demand today for pha sabai in all the areas of the T'ai Buddhist people, especially in Thailand where the fashion has rapidly increased in popularity as a result of the interest in traditional costume promoted by Queen Sirikit. There are now a huge variety of designs on pha sabai, some more suitable than others. The use of hem piece designs for the pha sabai, for example, is incongruous with traditional T'ai aesthetics.

Sin Mi Mai

The T'ai groups living in Huaphanh and Xiengkhuang traditionally had a tube skirt, known as *sin mi mai,* for dressing their female relatives after death and wearing at the funeral ceremony that is quite unusual and beautiful. The use of these skirts was restricted to the female relatives of the dead who would wear five or seven of these on top of one another for the ceremony. The dead were buried in a sacred area outside the village. This was the most important shamanistic ceremony in this area and a great deal of preparation was required for the weaving of the skirts and other related textiles.

These skirts were made in three parts: the waistband, the main body part, and the hem piece. The waistband was red, black, or white or a combination of these colors. It was wide enough to cover the breasts and was often secured above the breasts rather than at the waist. On rare occasions it was made in a supplementary warp weave known as *hoa buan.* (*Plate 3.7*) The hem piece was made of plain dark blue cotton using a compound weave to make a ribbon-like strip which was sewn to the main body of the skirt. In the main body of the pha sin wide ikat bands alternate in red and dark blue and are separated by supplementary weft patterns.

Similar skirts were used in Luang Prabang in the early part of the twentieth century, with adjustments to the structure. The wide waistband was replaced with a narrow striped waistband typical of Luang Prabang and the hem piece was changed to a decorative teen chok. The wearing of these skirts at the waist rather than over the breasts was likely a result of Western influence, while the addition of a decorated hem piece was a Buddhist/Indian influence. The skirts worn by the Buddhist T'ai groups usually have a decorative hem made with supplementary weft designs for ceremonial occasions.

Sin Tin Yai

Identification according to the style of hem piece is also possible for other types of pha sin that did not originally have decorative hem pieces, such as the *sin mok* and the *sin mi fai* of the T'ai Daeng. (*Plates 3.8, 3.9*) Changes in this regard are the effect of commercialization and Buddhist influences since modern Lao people as well as T'ai like to wear heavily decorated hem pieces to the temple as well as on social occasions.

The *sin tin yai* of the T'ai Daeng is a plain black or dark blue skirt with a wide decorated hem piece. This type of skirt was not mentioned by researchers in the early part of the century but appears to have been popular since 1940. The design of this hem piece is interesting for the plain horizontal stripes that border each piece at the lower edge. These are dark blue, red, and green stripes that always appear in this order on these pieces. The strictness with which this is adhered to is surprising since today hem pieces are often made in the same pattern as the main body part, so as to match it, as a result of the influence of western aesthetics. On interviewing weavers about the meaning and origin of the dark blue, red, and green stripes, I found that they knew nothing except that the structure indicates the purpose of the piece of cloth as a hem piece that was not to be used for anything else.

Pha Pok Long

When the first Indian cloths came to Southeast Asia they captured the imagination of the people as well as being given status by the royal courts of different kingdoms. These cloths were copied and imitated even in the most remote places. The most popular textile design was the patola from Gujarat. In many places in Indonesia these imported cloths were thought to have magical powers and in Thailand they were called *pha thai that,* meaning "cloth to free a slave." Many other names exist both in Thai and Lao languages for these cloths from India and their imitations. Their influence on textiles of the T'ai peoples is significant and varied. One of the most interesting uses of such textiles is as a funeral cloth, in which case they are referred to as *pha pok long.*

The name pha pok long is used as a classification by the various T'ai groups for different cloths used for covering the coffin. The textiles in question here are the silk ikat masterpieces that were woven in the patola structure by the T'ai groups living in Huaphanh and Xiengkhuang prior to the Second World War. The design of these textiles was originally used on textiles made for the Lao court (that had followed the Siamese court in the use of this design) for use by the royal family as *chongkraben* (long cloths or hip wrappers). The Thai pieces of this type were originally woven in Cambodia using very fine silk and a three-shaft weave. In Laos such cloths were made from a rougher silk with darker colors. They were woven in plain weave and dyed with natural dyes, indicating that they were made in the northeastern provinces of Huoa Phan and Xiengkhuang. Less decorative versions of these cloths were used as long cloths or hip wrappers by the ruling class and buried or burned with them at death.

Apart from their use at the court at Luang Prabang, these cloths were used by members of the T'ai Daeng, T'ai Khao, and T'ai Phuan upper classes and were kept and treasured by the Khmu in Huaphanh and Oudomxai as status symbols. The T'ai Phuan who moved to Muang Hun in Oudomxai province preserved the weaving of these textiles until they were evacuated to Luang Prabang during the Vietnam war. As the cloths became scarce and production of them virtually ceased, the existing cloths were used as shamans' costumes when they entered trances and as funeral cloths that were no longer destroyed, but passed down in the family. Such cloths were also seen among the heirlooms of the Lao Khrang in Thailand and were adapted for use as ordination cloths following their conversion to Buddhism in the late nineteenth century. Their color and design was not changed in newer pieces, but the central seam disappeared with the use of wider looms.

Conclusion

The adaptation of textile designs and structures among the T'ai in Laos and Thailand has occurred continuously in history, but never before at the speed at which it is taking place today. The examples given here are related to the requirements for cloths used in Buddhist ceremonies as well as changing attitudes towards rare textiles. The first three examples are of textiles that have been changed to adapt to a different use while the last example is of the elevation in status of a textile from garment to sacred decorative item without change in its structure, color, or design. Both of these developments are useful for the dating and identification of textiles. The destruction of original designs is a sad reality in the commercial era, but as shamanism disappears so do the textiles that were associated with its rituals. The symbols remain in an impotent form except for the work of a few inspired artists who continue the tradition inspired by myths and sacred power associated with the ancient textiles.

Note

1. Patricia Cheesman, Lao Textiles: Ancient Symbols, Living Art (Bangkok: White Lotus, 1988).

4

T'ai Lü Textiles: Cultural Reproduction

Songsak Prangwattanakun
and
Patricia Cheesman Naenna

The T'ai Lü have a distinctive tradition of textile production that has been passed on for generations and forms an important part of their cultural heritage. The T'ai Lü art of weaving includes an aesthetic sense as well as techniques of weaving and dyeing. It is an art form that has adapted in recent years to conditions in their contemporary environment.

It is remarkable that the art of weaving has survived at all in the various T'ai Lü communities that are scattered in Thailand, Laos, China, Vietnam, and Burma amidst the current winds of change. (*Plate 4.1*) Equally astonishing is that, despite modernization, T'ai Lü textiles not only possess a distinctiveness in regard to the Lü in general, but often are still identifiable as to place of origin among specific Lü communities. (*Plates 4.2, 4.3*)

T'ai Lü Women and Textiles

Like other T'ai women, T'ai Lü women in the past learned how to weave from their mothers, grandmothers, and other female relatives who trained them in artistic skills. Young girls started weaving with simple techniques and products such as plain natural cotton yardage that was used for a variety of purposes, small ritual cloths known as *pha chet noi,* and shoulder bags. Later they developed their skills to weave textiles that required complicated techniques such as supplementary weft and tapestry weave.

In the past, textiles in T'ai Lü society were considered indications of the virtues of a good woman. In addition, activities associated with weaving provided opportunities for young men and women to meet. As young women sat spinning cotton in the middle of the communal yard, in a custom called *long hang khong* young men would come to court them. If a young woman liked a particular young man she would lend him her shawl to wrap around himself on his way home, knowing that he would have to come back the following evening to return it to her. In this way relationships were established. Other types of textiles which communicated fondness between young men and women were cloths that the women wove and gave to their loved ones. These included a man's shoulder cloth, *pha chet,* and shoulder bags, *thung yam.*

Prior to marriage T'ai Lü women needed to prepare household items for their married life such as mattresses, pillows, bed sheets (*Plate 4.4*), blankets, mosquito nets, and curtains. Today these textiles no longer hold the importance that they once did for women upon their marriage since many of these items are purchased and commercially made.

The weaving skills of T'ai Lü women are no longer associated with their virtue in the sense discussed above, but have come to be regarded by men as an asset that women can contribute in supporting a family.

The Survival of T'ai Lü Weaving in Different Countries

Prior to the 1980s, the T'ai Lü in Thailand commonly avoided calling themselves Lü for fear of class discrimination. Despite such denial of identity, their textile traditions have survived more intact than those of the T'ai Lü of China and Burma. Is this a case of greater freedom of cultural expression in Thailand or more a need to maintain aspects of their culture in a new environment?

In China under communist rule the Lü experienced a period of cultural suppression which resulted in the widespread disappearance of home-woven fabrics, especially for personal dress, which were replaced by printed commercial fabrics. In recent years such suppression seems to have lifted and there are signs of a rebirth of cultural expression in the Sipsongpanna area. One of the expressions of this rebirth is in the production of handwoven textiles, but the weavers themselves are still reluctant to wear their products and produce them only for sale. In Don Thaen, Sipsongpanna, for example, women are weaving lengths of multi-purpose cloth for sale employing designs traditionally used for bed sheets (*pha lop*), banners (*tung*), and mattresses (*pha taeng salee*).

In Burma, the marketing of mass produced commercial cotton fabrics in Shan State during the period of British colonial rule was so successful that most villagers stopped weaving their traditional textiles and relied upon the commercial goods for everyday wear. Older women kept their traditional handwoven textiles for special occasions only.

In Laos the T'ai Lü initially migrated along the river courses of the Ou and Mekong in a natural migration pattern that may have commenced in prehistory. (*Plate 4.5*) The T'ai Lü of Luang Prabang province seemed to have enjoyed a high status and influenced local Lao groups. The classic woman's blouse of Luang Prabang made from imported Chinese satin or velvet and decorated with gold and silver yarns took its form from the T'ai Lü blouse. Many T'ai Lü weavers from Ban Pha Nom were employed by the Lao court to weave textiles for the royal court. Today Ban Pha Nom has become a tourist attraction where textiles from all over Laos are sold.

The T'ai Lü Cultural Resurgence in Thailand and the Return of a Strong Weaving Tradition

The assimilation of the T'ai Lü into national Thai culture was almost complete by the early post-war period. The T'ai Lü themselves sought to speak standard Thai, wore mainstream clothing, and built houses in Thai fashion. Some villages succeeded in eradicating any indicators of their T'ai Lü heritage.

The reversal of this process and the emergence of a profound interest in their own ethnic heritage came about as a direct result of outside forces, in particular the local educational centers, the local cultural centers, and civil servants in the north who were inspired by the Office of the National Culture Commission of the Ministry of Education to promote local cultures. Another strong influence was a growing market among tourists for handwoven textiles.

In response to these influences the T'ai Lü underwent a cultural revival and once again began producing tradition-inspired handwoven textiles. Rather than being extinguished it appeared as if their cultural traditions had merely lain dormant in the minds of the older generation.

T'ai Lü textile production initially received financial and moral support from many groups and subsequently has grown into a large cottage industry. In 1987 the Center for the Promotion of Art and Culture at Chiang Mai University (Work for the European Commission) (*Plate 4.6*), with support from the Chiang Mai office of the United State Information Service, arranged an exhibition of traditional Lan Na textiles and published a book called *Lan Na Textiles: Yuan, Lue, Lao*. This was the first event of its kind in Chiang Mai and had a profound influence on the fashion for wearing and collecting traditional textiles. The newly found knowledge caused a rush to purchase older textiles and within five or six years all of the older pieces had been purchased from the villages in the north, including the T'ai Lü villages. The disappearance of supplies of older textiles created a market for reproductions and, as will be discussed below, the adaptation of traditional designs.

Market Influences

The handwoven textile market in Thailand can be simplified into three main strata.

First, there is the high-class market. The interest in hand weaving by the élite in Thailand that has occurred since the mid-1970s is due to the patronage of Queen Sirikit and her leadership in the acceptance of handwoven garments for official wear. The style of wearing a traditional pha sin and carrying a basket has become the symbol of a high class woman. This is illustrated clearly in the Mae Fah Luang Foundation's annual festival in Chiang Rai which has become a stage for the upper classes to show off their beautiful textiles. Most of the textiles are produced by the most famous weavers and use the best raw materials with no skimping on cost. This gives some T'ai Lü weavers a wonderful opportunity to revive their most intricate designs and to receive handsome returns for their careful work. However, this élite market is quite small and in some cases designs have become over-decorated and the textiles have lost the crucial balance of attractive design associated with traditional T'ai Lü textiles.

The second stratum is the middle class market. This is the largest market and includes civil servants who wear traditional costumes to work on Fridays. The latter practice has been a great benefit to weavers and provided an important source of income. Many of the wearers have never previously worn traditional costumes and have had to learn how to do so. Previously the pha sin had come to be worn only by the lowest status of servants until it was lifted into the realms of both high and middle class.

The third stratum is associated with the lower-class market. Weavers today do not weave for themselves as they did in the past. Instead, the weavers wear cheap mass-produced clothing for work and occasionally keep a special example of their own work for show. The occasions when they have the opportunity to fulfill an order for a special textile are rare. The "bread and butter" income of most weavers comes from merchants who order low-cost synthetic fabrics for sale to the lower classes. The designs of these textiles are not necessarily T'ai Lü and the quality is poor.

General Aspects of Design Today

The main difference between the design of textiles today and in the past is that the weaver is no longer the designer. The buyer has become the designer and in many cases does not have a basic knowledge of design theory nor a knowledge of traditional T'ai Lü aesthetics. Today's T'ai Lü weaver readily weaves a design from another village, country, or ethnic group if there is a chance to sell such a textile. The ordinary village weaver does not have the capital to experiment with designs. It is a hand-to-mouth situation whereby designs made for a known market are preferred over the unknown. The weavers will take commissions even to the detriment of their traditional designs.

The exception to this general tendency is the group of textiles produced for the temple. These textiles, by and large, have maintained their original structures and functions and are still produced by women in most countries where the T'ai Lü live. Women can make merit for themselves in their next life by offering their handwoven cloths to the temple. These cloths include banners, small ritual cloths, sitting cloths, and other cloths needed for the everyday life of the monks. The only type of textile that is no longer being produced is the binders for the palm leaf book since the books are no longer produced.

Another type of cloth that is still woven by nearly all T'ai Lü households for their own use is plain white or natural cotton yardage. This is rolled up and stored until required. Sometimes it is dyed with indigo. Such cloth is made into clothing as well as used for linings and bed linen.

Changes in the Structure and Production of T'ai Lü Textiles in Thailand

The most commonly reproduced textile among the T'ai Lü in Thailand today is the *pha sin.*

One of the most notable features of these contemporary *pha sin* is that they are considerably larger than those made in the past. In fact, the traditional *pha sin* is so tiny that it will fit only a seven to ten year old child today. This is most likely a result of nutritional differences. Traditional pha sin were approximately fifty-five centimeters wide by seventy centimeters long. The modern ones are at least eighty centimeters wide by 105 centimeters long. The larger size ensures that there is plenty of fabric for tucking in and looking neat as well as to accommodate the larger size of the customer.

The greater size has given rise to the need to change the weaving equipment. At the same time, labor-saving devices have been introduced to speed production.

The traditional pha sin had a waistband made out of one piece of cloth, a main body section made out of two pieces of cloth, and a hem piece made out of another piece of cloth. These four pieces of cloth were joined together to make a tube. Today the weavers join only one or two pieces of cloth to make the tube. To allow the tube to be made out of a single piece of cloth, a loom has been designed in Ban Thung Mok, Tambon Chiang Ban, Chiang Khong district, to weave 160 centimeters wide. This loom must be worked by two weavers. This is not a common situation and most pha sin today are made from two pieces of cloth. Such *pha sin* still therefore require two side seams like traditional pha sin, but they are made with an integral waistband and hem piece. This was not practical in the past since waistbands and hems wore out easily and needed to be replaced, but now *pha sin* are only worn on special occasions and discarded when considered too old. In the past, old *pha sin* were used as under garments, bathing garments, work clothes, and even cut up to make diapers for babies.

By far the most obvious innovation in T'ai Lü weaving techniques is the use of vertical heddles (*Plate 4.7*). In the past supplementary weft and tapestry designs were introduced into the weave by hand with the use of shed sticks. This was slow but very creative and resulted in a great variety in the rendering of traditional designs due to the individual counting of warp yarns. The vertical heddle system is used to lift the warp yarns in a set pattern, thus speeding up production of *khit* (continuous supplementary weft), *chok* (discontinuous supplementary weft), and tapestry woven patterns and even enabling unskilled weavers to weave complex designs set into the heddles by a skilled weaver. The exact date of the introduction of these devices has not been recorded, but in Ban Don Chay, Bua district, Nan province, for example, the use of vertical heddles first began about 1985. This technique was probably introduced from Isan, where it has been in use since the 1940s. The use of the heddles creates set patterns which invariably repeat themselves, thus losing the innovative spirit of the traditional textiles.

The traditional T'ai Lü design for the *pha sin* was to have a red waist band, below which was a section of even horizontal stripes in green, purple, orange or red, then a band of special designs made in chok, khit, tapestry, and some weft ikat weave, and at the bottom more horizontal stripes. The band of special designs fell in the center of the textile which was on the hip when worn. The hem was very wide and made up at least one-third of the whole *pha sin* and was plain black, indigo, or green. Contemporary weavers have responded to market demands for greater patterned areas and altered the balance of the original design by enlarging the amount of space devoted to such designs while reducing the portion that is plain or striped.

The use of color in *pha sin* and other T'ai Lü textiles has gone through three major stages. During the nineteenth century most T'ai Lü weavers used natural dyes made from plants and animals to dye handspun cotton warps, wefts, and some silk wefts. The T'ai Lü upper classes at this time were able to purchase chemical dyes that were probably Chinese in origin to dye the bright pinks and purples which came into their palette prior to the aniline dyes of the West. They also had access to Chinese ribbons, gold and silver threads, and satins, which they used to decorate their handwoven textiles.

Aniline dyes were created in the late nineteenth century and began filtering into T'ai Lü villages in the early twentieth century as Thailand's trade with the West increased. These dyes were introduced in the form of ready-dyed yarns which were very convenient for the weavers and were considered attractive because they had bright reliable colors. Thus, a group of textiles employing such imported threads were woven for a period of over forty years dating from the early twentieth century until shortly after the Second World War. After this period weaving came to a low point as the T'ai Lü purchased newly available cheap commercial goods for everyday clothing.

The recent revival of handmade textiles, starting in the 1980s, differed in terms of color and the raw materials used—according to which of the three main market categories they were intended for. Textiles for the high classes employ silk dyed with both natural and aniline dyes and metal threads for decorations. Textiles for the middle-class market include cloth made of naturally dyed handspun cotton as well as cloth made of aniline-dyed commercial cotton, which is sometimes pre-dyed. The lower-class market requires the cheapest cloth, made from pre-dyed synthetic threads.

Other forms of traditional textile that are being reproduced today by the T'ai Lü include blankets, *pha lop, pha laep, pha chet,* pillows, and blouses. These textiles follow the general changes described above in their adaptation of size for modern use and the techniques for faster production.

There is also a new group of textiles being developed for new end uses, but employing tradition-based T'ai Lü patterns and designs. For example, shawls are being made using bed sheet patterns, *pha sabai* are being made for central Thai customers using patterns from *pha chet luang* and *tung*, and floor rugs and wall hangings are being made based on patterns from traditional *pha sin*.

Conclusion

The revival of T'ai Lü weaving in Thailand is especially interesting in that it has taken place largely because of outside national and international influences—forces that often lead to the disappearance of distinctive weaving traditions. It is important to recognize, however, that there are many differences between the textiles produced today and those made in the past in terms of how they look and their role in T'ai Lü society. In the past, textiles were produced primarily for local use and were an integral part of T'ai Lü society. Today they play a less important cultural role for the T'ai Lü and are more an export-oriented product made to suit external market demands rather than internal cultrual considerations. Thus, the new textiles may be important to the T'ai Lü, but this importance is more economic than cultural in nature.

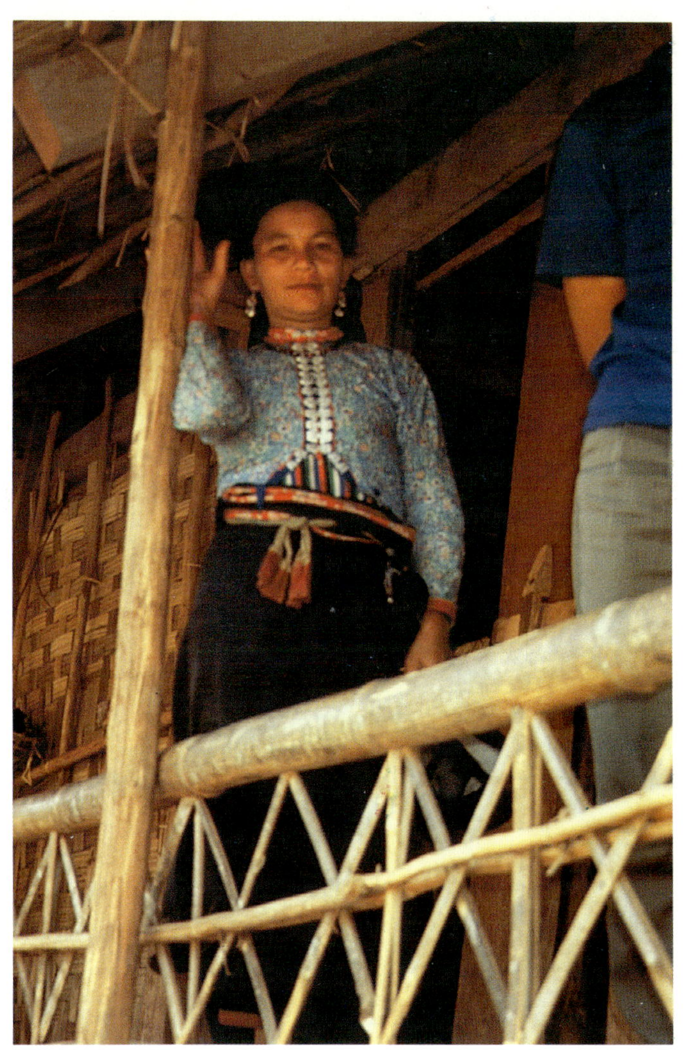

2.1. Kho-mú woman in Lai Châu province in traditional T'ai-inspired dress.

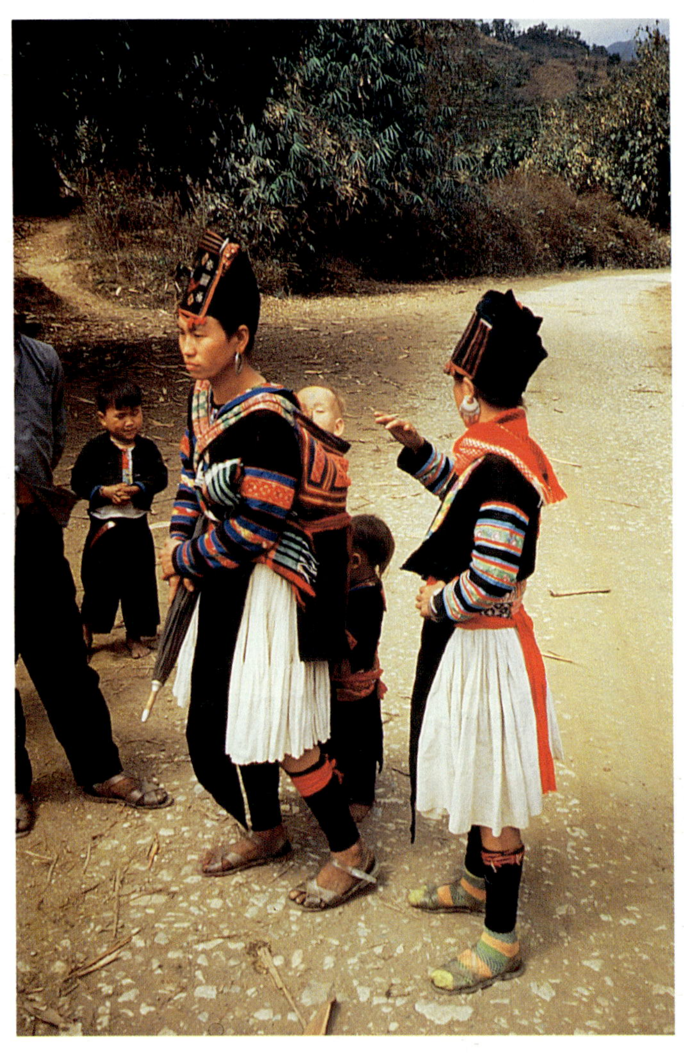

2.2. White Hmông women in Lai Châu wearing headcloths purchased from T'ai Dam that are woven in T'ai Dam style but worn in a distinctive fashion.

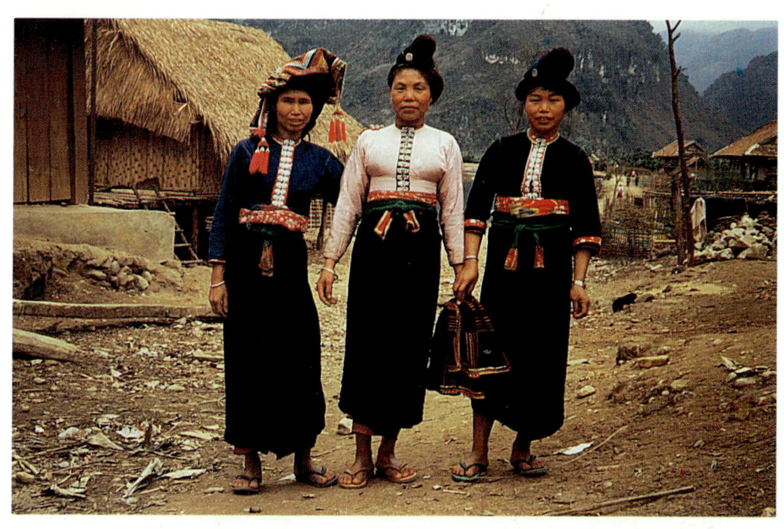

2.3. T'ai Dam women near Tuân Giáo, Lai Châu province, wearing traditional dress.

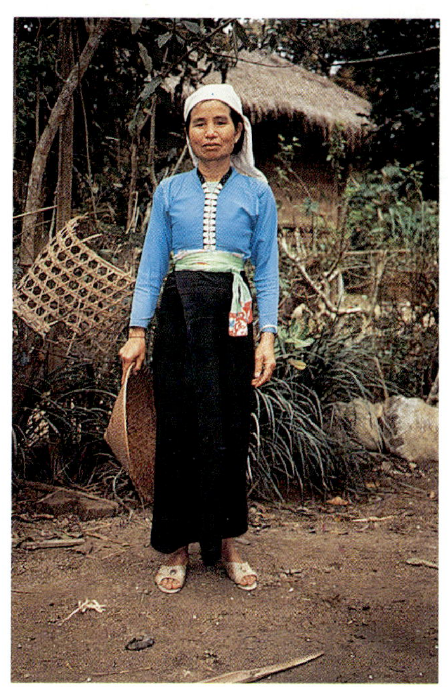

2.4. T'ai Khao woman of Ban Phuong Danh, Lai Châu province, in traditional dress.

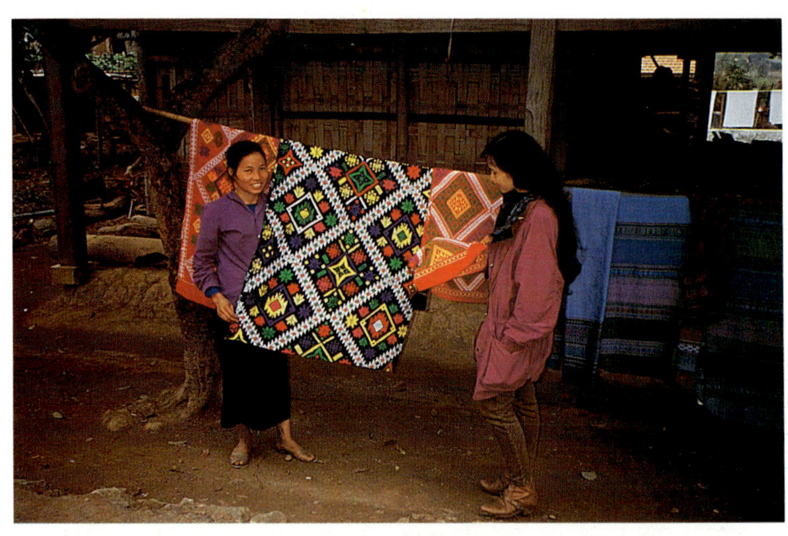

2.5. Cloth woven in Ban Lác, Mai Châu, for sale to tourists and buyers for the Thai market.

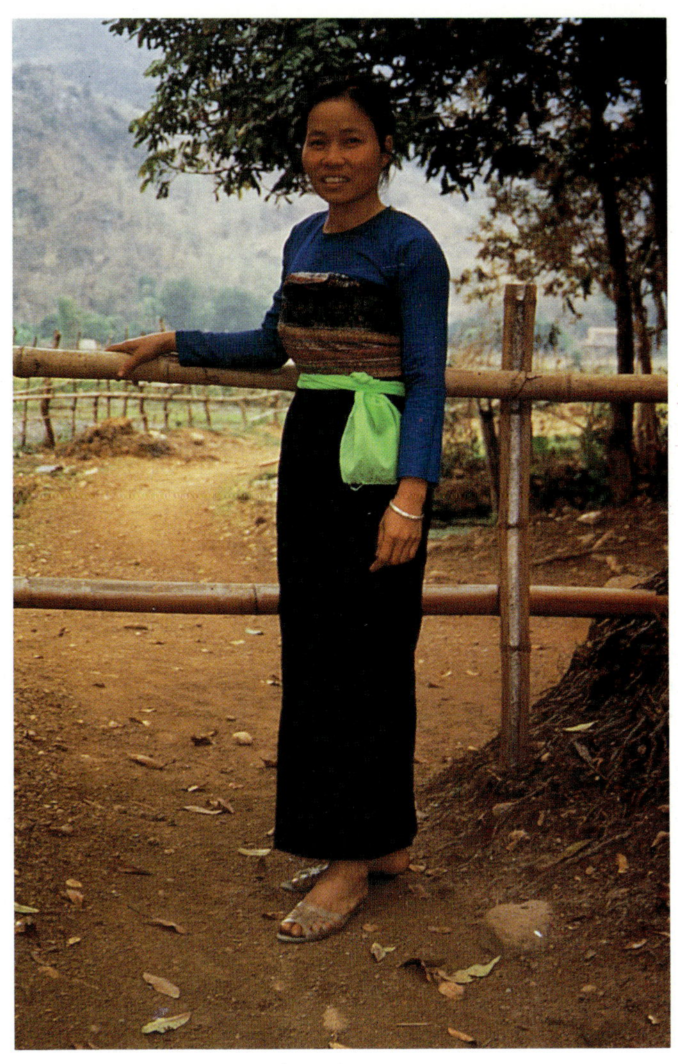

2.6. T'ai Dón woman of Ban Lác, Mai Châu, wearing dress similar to neighboring Muòng.

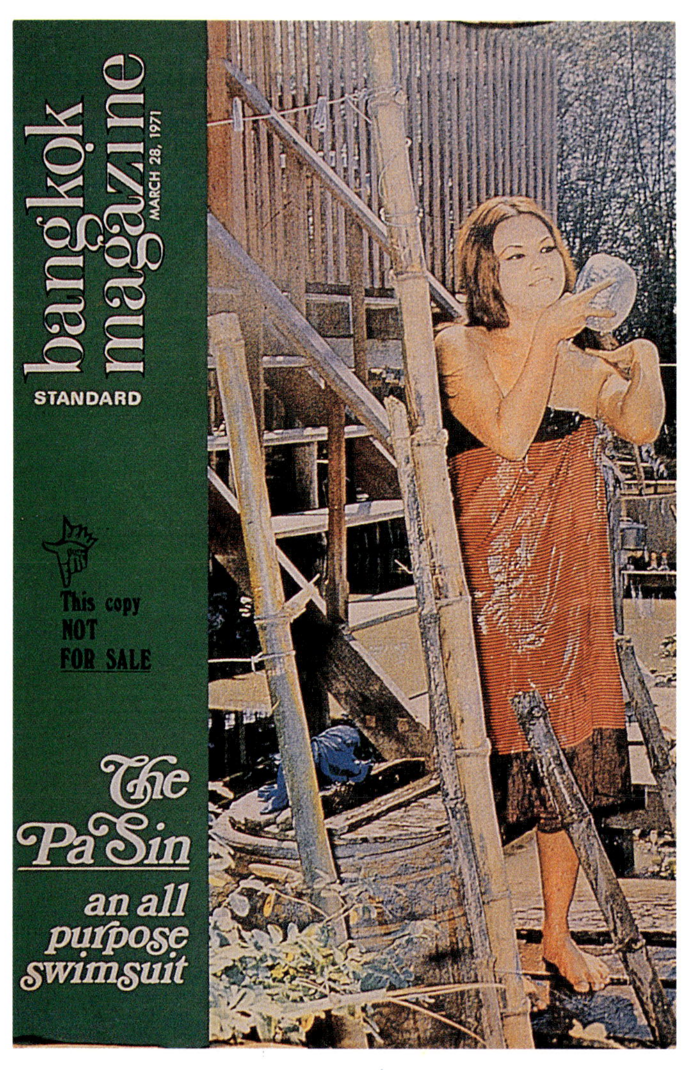

2.7. An image of the *pha sin* among urban Thais in the 1970s.

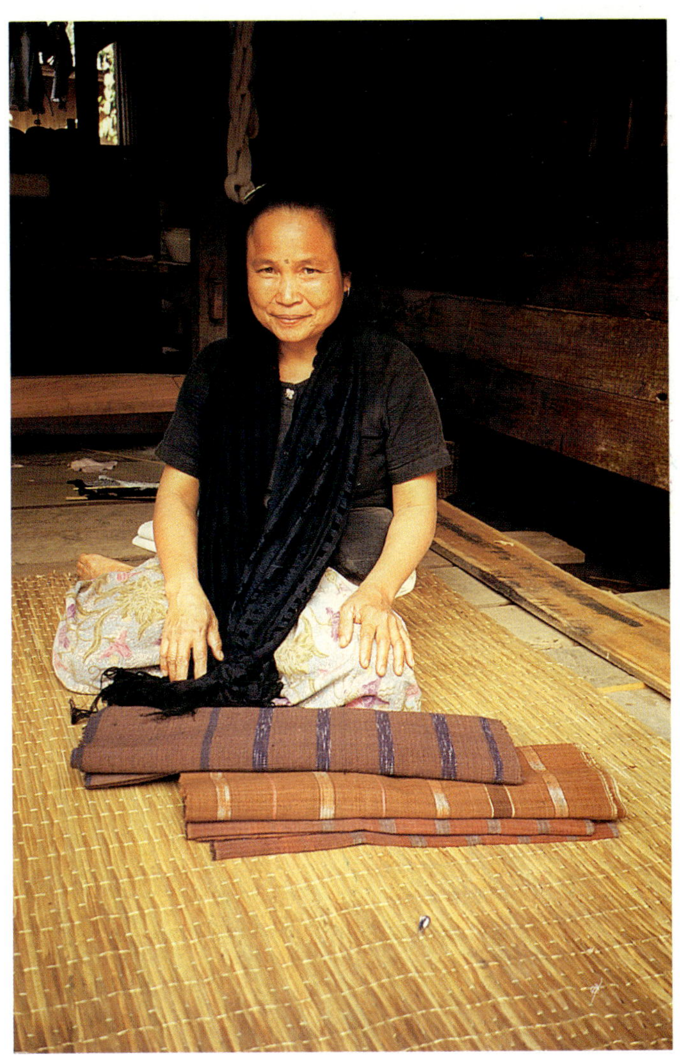

2.8. T'ai Yuan woman of Ban Kong Kaek, Mae Chaem, with cloth that was woven with support from the village weaving cooperative.

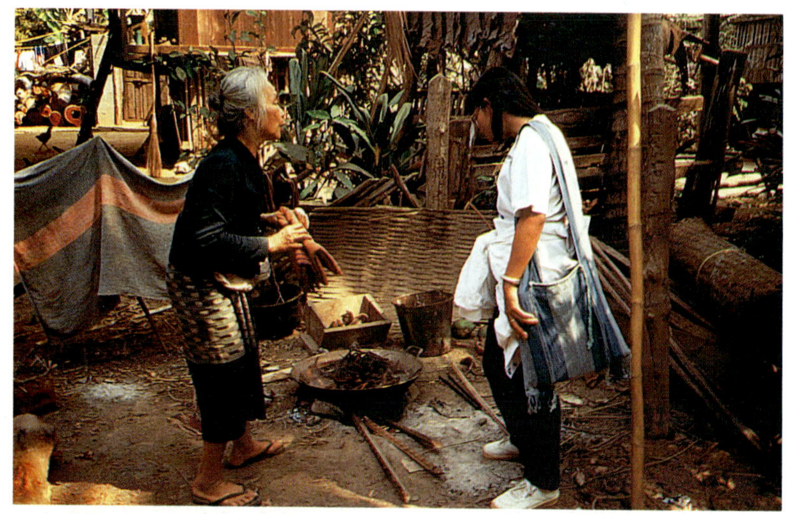

2.9. T'ai Yuan woman of Ban Kong Kaek, Mae Chaem, holding cloth she has recently woven for the village weaving cooperative, and discussing natural dyes.

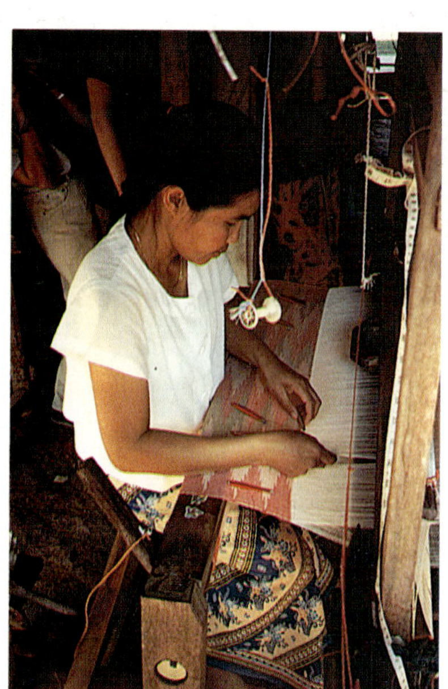

2.10. T'ai Lü weaver in Nan province producing cloth for Thai and foreign markets.

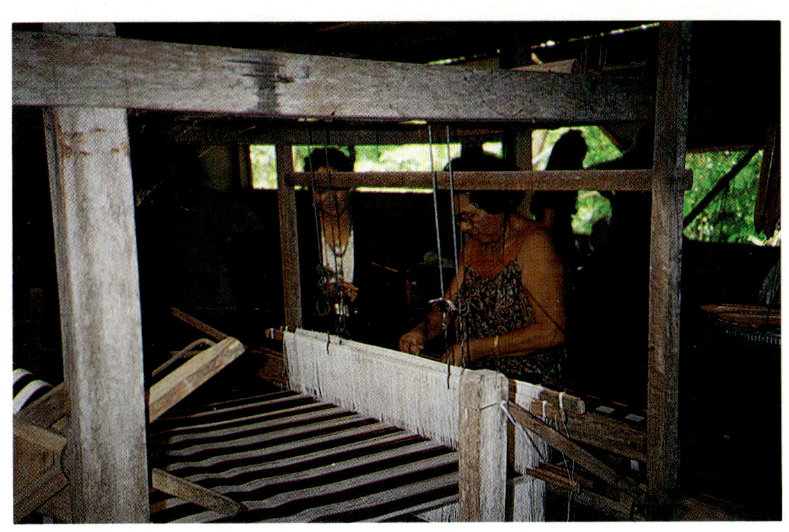

2.11. Weaver on Ko Yor discussing her plans to give up commercial weaving.

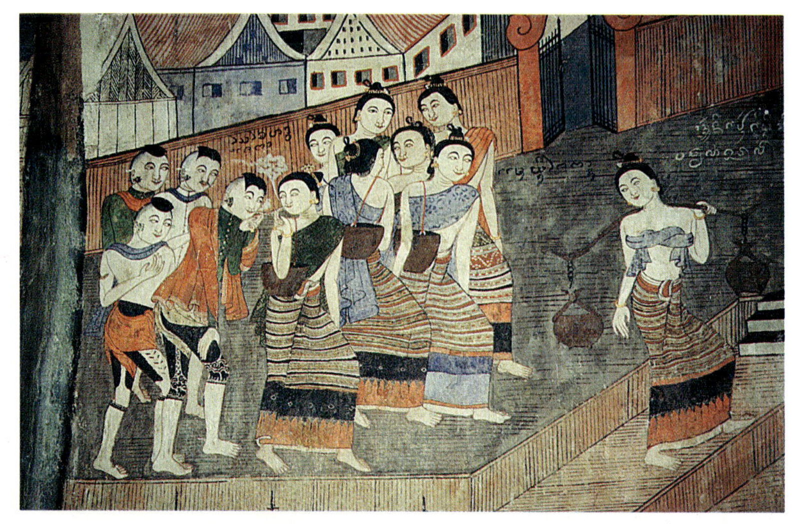

2.12. Mural from Wat Phumin, Nan, depicting people in traditional *Lan na* dress.

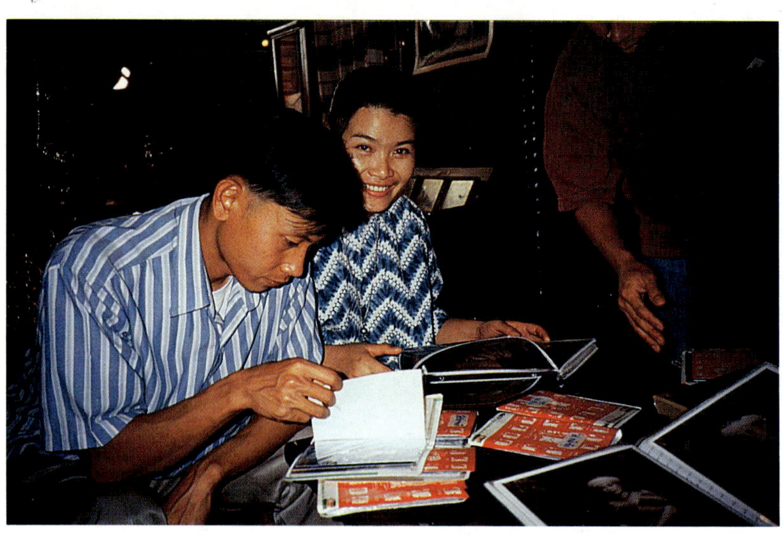

2.13. Customers at a portrait studio in Chiang Mai's Night Bazaar selecting traditional costumes to wear.

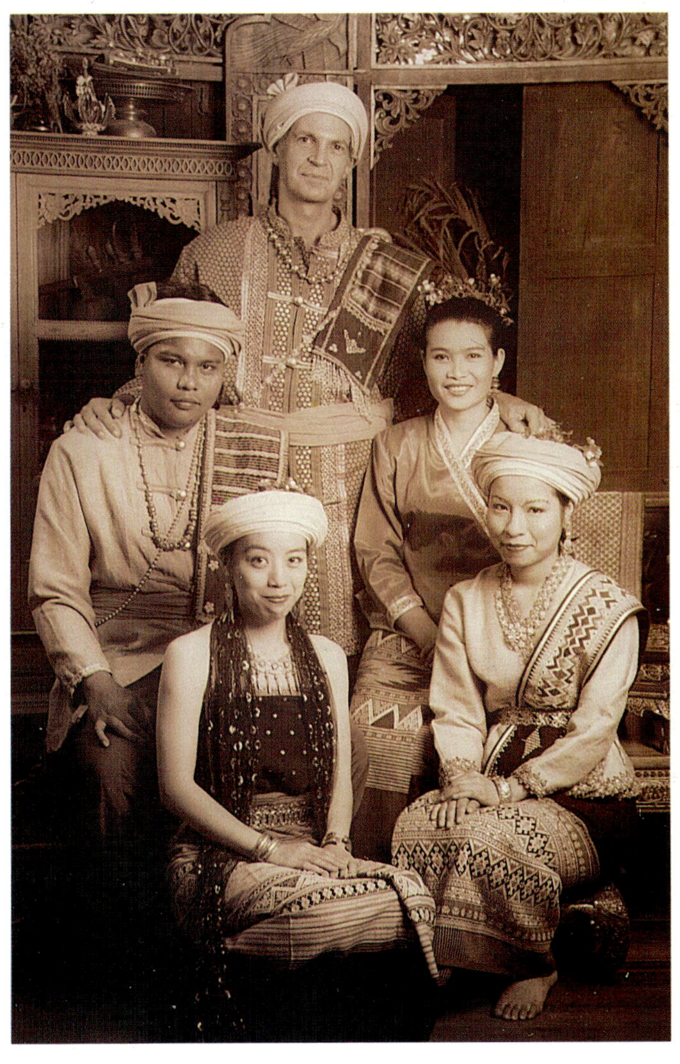

2.14. Portrait of the author and friends in traditional northern dress taken at a Chiang Mai Night Bazaar studio.

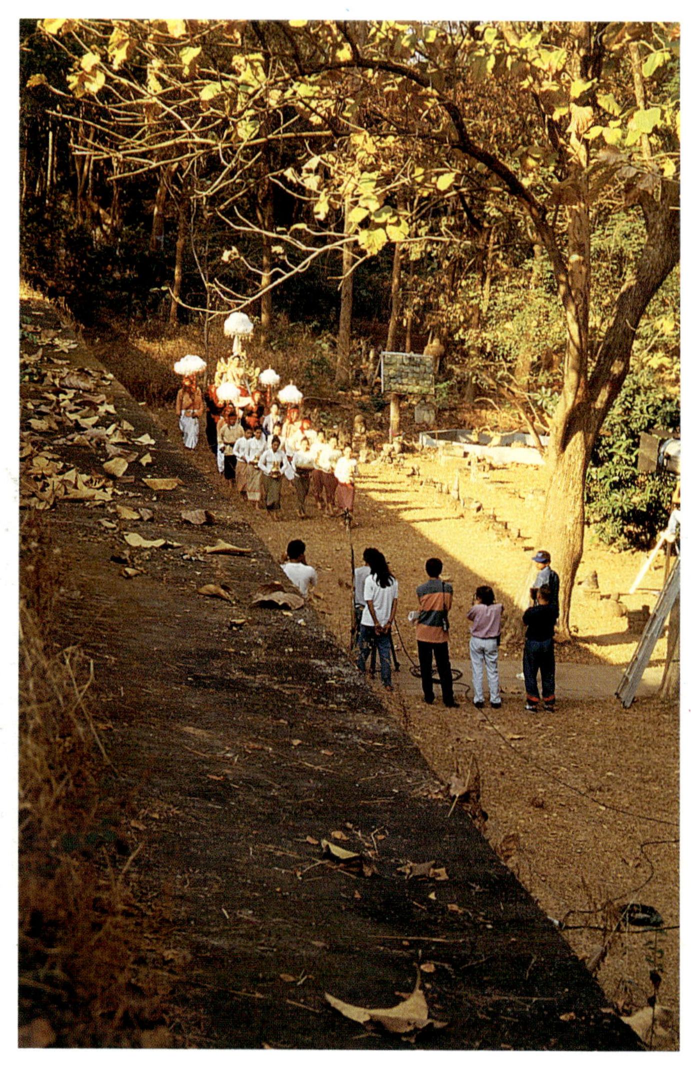

2.15. Filming of a historical costume drama for television at Wat U Mong, Chiang Mai.

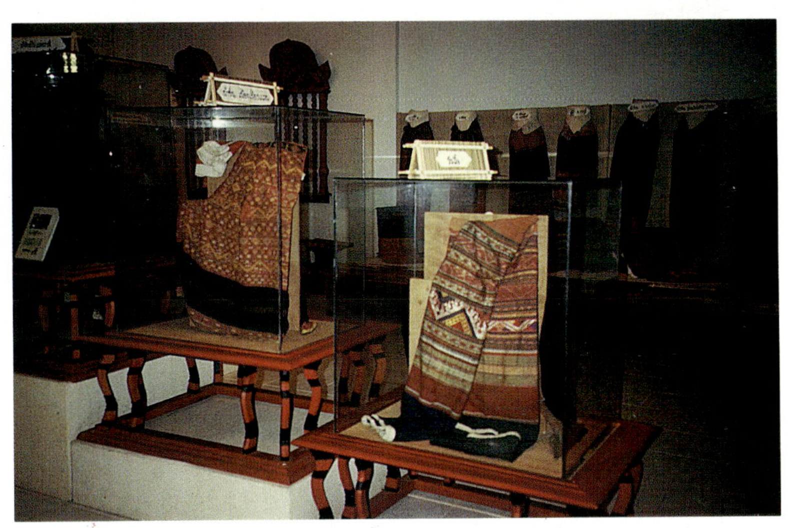

2.16. Private museum in Phrae associated with a company dealing in new traditionally-inspired handwoven cloth.

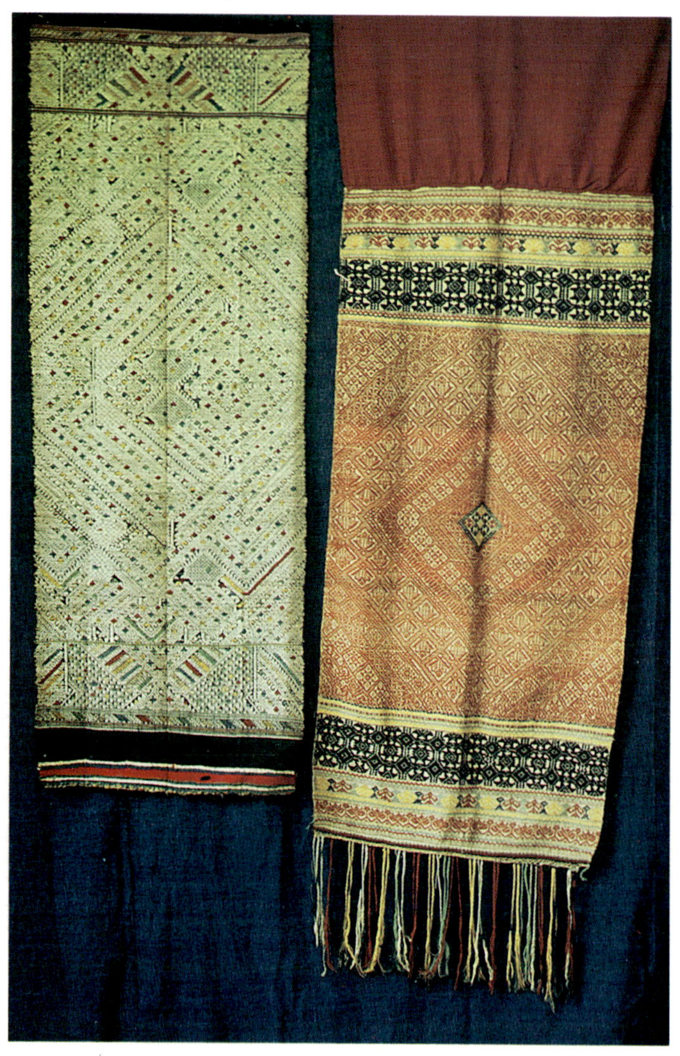

3.1. Left: *Pha khan soeng* from Huaphanh made by T'ai Daeng as a healing cloth (early twentieth century). Right: *Pha phi mon* from Huaphanh made by T'ai Daeng as a shaman's cloth (late nineteenth century).

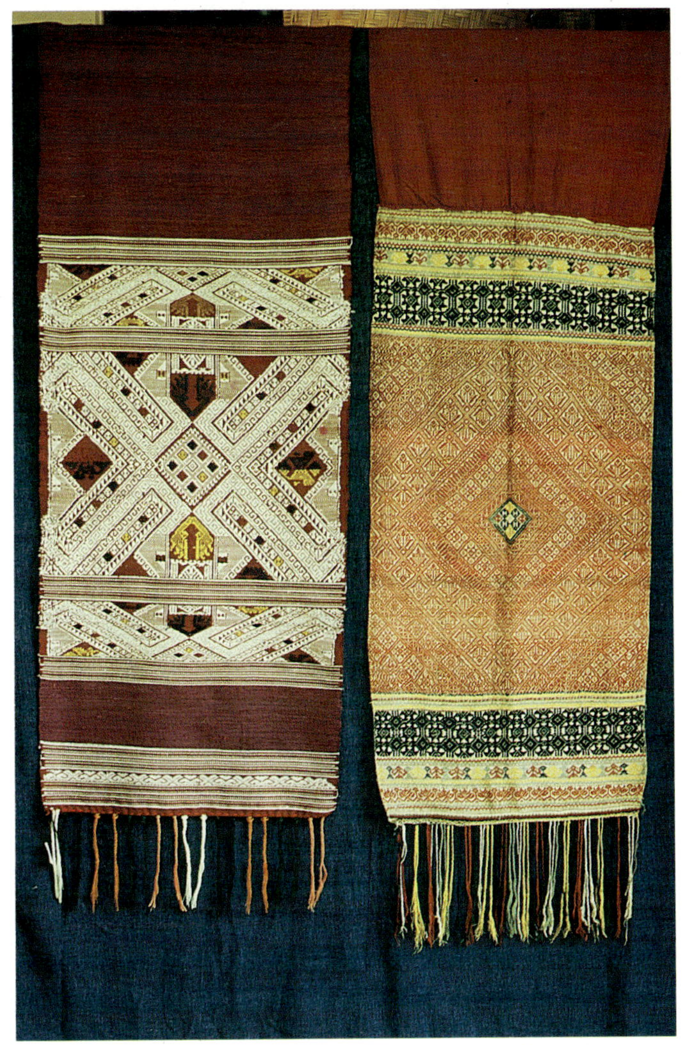

3.2. Left: New *pha biang* made in Vientiane with designs from *pha khan soeng* (1995). The rendering of the design is modern, using synthetic dyes and is not detailed. Right: *Phan khan soeng* from Huaphanh made by T'ai Daeng as a healing cloth (early twentieth century).

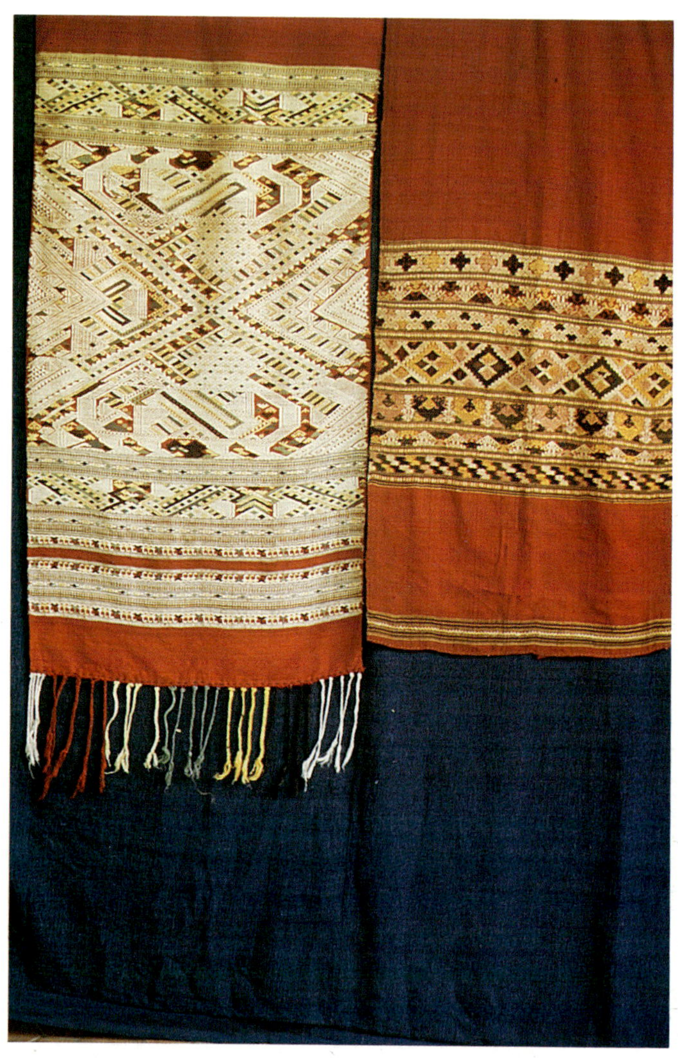

3.3. Left: New *pha khan soeng* from Huaphanh made in the old tradition with natural dyes and homespun silk by T'ai Daeng as a healing cloth (early twentieth century).

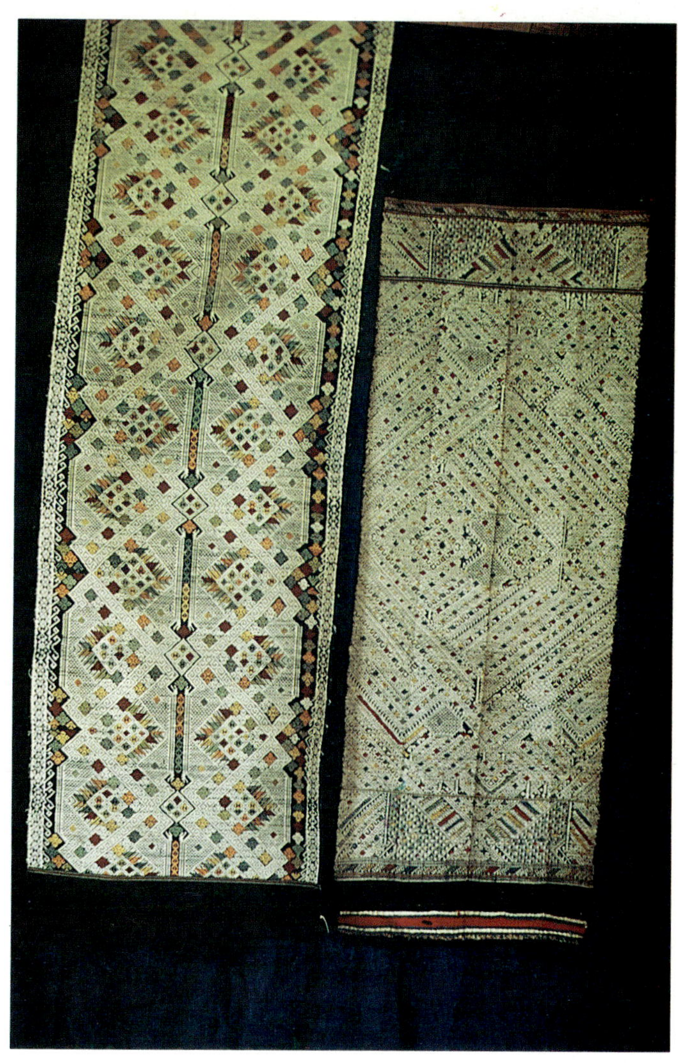

3.4. Left: New *pha biang* from Vientiane made with designs from *pha phi mon* (1995). Right: *Pha phi mon* from Huoa Phan made by T'ai Daeng as a shaman's cloth (late nineteenth century).

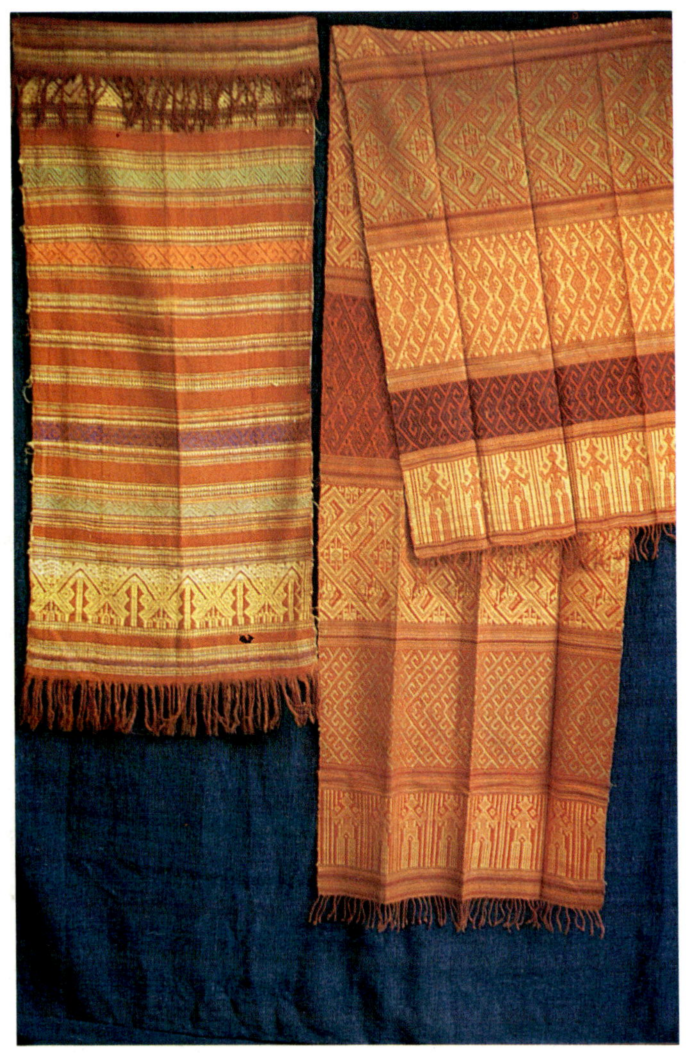

3.5. Left: *Pha phae kep* from Xiengkhuang made by T'ai Phuan as a man's cloth (mid-twentieth century). Right: *Pha bing* from Isan made by T'ai Phuan as a woman's cloth (mid-twentieth century).

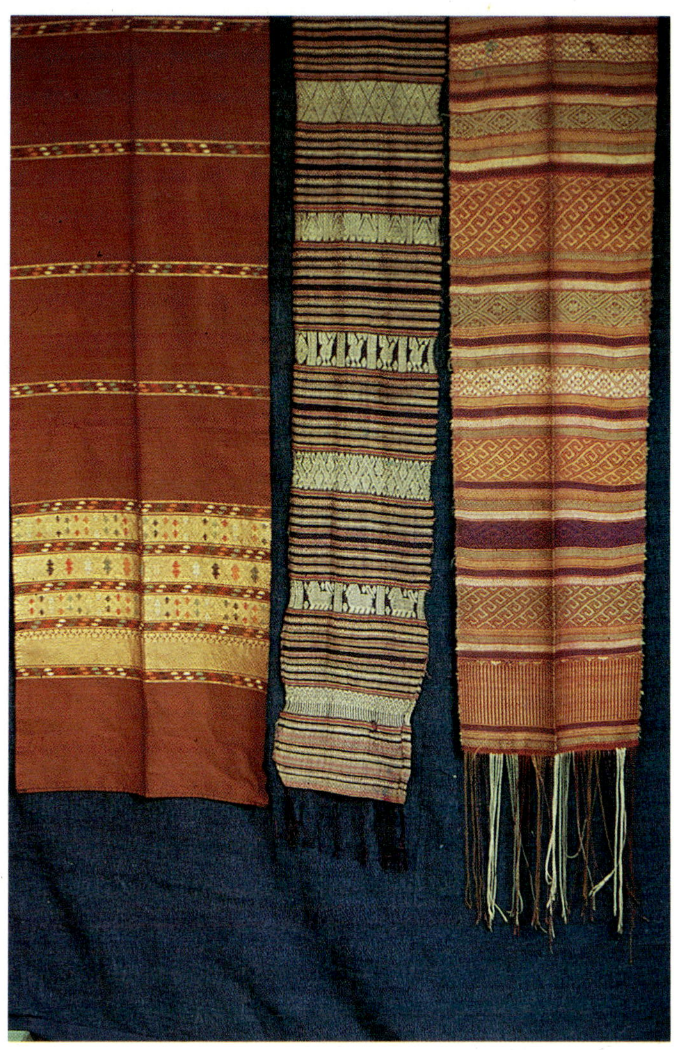

3.6. Left: Silk *pha biang* from Luang Prabang (late twentieth century). Center: Silk *pha biang* from Luang Prabang made in the style of a *pha phae kep* (early twentieth century). Right: Silk *pha bing* from Savanakhet made by Phutai (mid-twentieth century).

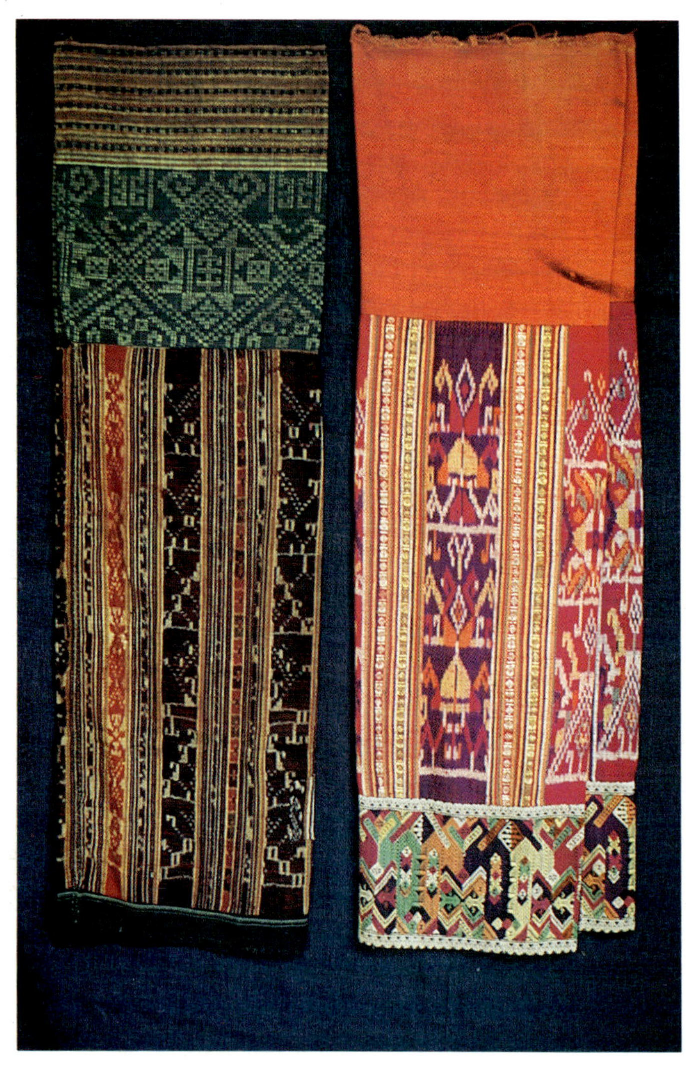

3.7. Left: *Sin mi hoa buan* from Huaphanh made by T'ai Daeng (late nineteenth century). Right: *Sin me teen chok* from Bolikhamxai made by T'ai Moei (late twentieth century).

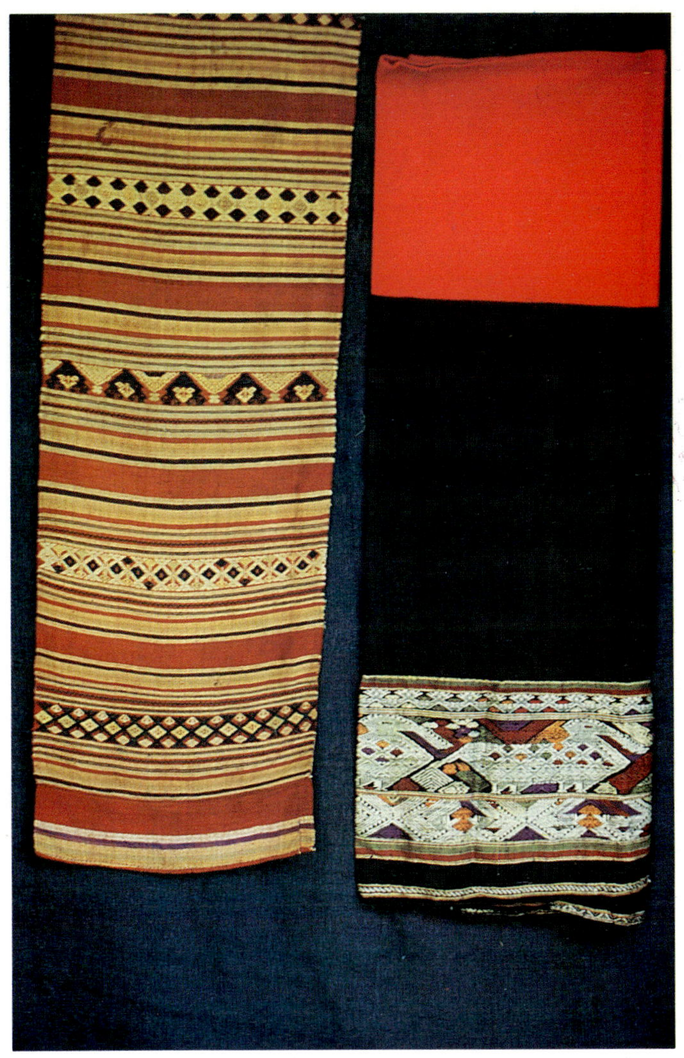

3.8. Left: All-purpose cloth from Huaphanh made by T'ai Daeng (mid-twentieth century). Right: *Sin tin yai* made by T'ai Daeng from Huaphanh (late twentieth century).

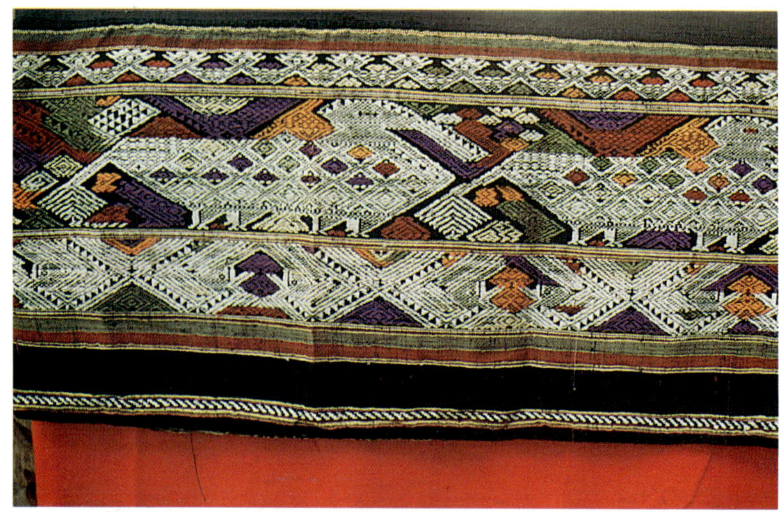

3.9. Detail of a hem piece from a *sin tin yai* made by T'ai Daeng from photo 3.8 showing the dark blue, red, and green stripes that identify this as a hem piece.

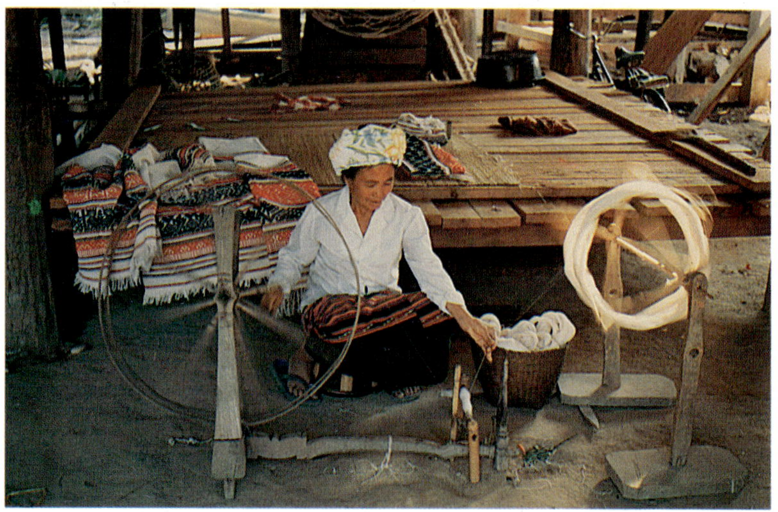

4.1. T'ai Lü spinner in Ban Hat Bai, Chiang Khong district, Chiang Rai province. The T'ai Lü in this community migrated from Laos. The women still wear traditional *pha sin* (tubeskirts).

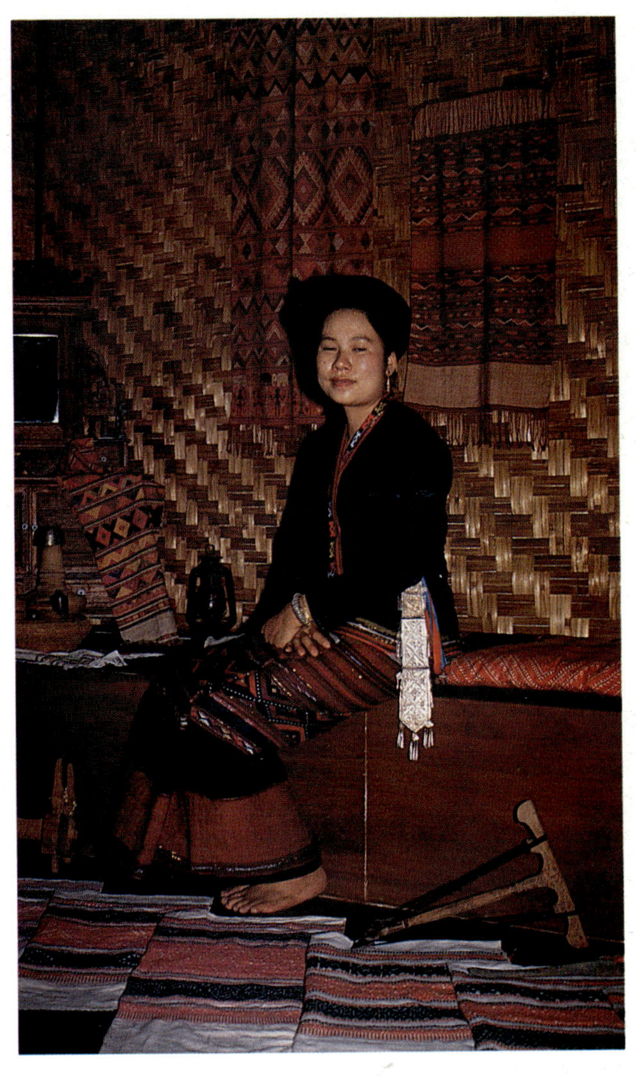

4.2. T'ai Lü weaver from Ban Lai Thung, Thung Chang district, Nan province. The costume is *muang ngaen* style.

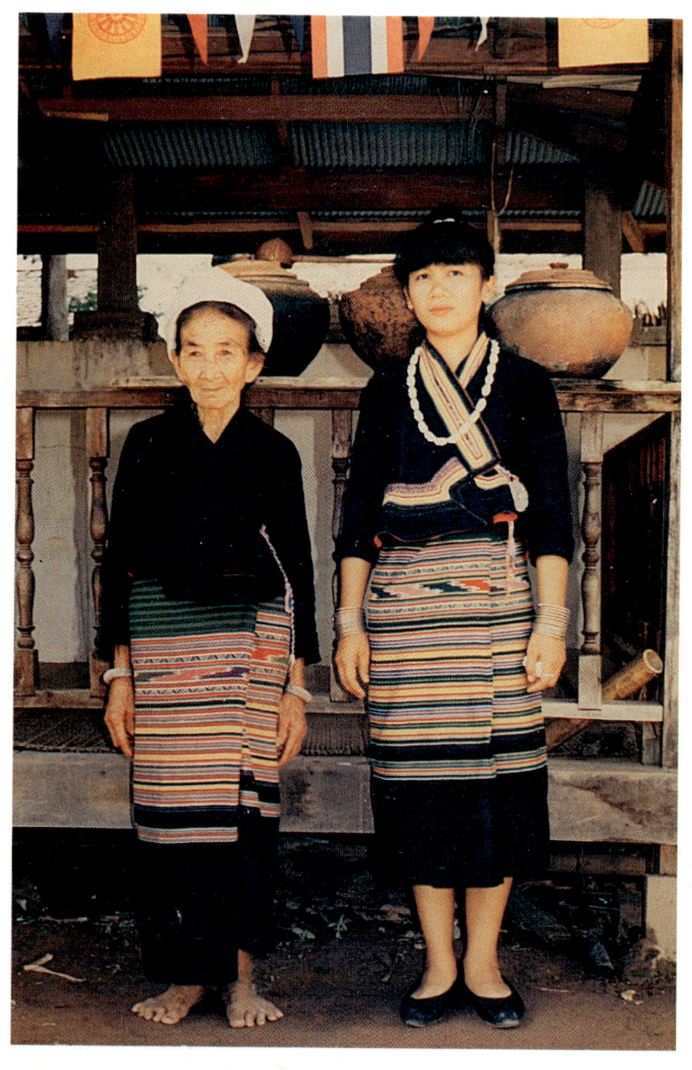

4.3. T'ai Lü women's costumes from Ban That, Chiang Kham district, Phayao province.

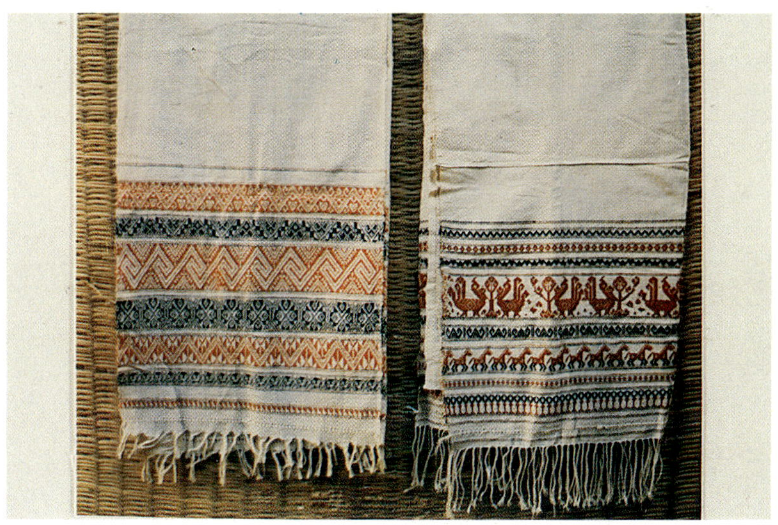

4.4. T'ai Lü bed sheets: left from Chiang Khong, Thailand; right from Chiang Pom, Sipsongpanna, China.

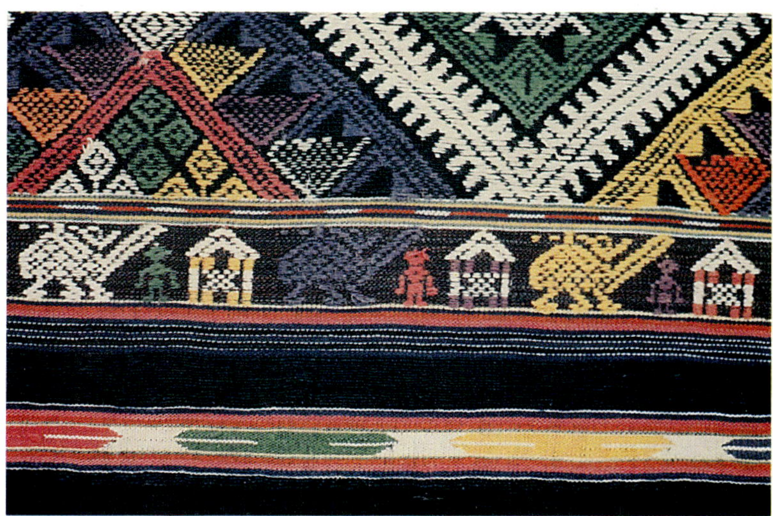

4.5. Helicopters, houses, and humans appear as motifs on T'ai Lü *pha sin* from Ban Na Lae, Laung Nam Tha, Laos.

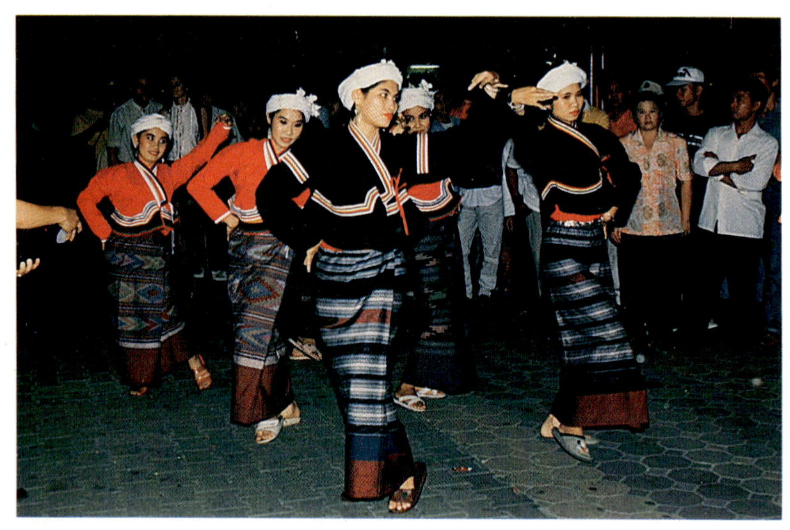

4.6. Chiang Mai University students in T'ai Lü cultural performance.

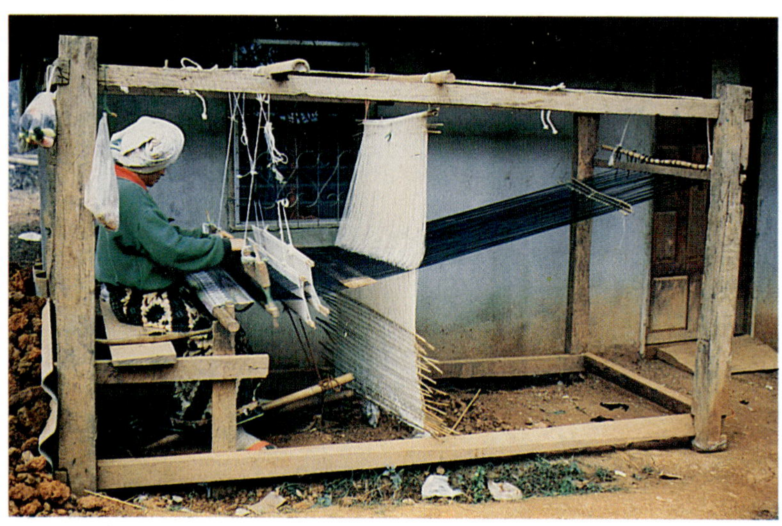

4.7. Vertical heddles that help make the weaving faster. Ban Hat Bai, Chiang Khong district, Chiang Rai province.

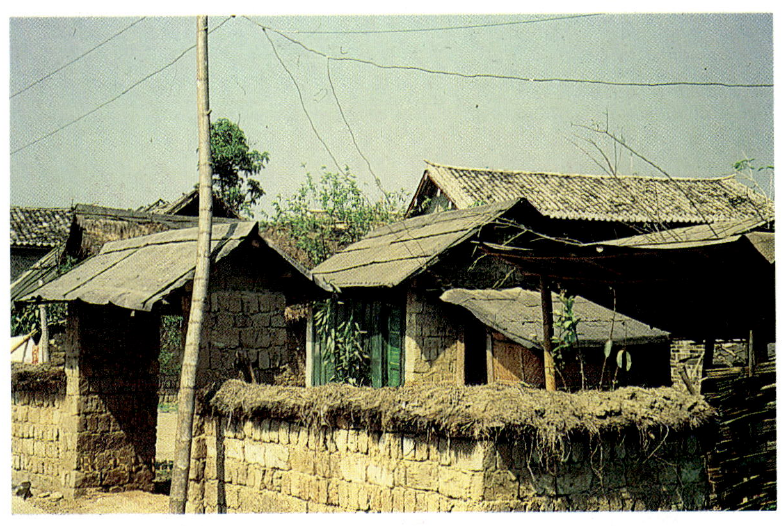

5.1. The T'ai Mao community of Muang Mou Luang, Burma.

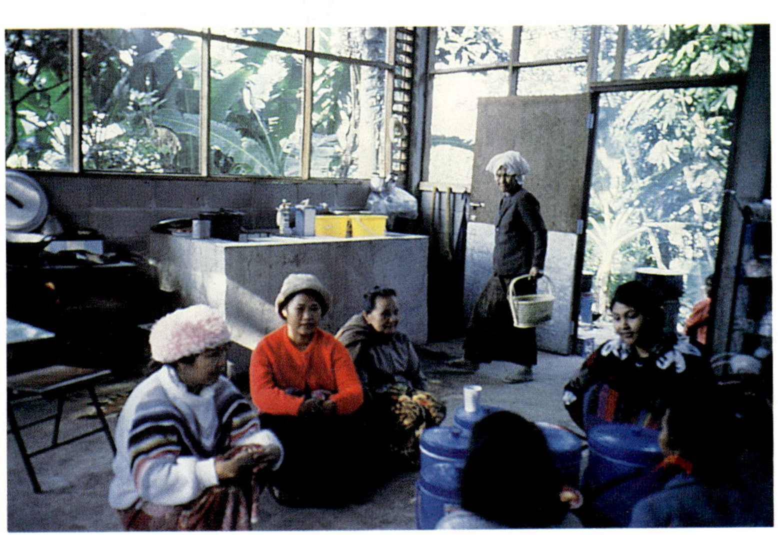

5.2. T'ai Yai in Ban Mai, Fang district, Chiang Mai province, Thailand.

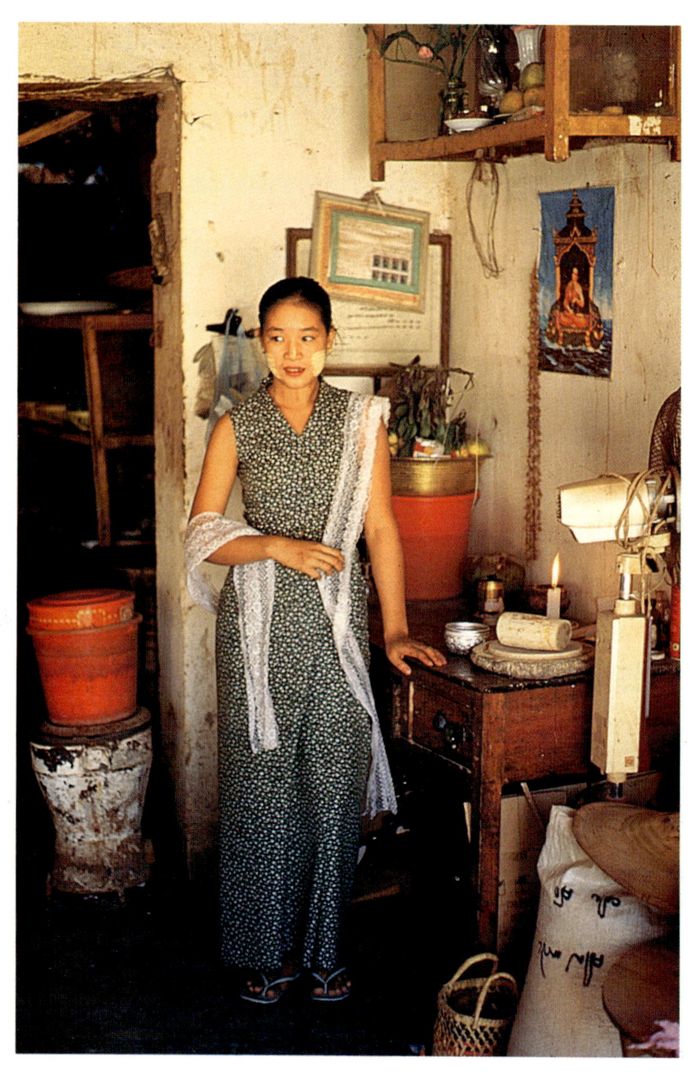

5.3. T'ai Mao woman dressed in contemporary Burmese fashion.

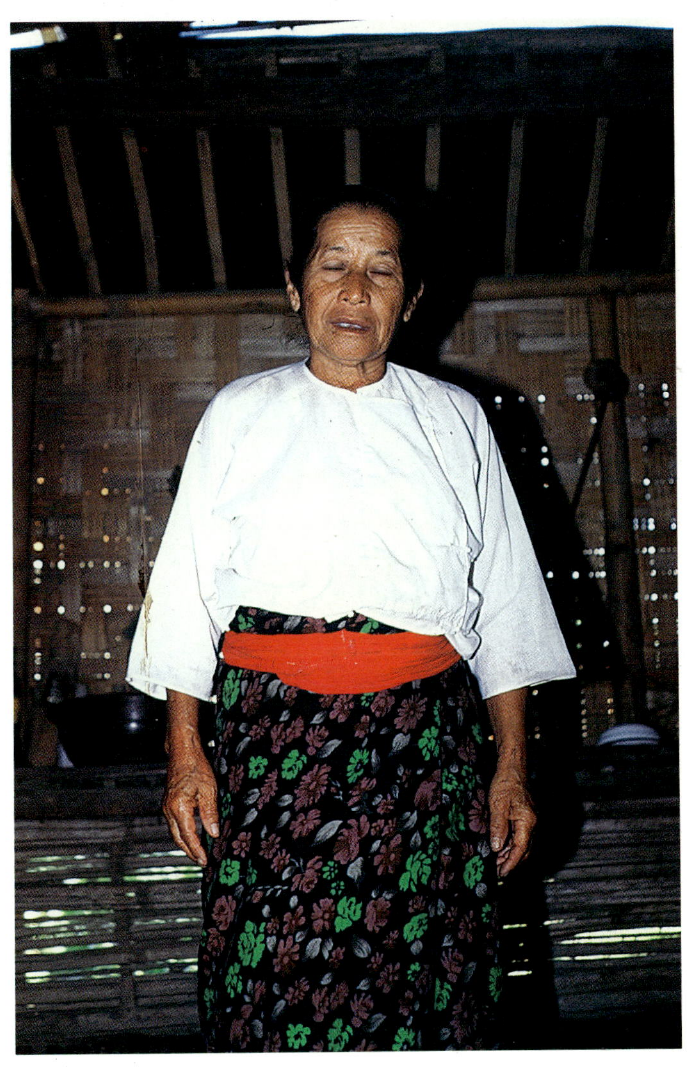

5.4. T'ai Mao woman wearing Burmese style clothing, but with a red sash around her waist in T'ai Mao fashion.

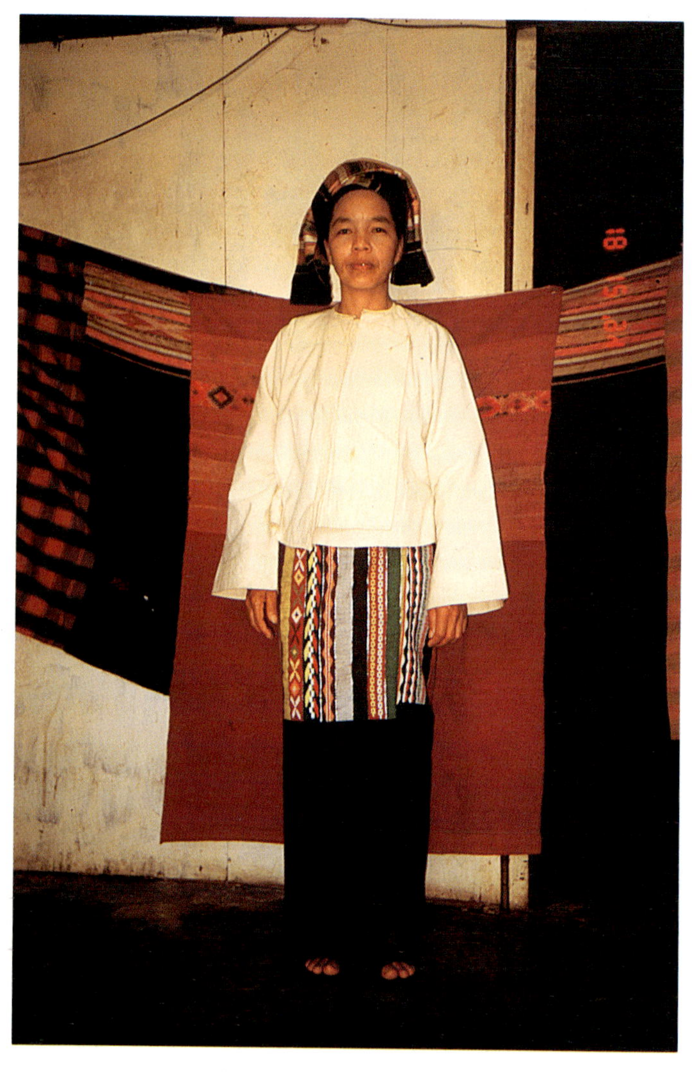

5.5. Woman wearing a T'ai Mao skirt decorated with *naka* scale designs.

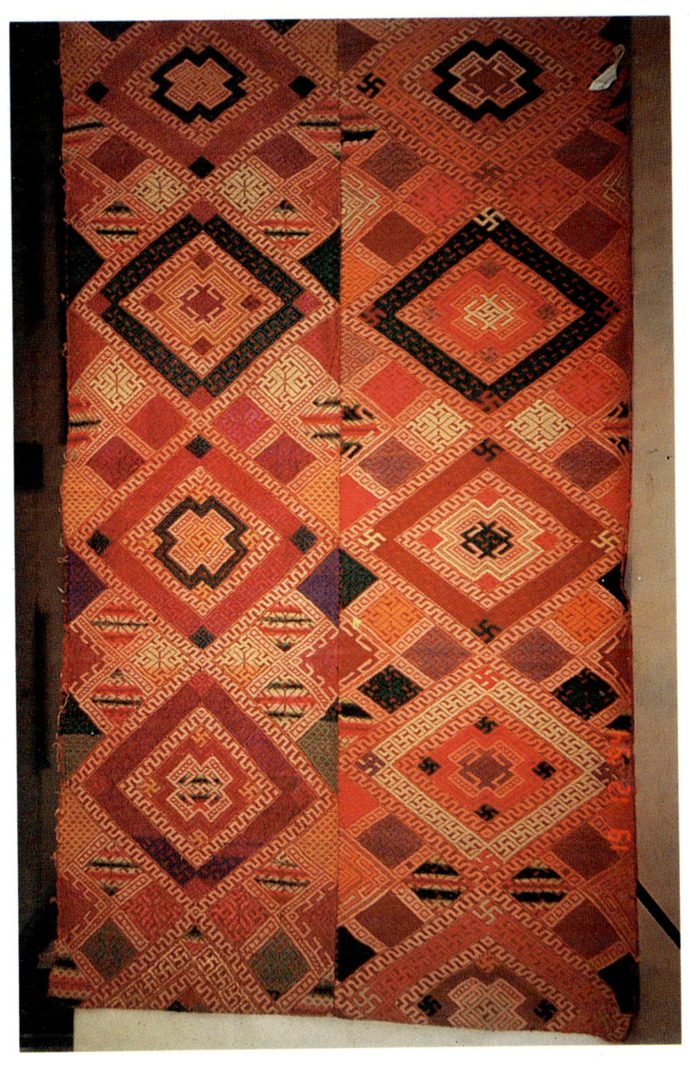

5.6. Detail of *naka*-scale designs from a T'ai Mao textile, Pangkam village, Jelan, Burma.

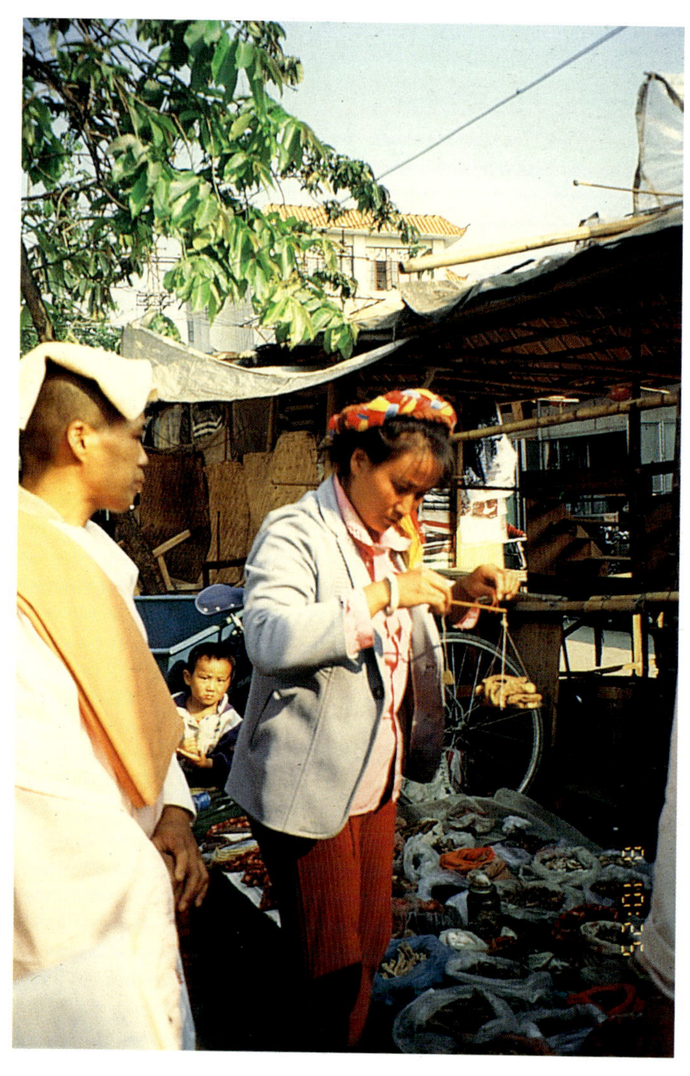

5.7. T'ai Mao Buddhist nun in Burma wearing characteristic T'ai Mao yellow sash over a Burmese-style pink robe.

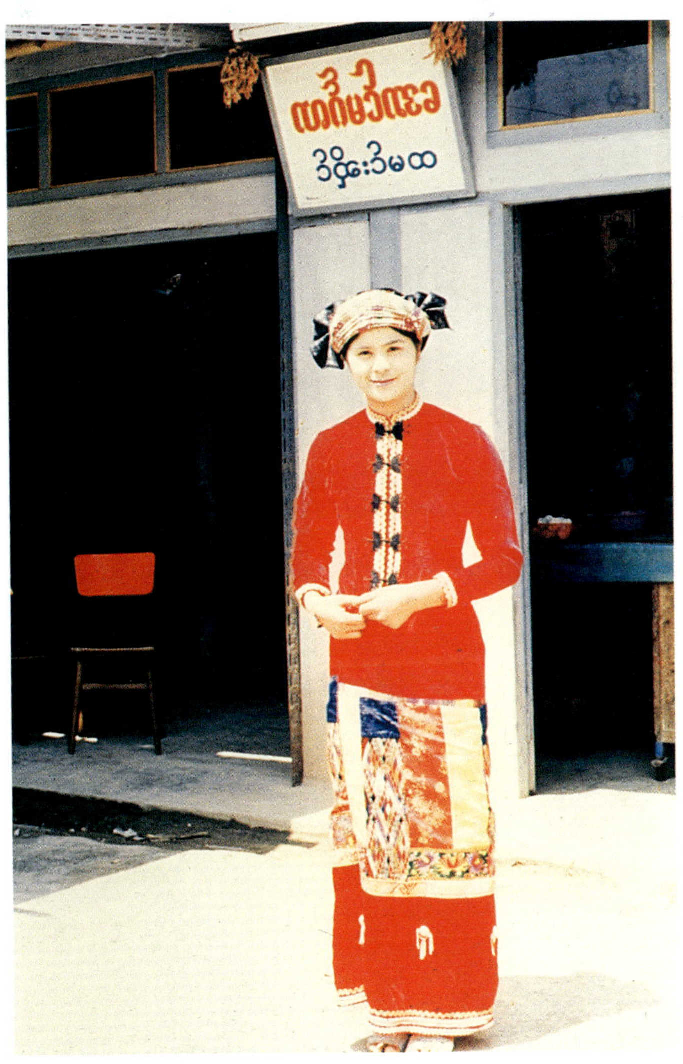

5.8. T'ai Mao woman wearing a traditional T'ai Mao costume associated with upper-class women.

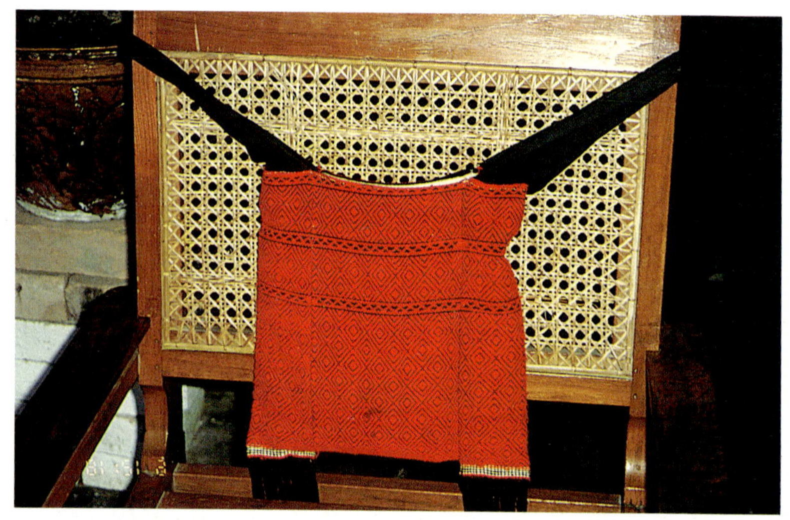

5.9. Contemporary T'ai Mao shoulder bag, Muang Nam Khung, Burma.

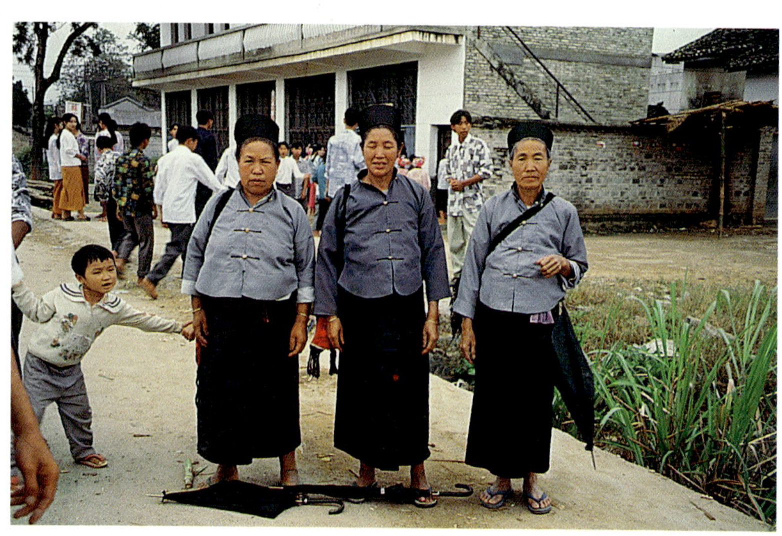

5.10. T'ai Mao women in distinctive T'ai Mao traditional dress, Muang Khorn (Muntzi), China.

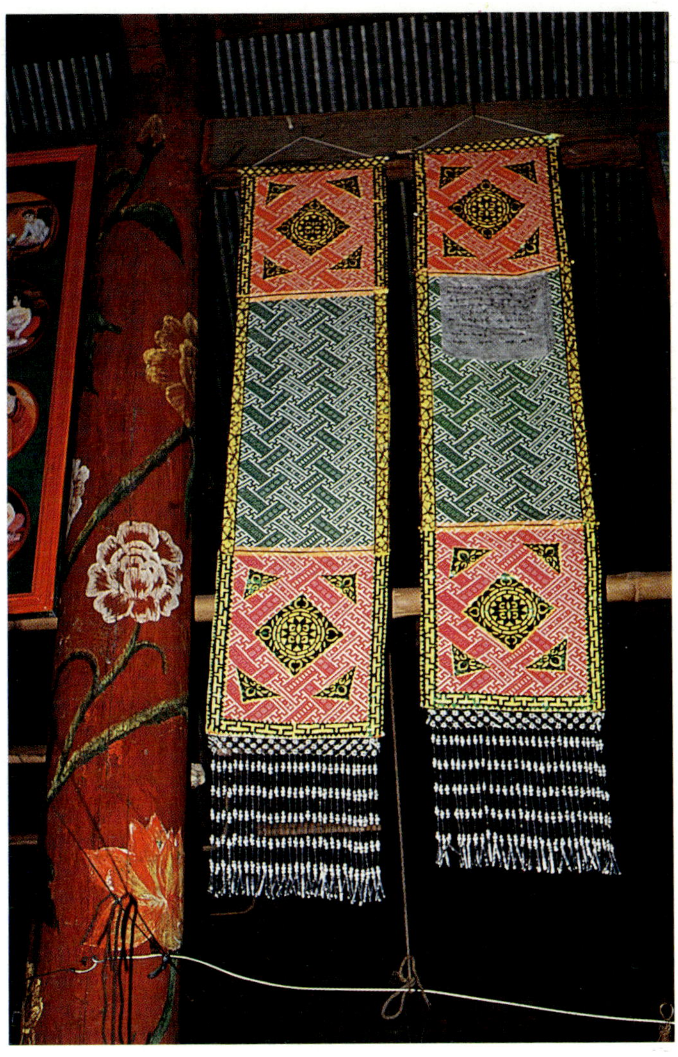

5.11. Contemporary T'ai Mao *tung* made of a piece of commercial Chinese cloth decorated with pieces of T'ai Mao woven cloth.

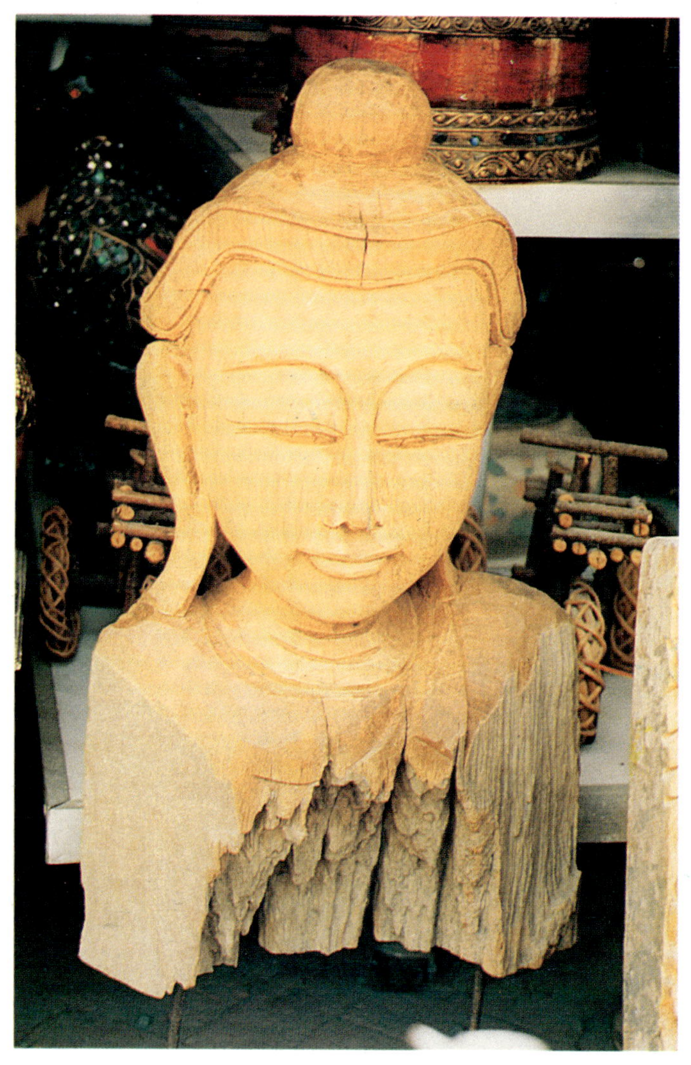

6.1. Ban Thawai, Buddha image carved of old teak (1995).

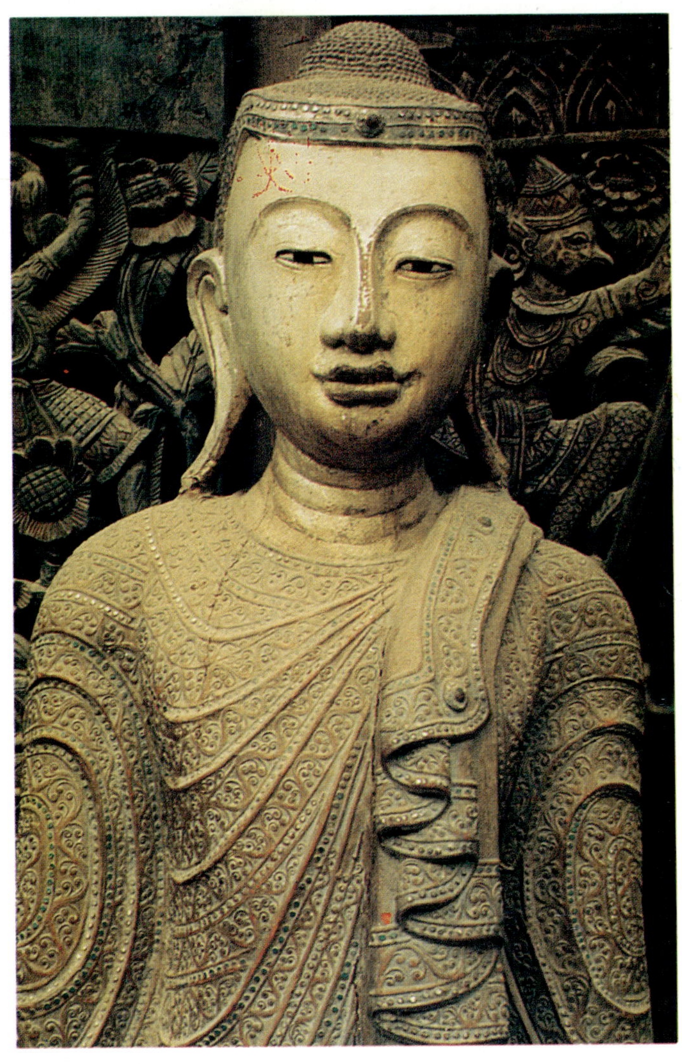

6.2. Ban Thawai, Burmese style Buddha image, decorated in pattern of carved embossed lines (1991).

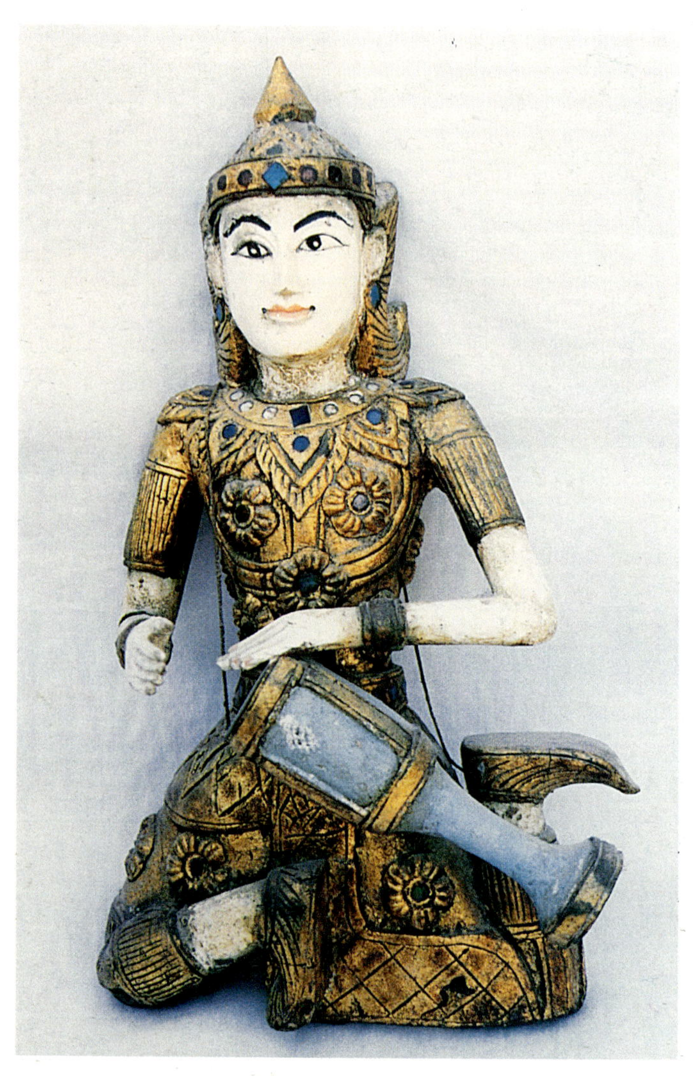

6.3. Ban Thawai, gilded figurines of traditional Thai musicians (late 1970s).

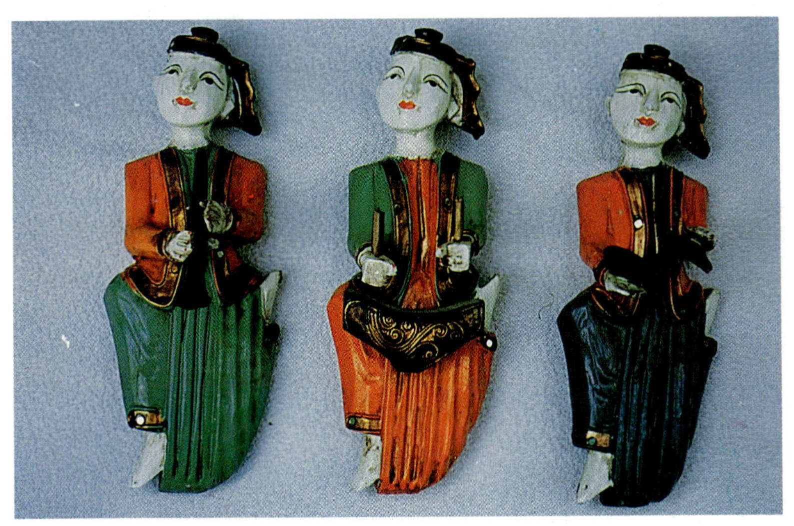

6.4. Ban Thawai, painted figurines of traditional Thai musicians (1996).

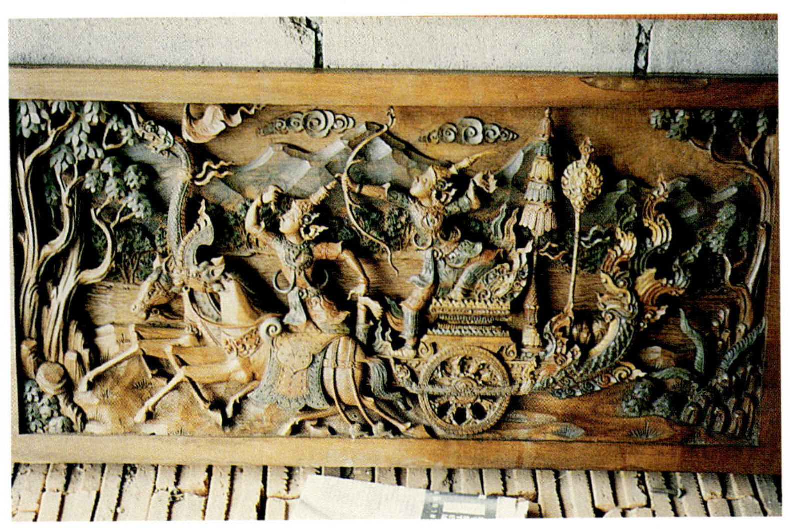

6.5. Ban Thawai, relief with Ramakien (Thai Ramayana) theme (1992).

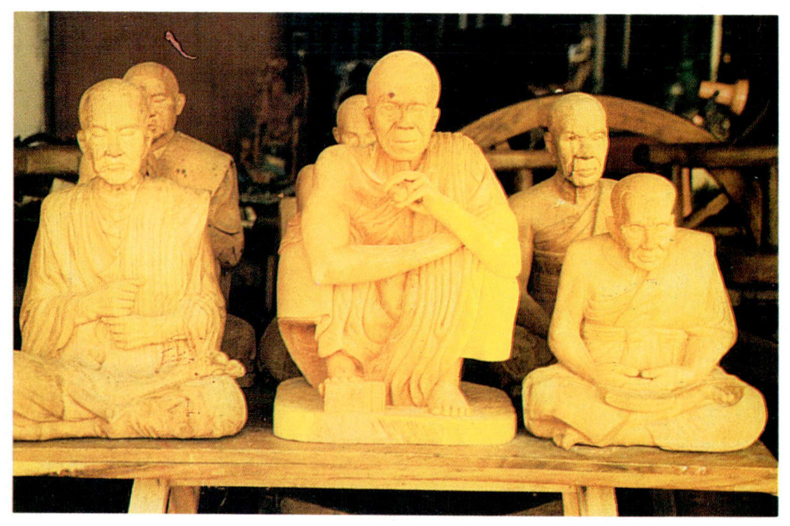

6.6. Ban Thawai, sculpture of Luang Pho Koon (center), a venerated northeastern monk (1995).

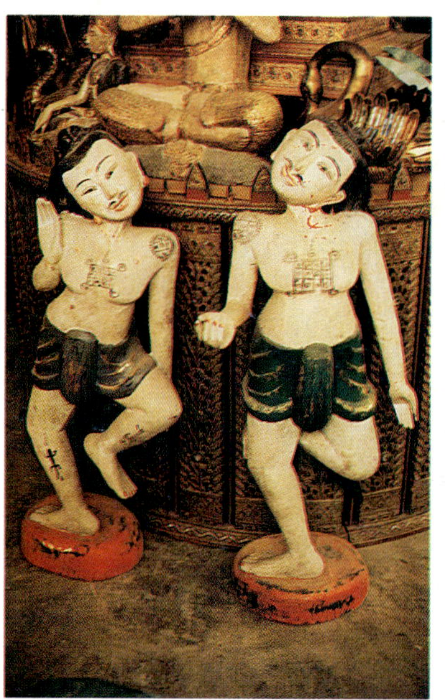

6.7. Ban Thawai, figures of Burmese dancers (1992).

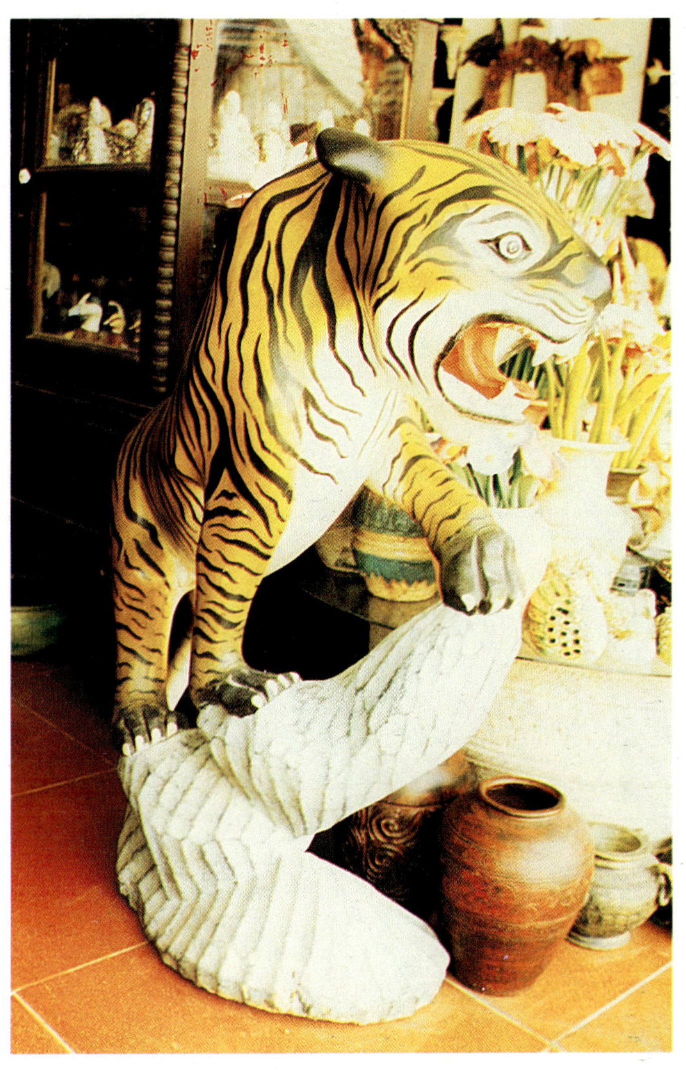

6.8. Ban Thawai, sculpture of tiger in shop in market (1996).

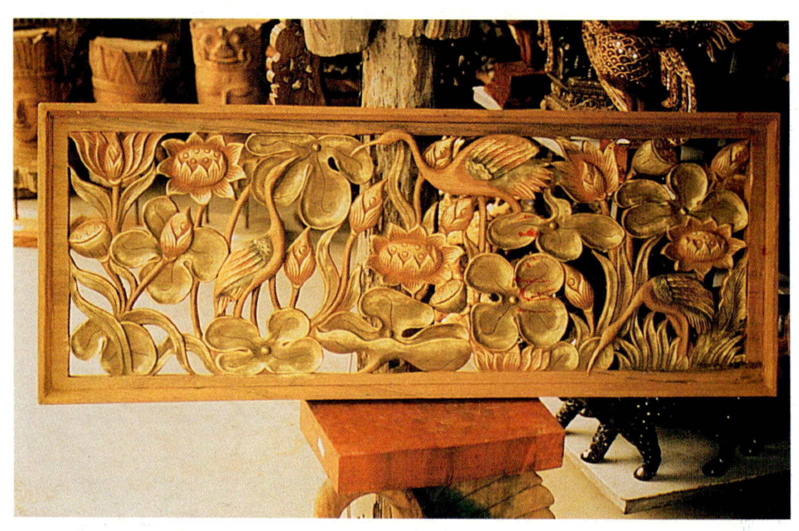

6.9. Ban Thawai, bird and flower relief (1995).

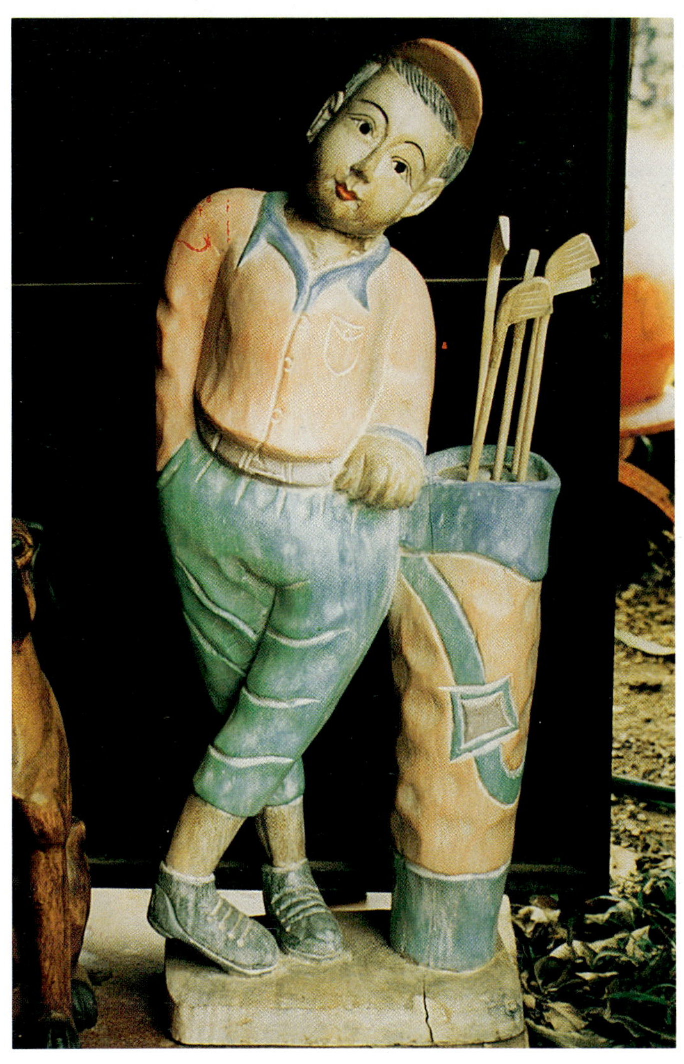

6.10. Ban Thawai, figure of golf player (1993).

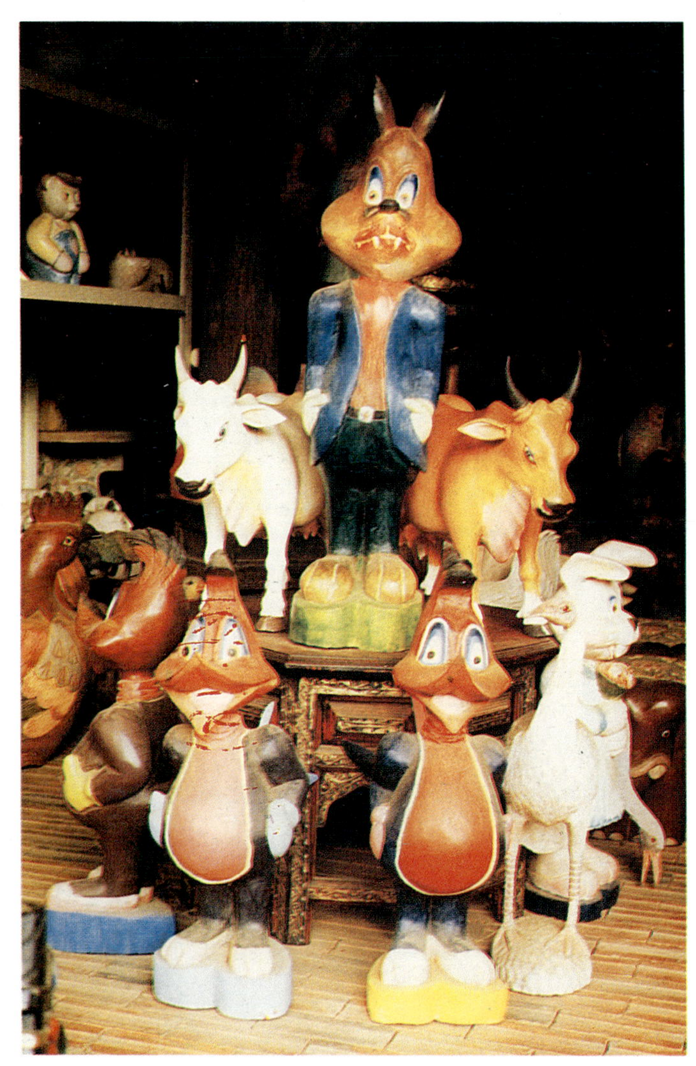

6.11. Ban Thawai, Disney film figurines (1992).

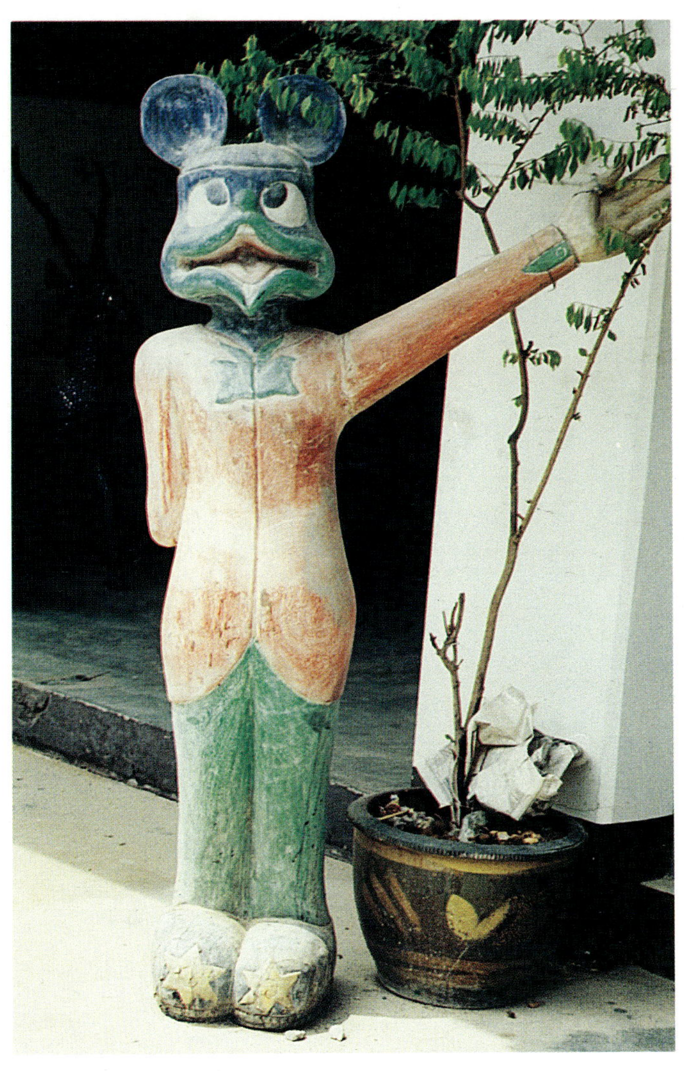

6.12. Ban Thawai, Mickey Mouse figure (1996).

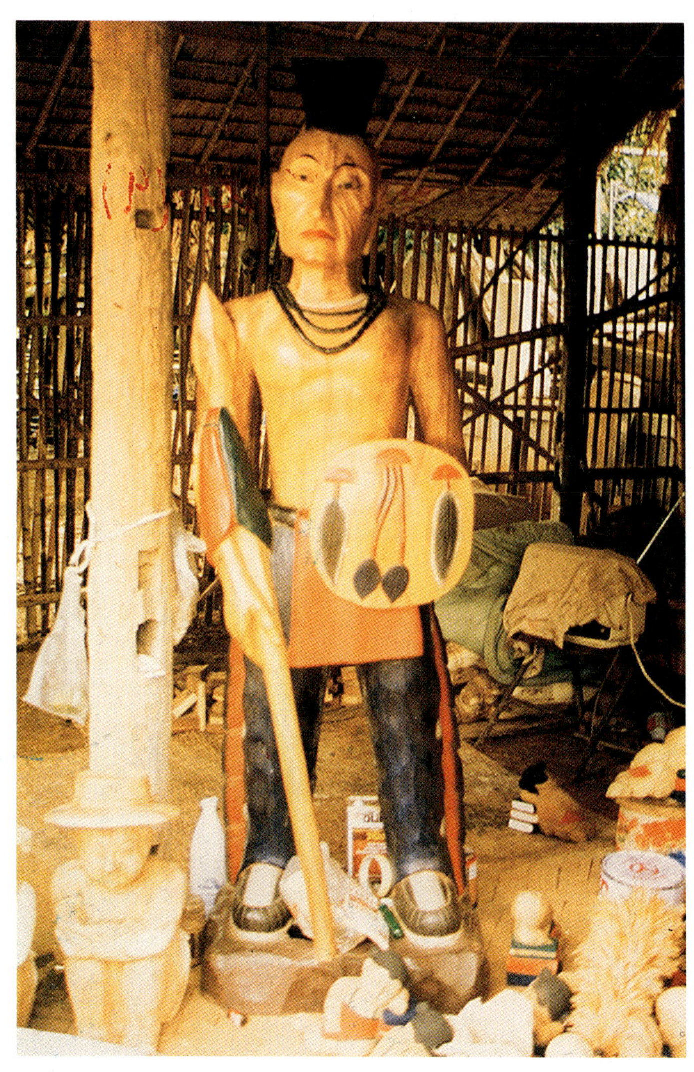

6.13. Ban Thawai, figure of Apache Indian (1995).

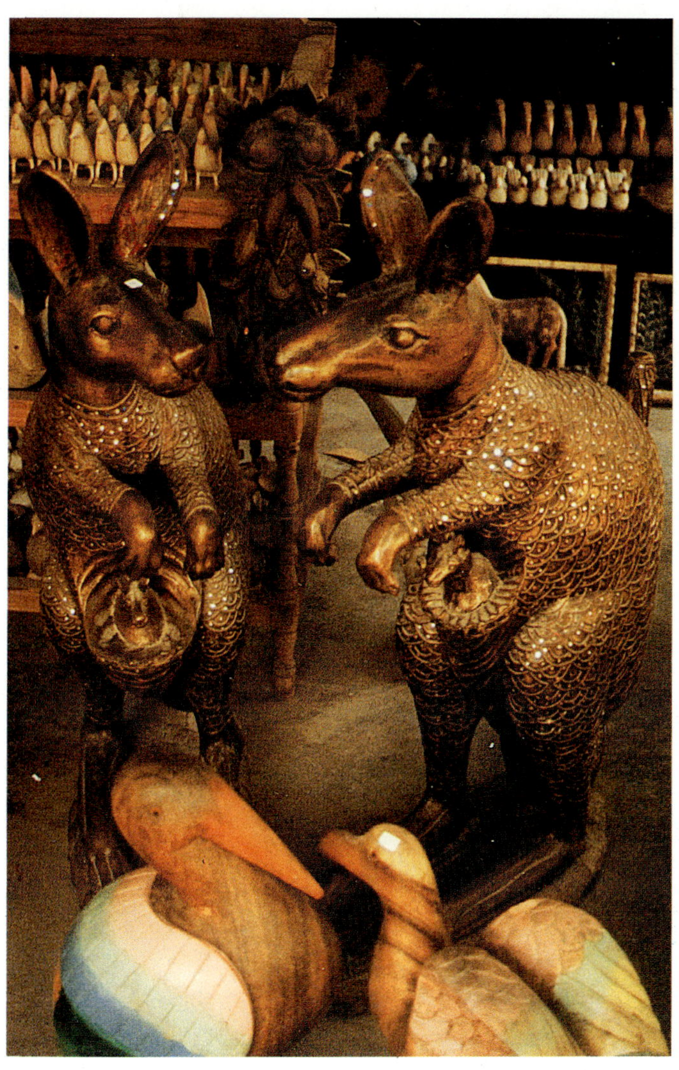

6.14. Ban Thawai, pair of kangaroos decorated in pattern of curved embossed lines (1992).

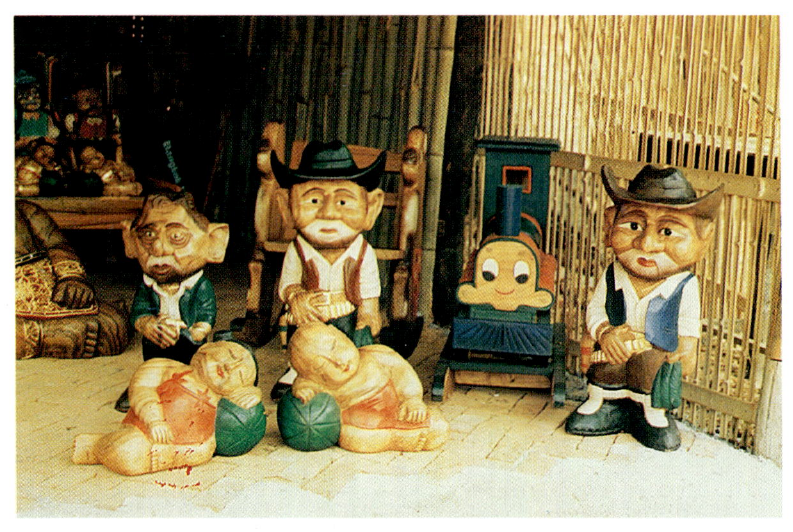

6.15. Ban Thawai, partly painted and partly varnished carvings (1995).

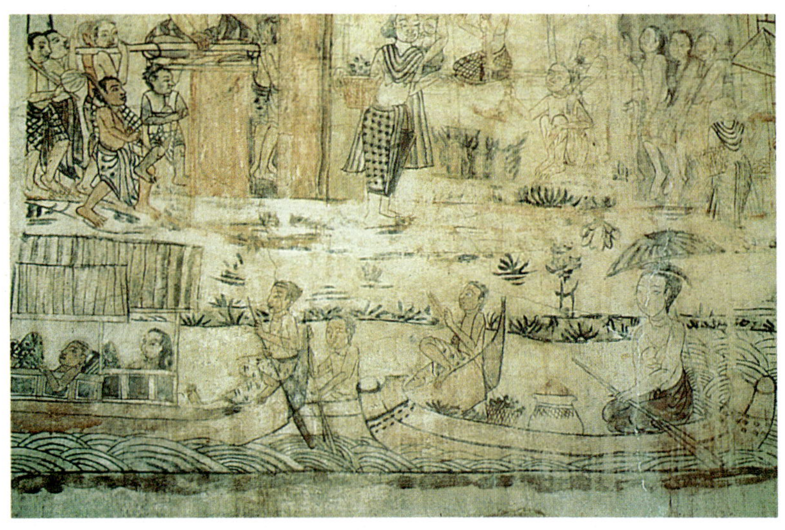

7.1. Vending from boat and on land, Wat Ko Kiauw, Phetchaburi province (*c.* 1670 AD).

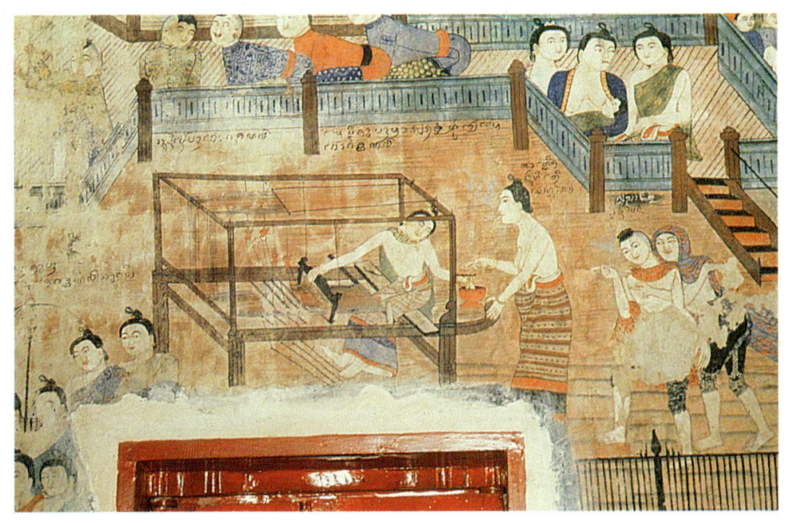

7.2. Weaving, Wat Phumin, Nan province (*c.* 1890 AD).

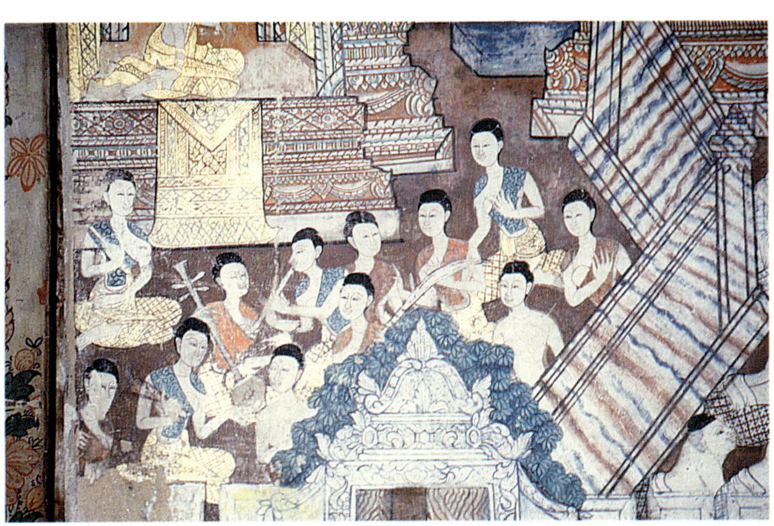

7.3. Court musicians, Wat Khongkharam, Photharam district, Ratchaburi province (*c.* 1780 AD).

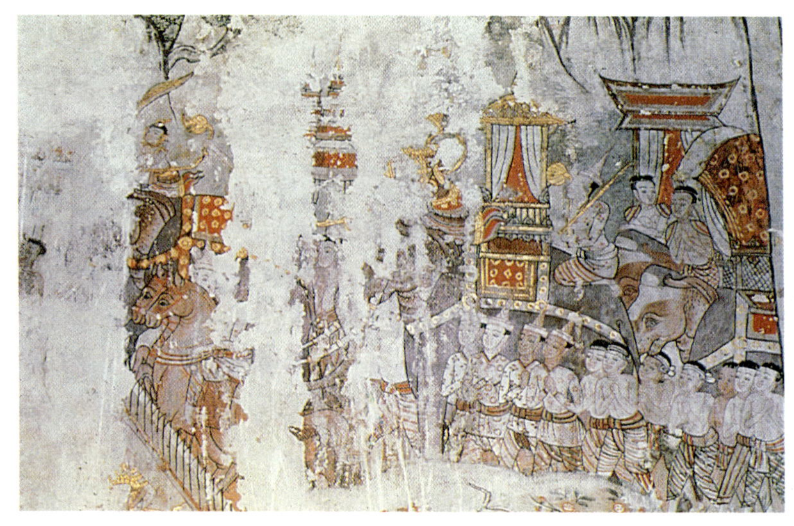

7.4. Female elephant mahout, Wat Chong Nonsi, Bangkok (*c.* 1670 AD).

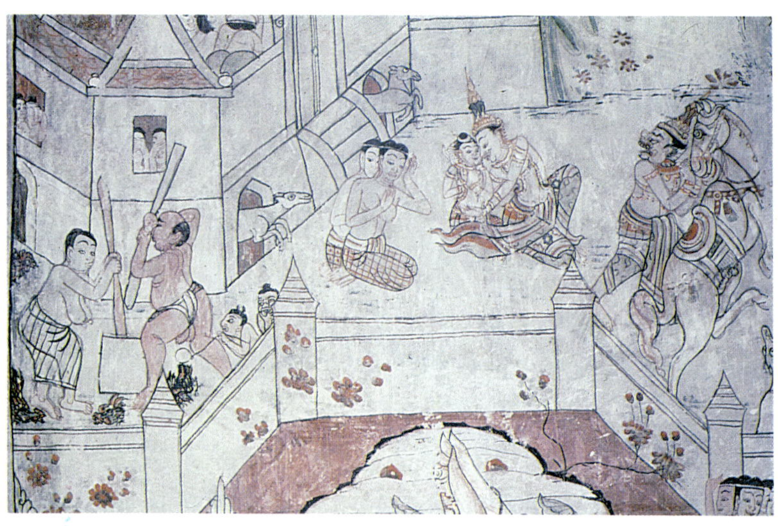

7.5. Male pounding rice, Wat Chong Nonsi, Bangkok (*c.* 1670 AD).

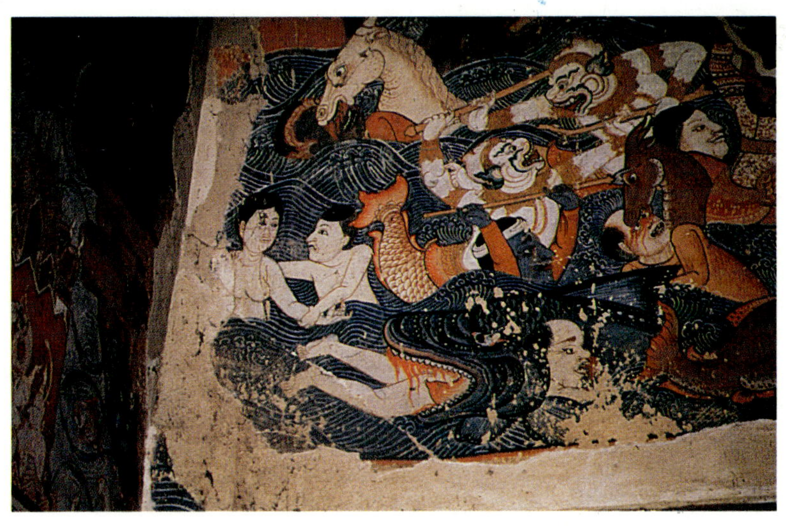

7.6. Tenderness, Wat Khongkharam, Photharam district, Ratchaburi province (*c.* 1780 AD).

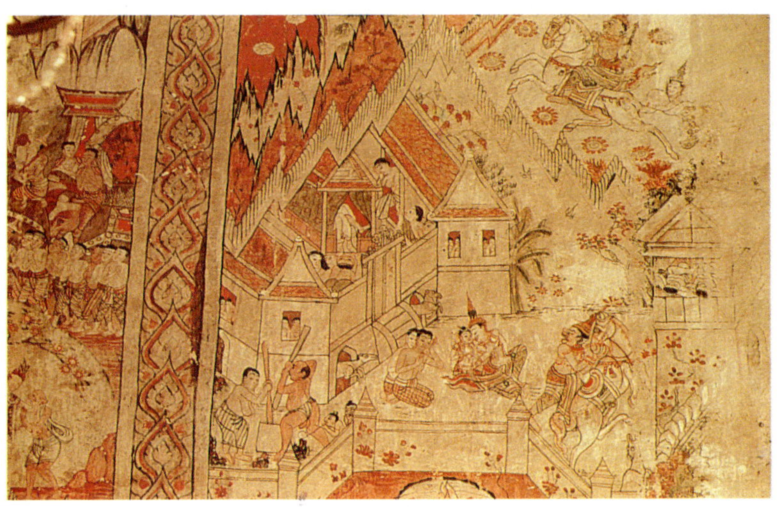

7.7. Scene from Vidhura Pandit Jataka, Wat Chong Nonsi, Bangkok (*c.* 1670 AD).

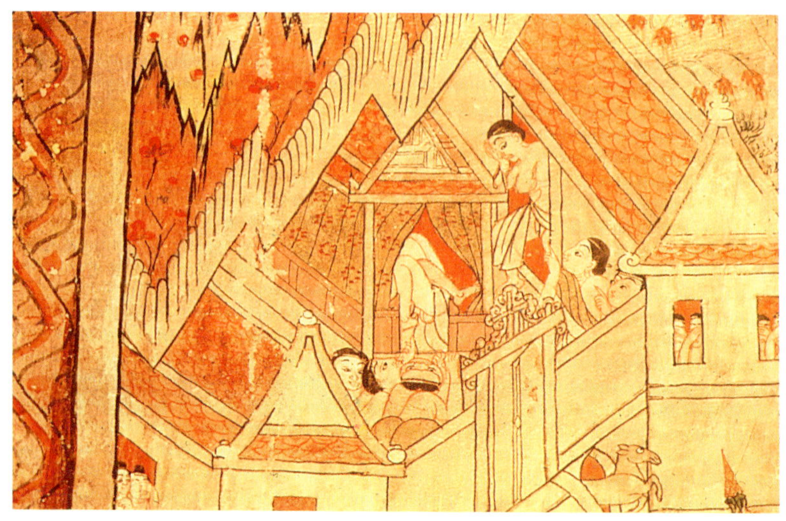

7.8. Sexual activities, Wat Chong Nonsi, Bangkok (*c.* 1670 AD).

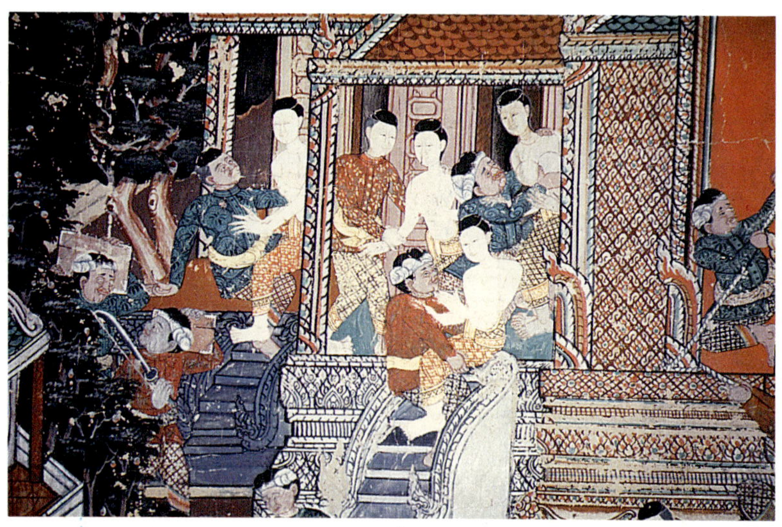

7.9. Scene of women being taken, Wat Khongkharam, Photharam district, Ratchaburi province (*c.* 1780 AD).

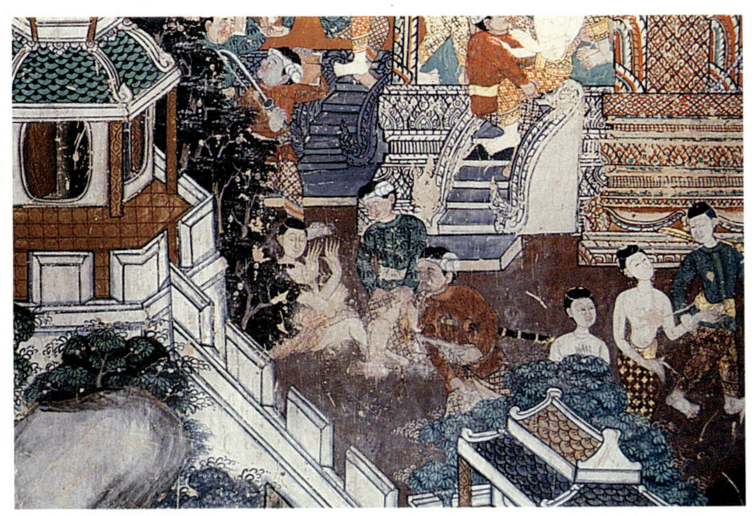

7.10. Sexual intercourse with abducted women, Wat Khongkharam, Photharam district, Ratchaburi province (*c.* 1780 AD).

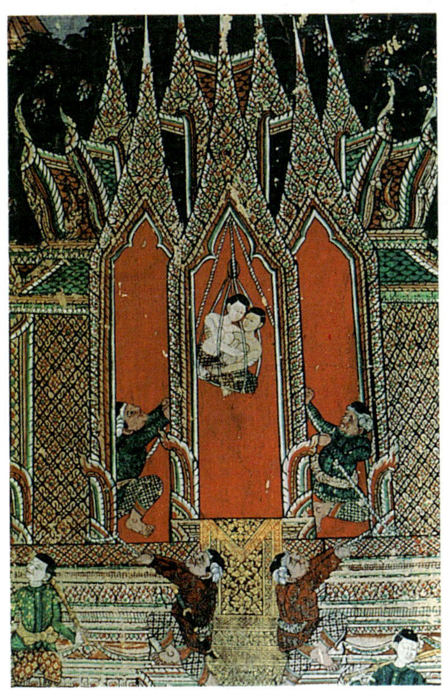

7.11. Women being punished, Wat Khongkharam, Photharam district, Ratchaburi province (*c.* 1780 AD).

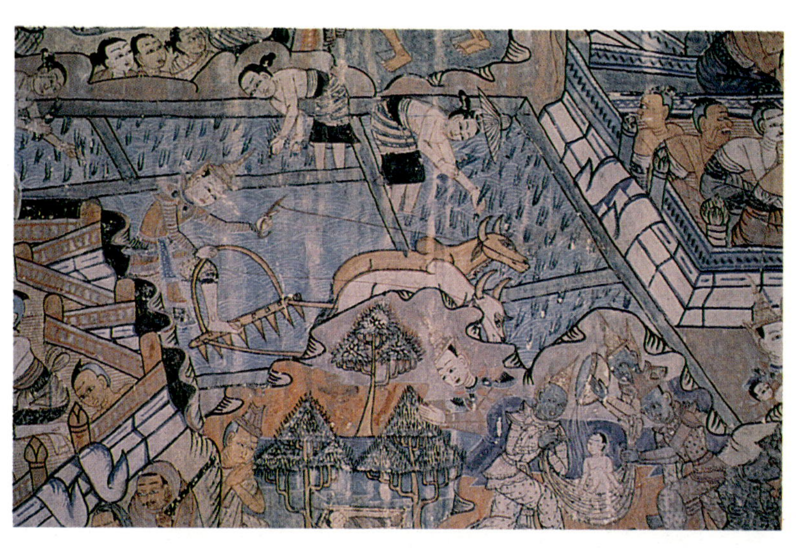

7.12. Rice planting scene, Wat Pa Daet, Mae Chaem district, Chiang Mai province (*c.* 1900 AD).

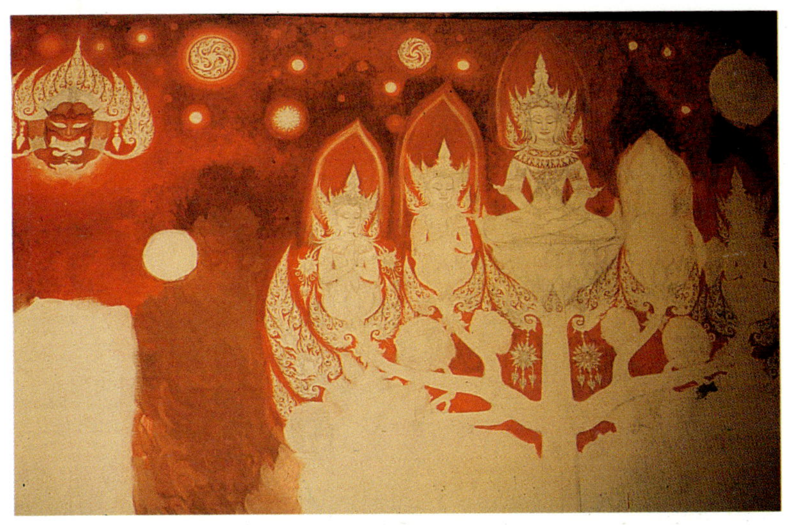

8.1. Angkarn Kalyanapong, temple mural at Phayao.

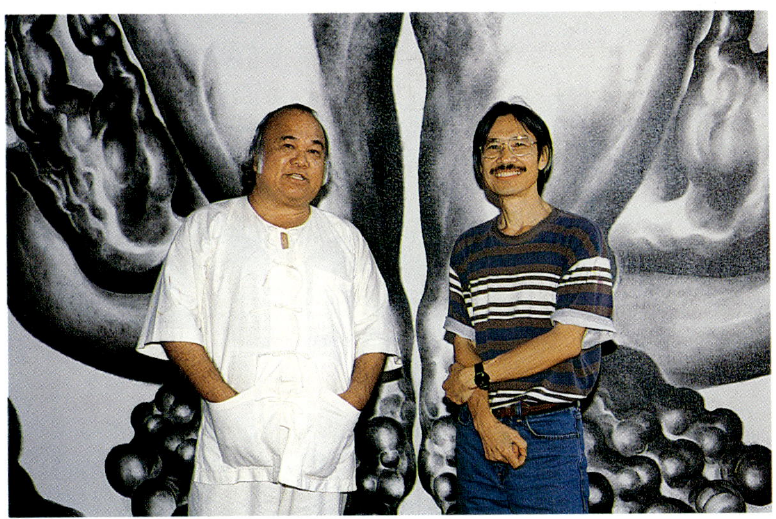

8.2. Artists Thawan Duchanee and Wattana Wattanapun standing before a mural being painted by Thawan in Chiang Rai to be installed in Bangkok upon completion (1996).

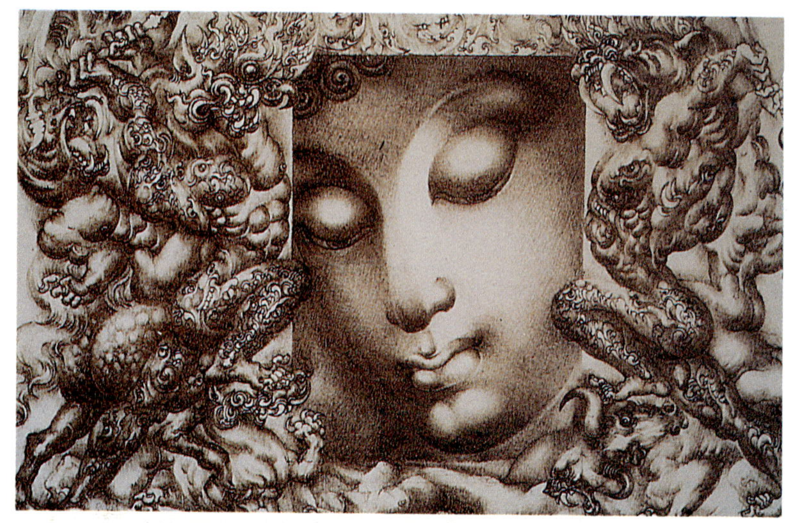

8.3. Thawan Duchanee, ball-point pen on paper.

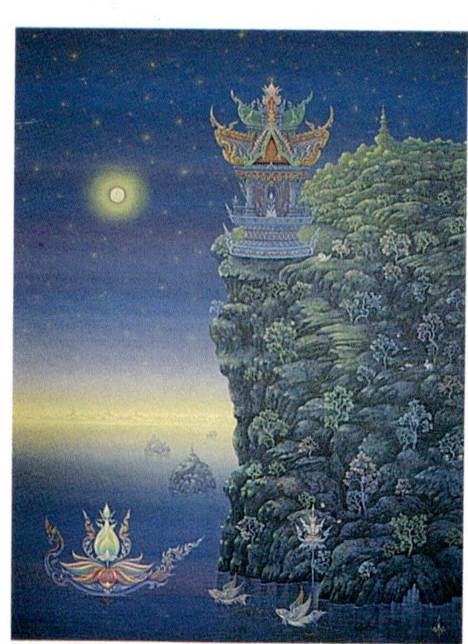

8.4. Chalermchai Kositpipat, “Detachment”, acrylic on canvas (1992).

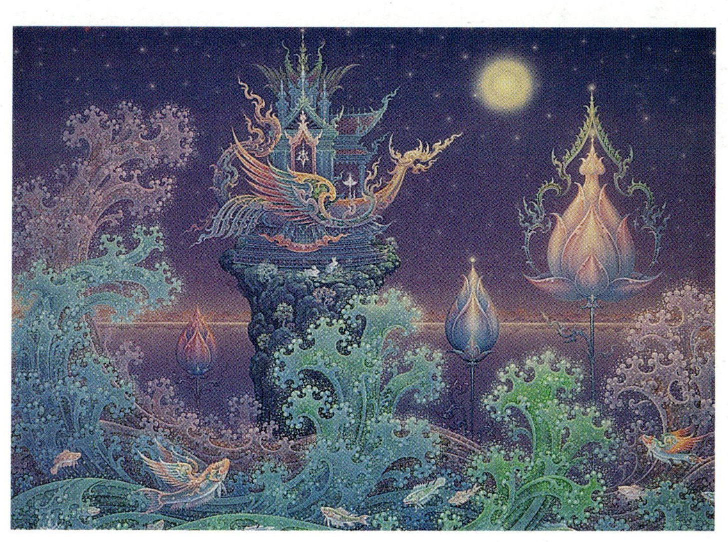

8.5. Chalermchai Kositpipat, "Serenity", acrylic on canvas (1992).

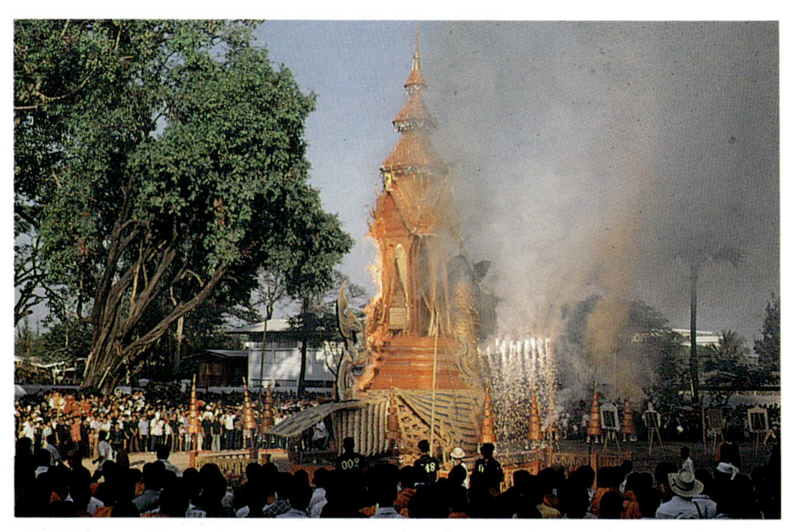

8.6. Prasat cremation.

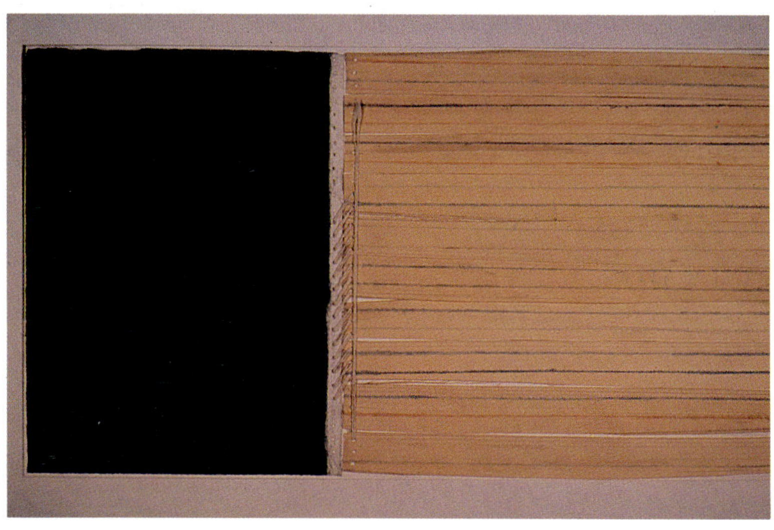

8.7. Kamol Tasnanchalee, from “Nang Yai” series.

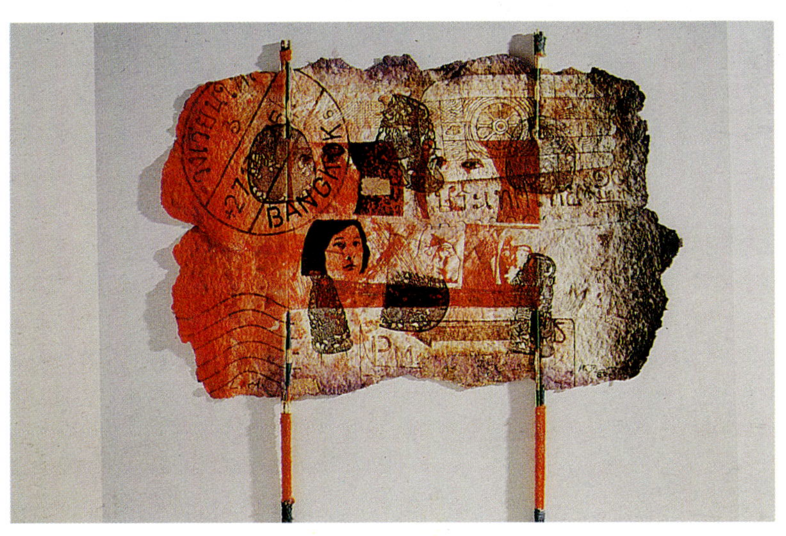

8.8. Parawat Laucharoen, “Infinitude II” (1983).

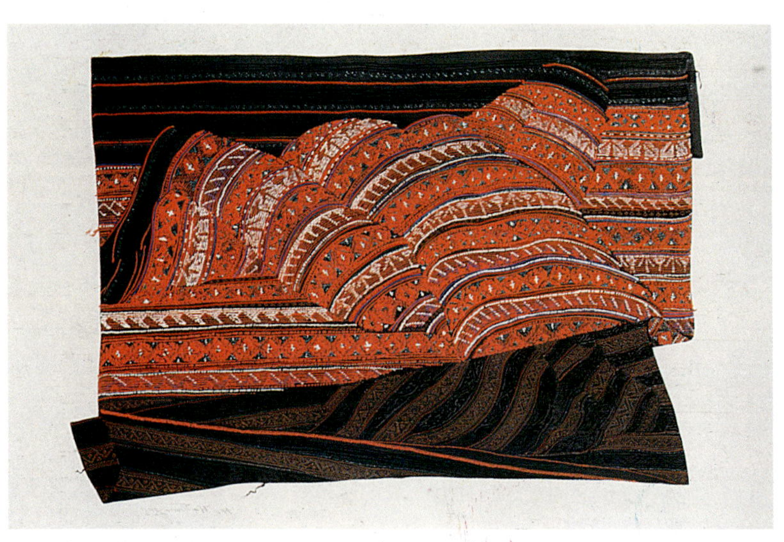

8.9. Wattana Wattanapun, unnamed, acrylic on paper. This painting is from Wattana's textile series that is part of the *Sun, Sand, Silk, Sex* series that he began in 1989 as a critical commentary on social changes associated with the Visit Thailand Year. The textile images were inspired by Wattana's interest in northern Thai crafts.

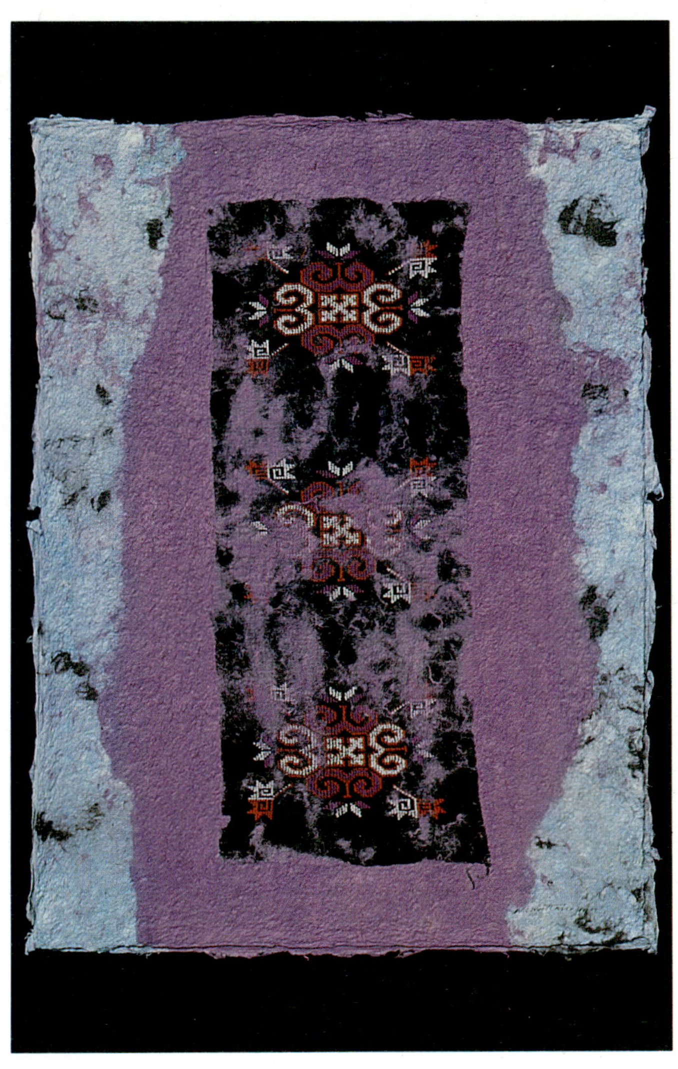

8.10. Wattana Wattanapun, "Emerge-Submerge", cloth on handmade paper. This is part of a series of works using handmade paper that Wattana began in 1992, inspired by his interest in northern Thai crafts.

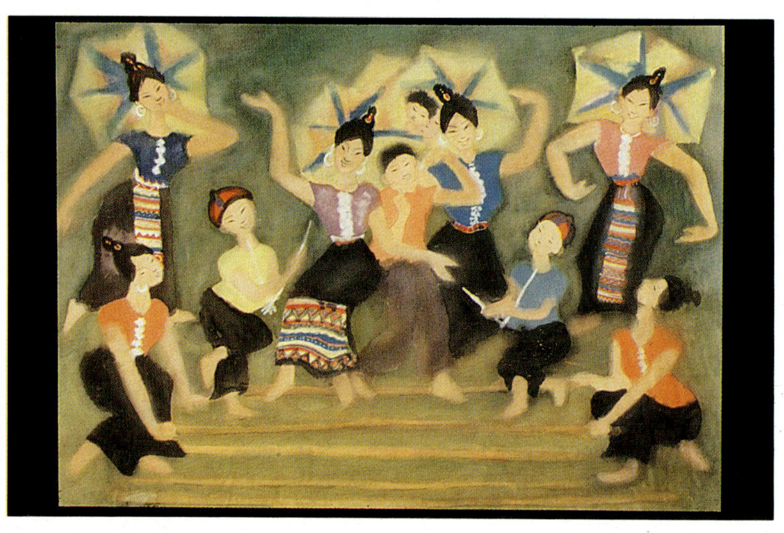

9.1. Painting of T'ai Dam bamboo dance by Chu Thi Thánh. Chu Thi Thánh herself is of the Nung ethnic minority and is one of the few painters in Vietnam from one of its ethnic minorities.

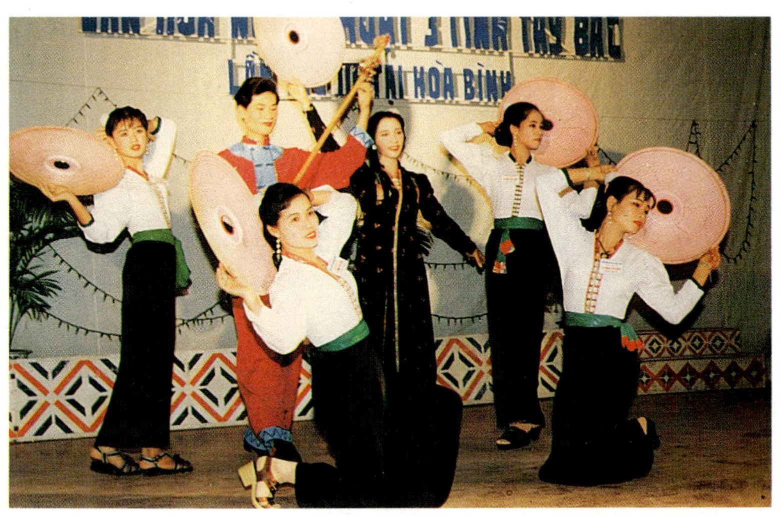

9.2. T'ai Khao hat dance performed by dancers from the Lai Châu Culture House (Nhà Van Hoá Tinh Lai Châu) in 1996 at a dance competition in Hòa Binh involving dance troupes from Lai Châu, Son La, and Hòa Binh provinces.

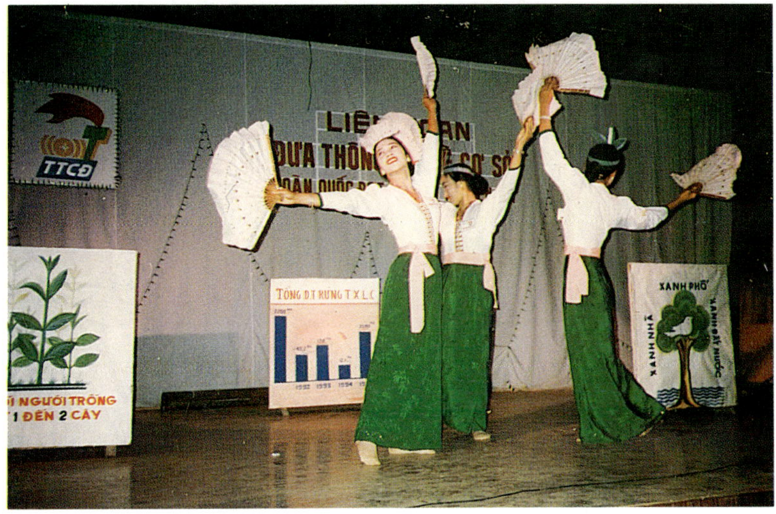

9.3. The *muá quat* (fan dance) performed at a government-sponsored festival in Lai Châu town, involving people from throughout Lai Châu province.

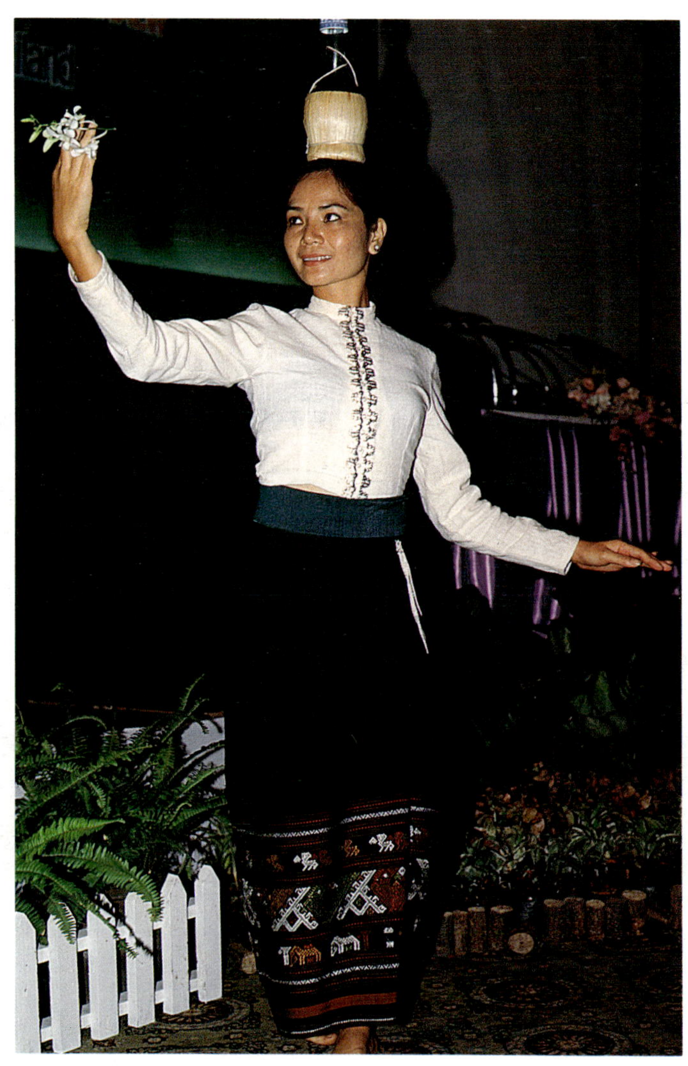

9.4. Be Kim Nhung performing a T'ai Khao greeting dance, the *muá moi lâu* (invitation to drink) at the October 1996 International Thai Studies Conference in Chiang Mai. This dance was first performed in the early 1950s in Lai Châu.

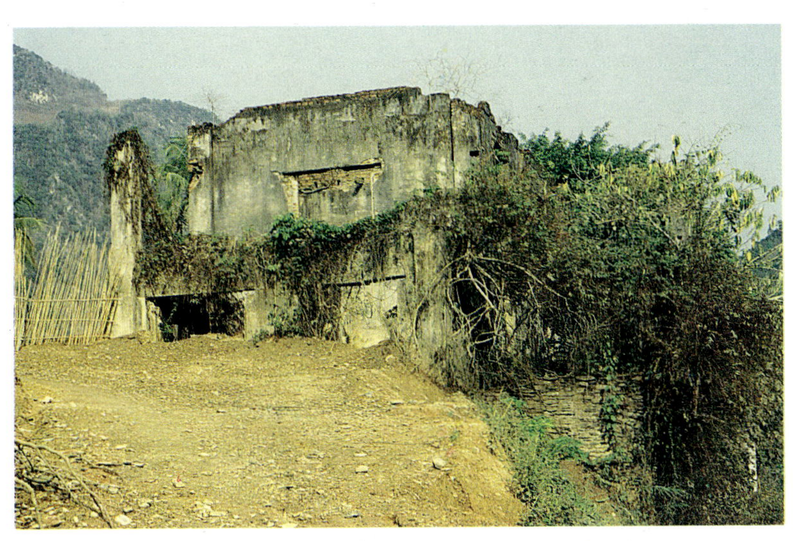

9.5. Ruins of the palace of the T'ai Khao king, Deo Van Long, located a few kilometers north of Lai Châu town.

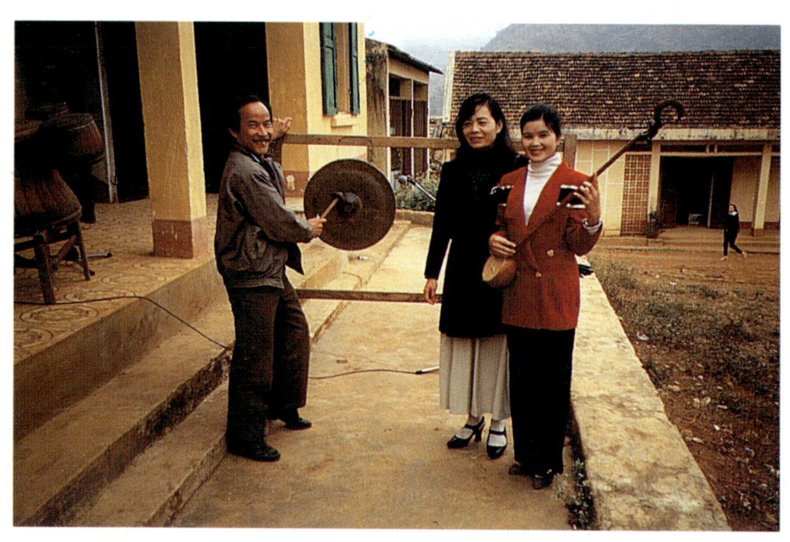

9.6. The director of the Son La dance group, Yu Hoài, with two members of the troupe.

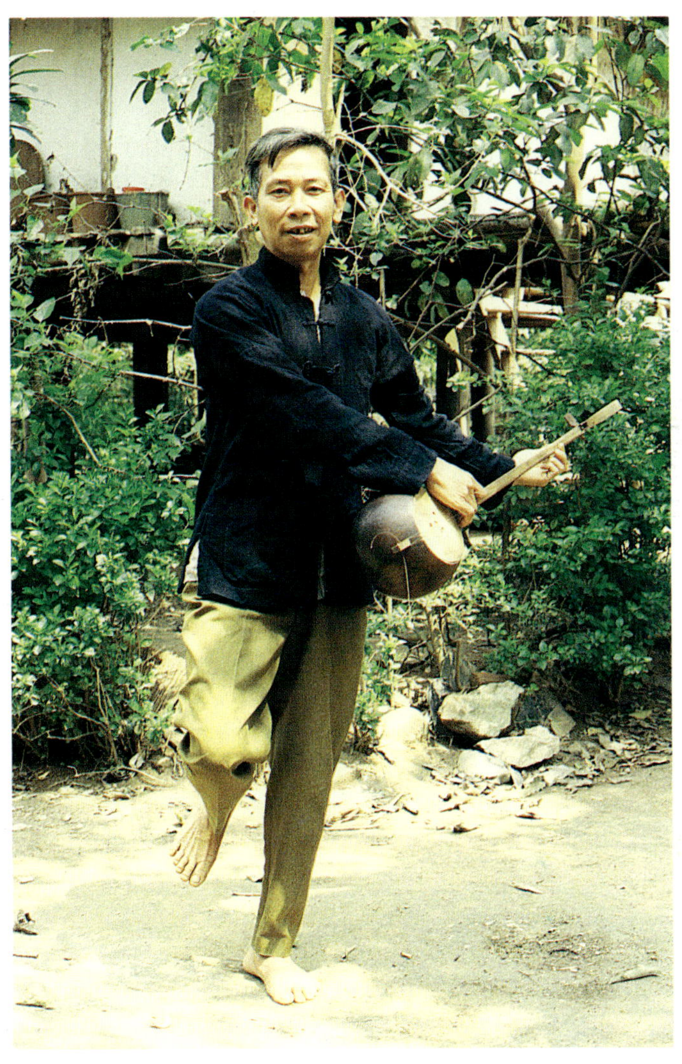

9.7. Dieu Van Sam illustrating a traditional T'ai Khao dance that is performed by male musicians, Ban Dan (1997).

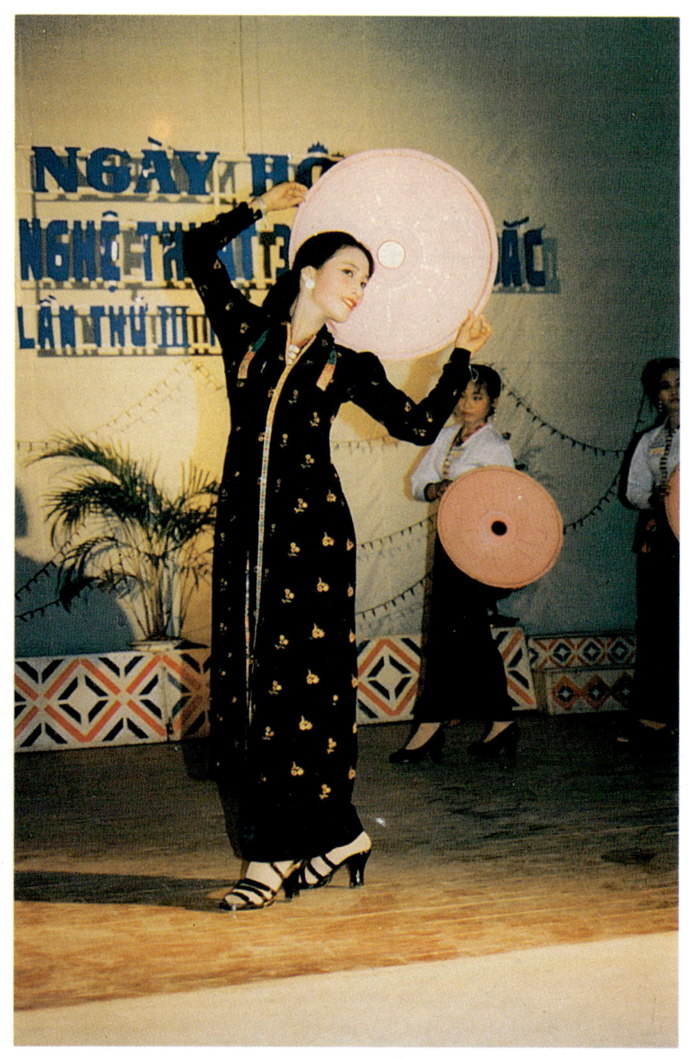

9.8. Dieu Thi Chuyên, wearing a dance costume of her mother's made around 1956, at a dance competition in Hòa Binh involving dance troupes from Lai Châu, Son La, and Hòa Binh provinces, at which she won the gold medal for her performance.

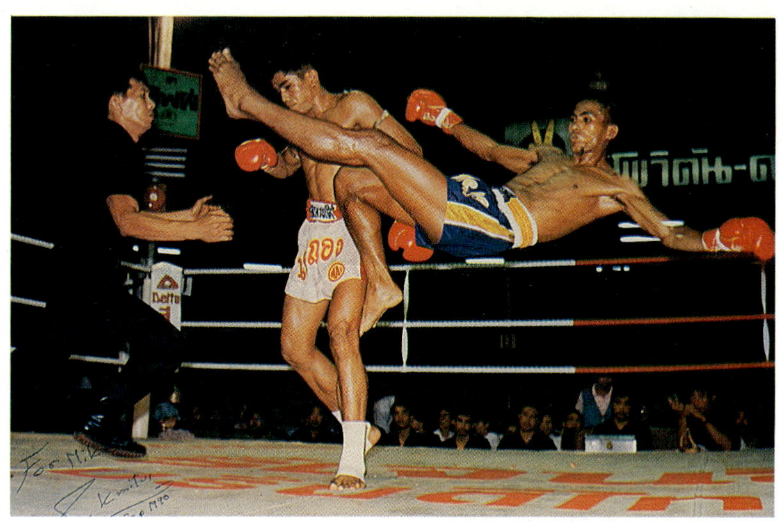

10.1. Fight action at a Bangkok stadium.

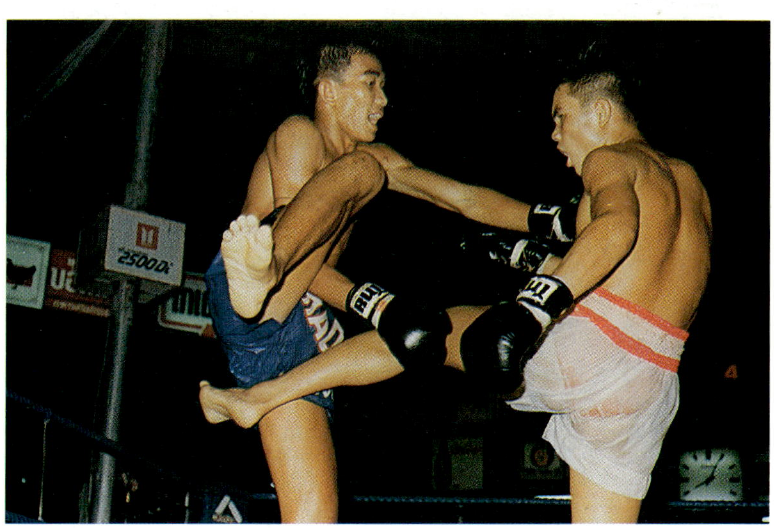

10.2. Fight action at a Bangkok stadium.

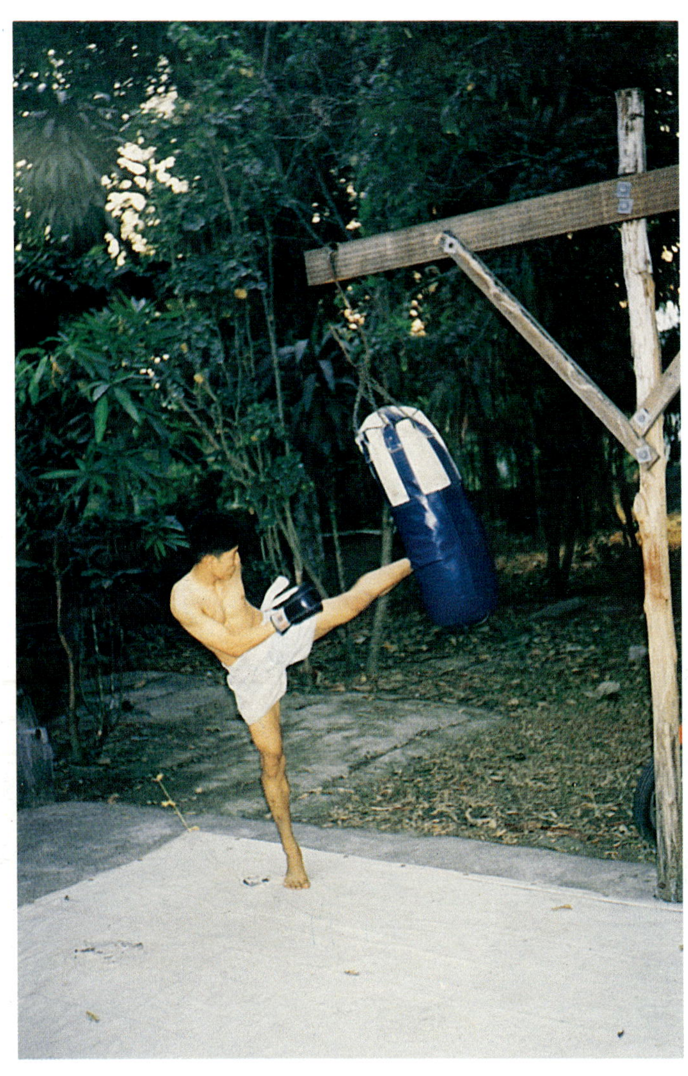

10.3. Boxer during his daily practice at the Sau Pattanasak gym in Chiang Mai.

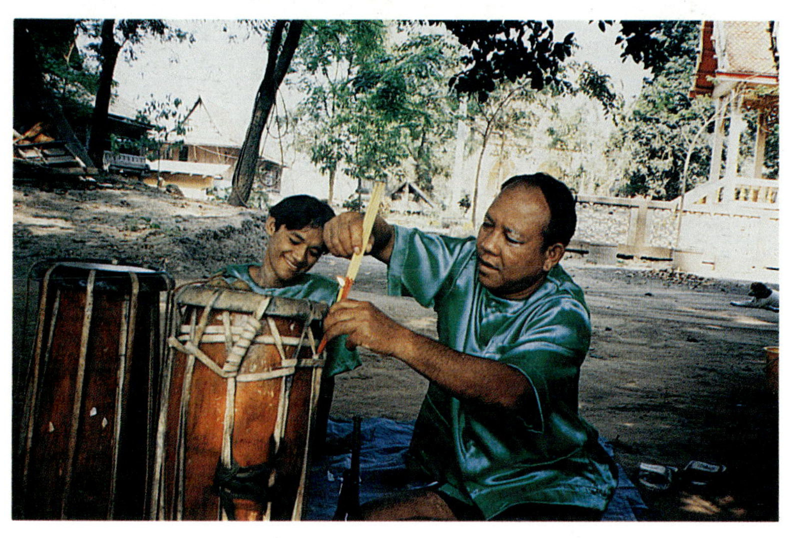

10.4. Musicians getting ready to perform before a *muay Thai* demonstration.

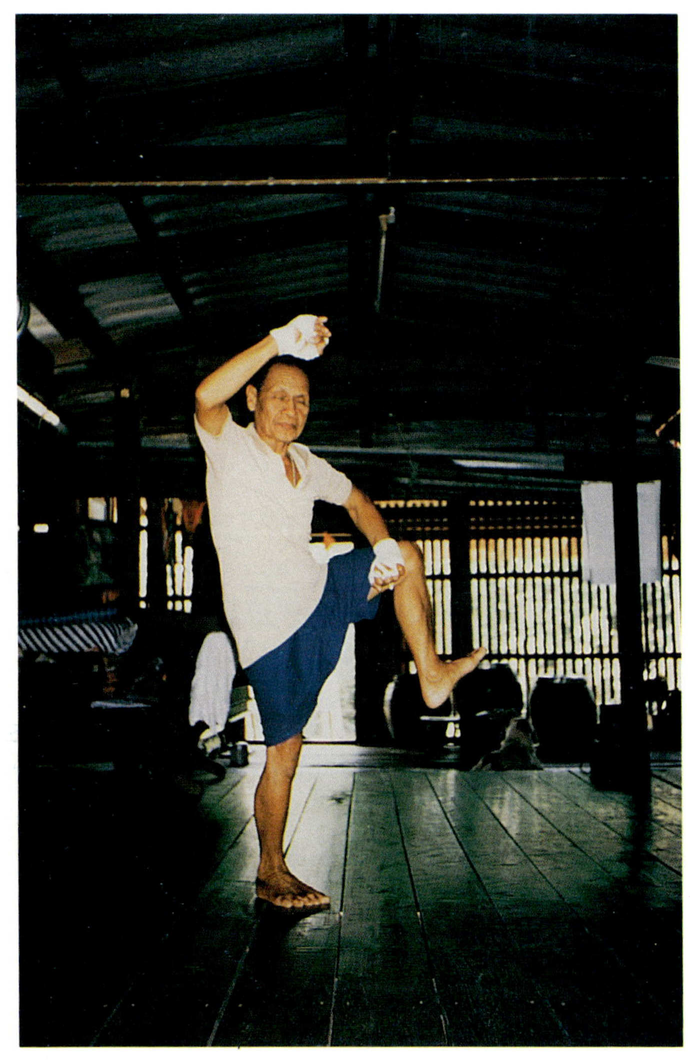

10.5. Kru Boonchoi Suppaiboon demonstrating the *yang sam khun* movement from the *ram muay* ceremony, Ayutthaya.

5

The Effects of Socio-cultural Change on the Textiles of the T'ai Mao from Muang Mou Luang, Burma

Raynou Athamasar

The present study is based on research conducted in the course of two brief trips to study the T'ai Mao (a sub-group of Shan) of Muang Mou Luang (*Plate 5.1*) on the border of China and Burma in 1996 as well as research conducted among T'ai Mao and other Shan (or T'ai Yai) living in northern Thailand in the districts of Fang and Mae Aye over the past few years.[1] In regard to the Shan living in Thailand, I paid particular attention to more recent migrants from Burma. The focus of the research was on how sociocultural changes affecting the Shan in these various settings have influenced their production and use of traditional textiles. The research conducted so far is very preliminary in nature and further research on this topic in the future is anticipated.

The T'ai Mao of Muang Mou Luang

The terms Shan and T'ai Yai refer to T'ai-speaking peoples living primarily in Burma's Shan State and in the adjacent territory across the border in China. Collectively, in the past their homeland comprised what was commonly referred to as the Shan States. The Shan initially settled in this area possibly as early as the sixth century AD, around which time they founded the polity of Muang Morong.[2] In 1215 the Shan founded the kingdom of Mao. Mao's control and influence extended into southern Yunnan and throughout much of what is today Shan State and some adjacent areas of Burma. In 1364 Burmanized Shan from this region established a capital in the lowlands at Ava. Mao was defeated by the Chinese in 1604. Following the fall of Mao, the Shan were divided into numerous small principalities ruled by *sawbwas.* Some of these principalities came under Chinese influence, others under Burmese influence, while still others retained a fair degree of autonomy. The center of Burmese influence was to the south at Mong Nai.

The Shan of Muang Mou Luang belong to a sub-group known as T'ai Mao. T'ai Mao speak a distinct dialect of Shan and have their own script that differs from that of the Southern Shan. In 1990 there were an estimated 350,000 T'ai Mao in Burma out of a total Shan population of over 3,000,000. The T'ai Mao are also known as Mao, Maw, Mau, T'ai Long, Northern Shan, and Chinese Shan. British sources during the nineteenth and early twentieth centuries referred to the T'ai Mao as Chinese Shan or Eastern Shan and the Burmese referred to them as Shan Tayok (possibly referring to the old kingdom of Nanchao). T'ai Mao living in Yunnan in the past were grouped with all Shan by the Chinese under the name Pai-i.

Seidenfaden states that the muong of the Chinese Shan or T'ai Mao were once part of the kingdom of Nanchao and were incorporated into the Chinese empire under the Ming dynasty in the middle of the fifteenth century.[3] Many of the Chinese Shan later migrated to Burma settling in the Bhamo and Myitkyina districts, where they mixed with Burmese Shan and Burmese. Leach states that these Chinese Shan were relatively recent migrants to Burma.[4]

British control of what is now Shan State in Burma was achieved between 1885, following the capture of Mandalay, and 1887. The British established administration over the Shan States between 1880 and 1890. Their administrative center in the area, too, was at Mong Nai. By and large, British administration of the Shan took the form of indirect rule, with local sawbwas retaining considerable independence. In 1892 the British recognized Chinese control of Sipsongpanna and, with the delimiting of the boundary between British Burma and China, the T'ai Mao such as those of Muang Mou Luang found themselves divided between the two states.

The T'ai Mao in this area subsequently have been under the influence of the governments of two different states: Burma, ruled by the British and later independent, and China. Initially this had relatively little direct impact on the lives of the T'ai Mao, as Chinese and British administrative control over this area was relatively weak. However, during the decades following the Second World War, as the governments of independent Burma and Communist China sought to increase their control over the frontier areas under their respective jurisdictions, the situation changed. Both governments pursued policies that differed in detail, but that in general aimed at enhancing national integration and acculturating ethnic minorities.

As a result of these government policies, many of the distinctive characteristics of T'ai Mao society disappeared from public view. This was particularly the case in China, where T'ai Mao cultural expression, as was the case with other ethnic minorities, was suppressed during the period of the Cultural Revolution (1966-1976) in a dramatic and often harsh manner. Thus, the Red Guards destroyed temples and other material representations of Buddhism among the T'ai Mao and forbade cultural practices associated with Buddhism, including temple rituals. One T'ai Mao who had become a member of the Red Guards told me of being forced to destroy temple paintings and of crying in private afterwards. In Burma, the T'ai Mao were affected by political struggles between government authorities and Shan and other separatists and the Communist Party of Burma. The resulting political situation placed considerable pressure on the T'ai Mao to adopt many aspects of Burmese culture. Temple rituals were curtailed and novices were only able to enter the temples in secret.

Despite such efforts to suppress T'ai Mao culture, some aspects of traditional T'ai Mao culture have survived—in large part by going underground over the past few decades. Memories of past practices and beliefs were retained in people's minds. Some items of material culture, including textiles, were hidden—in some cases buried—to order to keep them safe. More tolerant policies in China towards minority cultures in recent years have allowed greater public expressions of traditional cultural practices among the T'ai Mao in that country. However, what has emerged is a mere shadow of what existed prior to the Cultural Revolution. In the case of Burma, acculturative pressures on the T'ai Mao have been strongest in the towns and less isolated villages and traditional practices have survived best in the more remote areas. In both countries, the influence of Buddhism within T'ai Mao culture remains strong and there is evidence of a revival of activities reflecting their Buddhist traditions, but much has been lost. This loss is especially evident in the realm of material culture, including the production of textiles for use in ceremonies and for making traditional costumes.

Mention should also be made of the T'ai Nüa who live in the vicinity of Muang Mou Luang. Most T'ai Nüa live in China, but they are found on both sides of the border in the valley of the Mekong and part of the Salween valley as well as in the mountainous area between the two rivers.[5] Officially they are placed in the Dai nationality in China. Those living in Burma migrated from China.

Burmese political control and British commercial interests associated with the teak industry in what is now northern Thailand and later adverse political conditions in Burma and China resulted in the migration of Shan to northern Thailand over the years. The majority of Shan found in northern Thailand today are of southern Shan origin, but there are also some northern Shan or T'ai Mao. Among the latter are some people from Muang Mou Luang. (*Plate 5.2*)

Traditional T'ai Mao and T'ai Nüa Textiles

There are several sources from the early part of this century that provide descriptions of traditional Shan, T'ai Mao, and T'ai Nüa textiles. Both T'ai Mao and T'ai Nüa men traditionally wore trousers, a jacket, and a turban. However, as noted by Scott and Hardiman concerning the Shan in general, the style of the trousers in particular varied a great deal: "Sometimes they are practically of the Chinese pattern with well defined legs, but among the better-to-do classes the seat is frequently down about the ankles and the garment generally is so voluminous as to look more like a skirt than a pair of trousers."[6] They also mention that Chinese Shan (T'ai Mao) men's turbans were usually indigo, while those in the northern Burmese areas tended to be white, and further south were of various colors.[7]

Seidenfaden provides a brief description of the dress of the women of the various T'ai-speaking groups in the Shan States. He notes that while some Shan women wore a scarf folded across their chest, others, especially T'ai Lü and T'ai Khün (as he calls the T'ai Mao) wore "a white bodice with long and tight sleeves."[8] He also mentions that in the north of Shan State the women wore large turbans, while in the south they wrapped a scarf around their heads. Seidenfaden does not provide much of a description of everyday women's skirts, but he does remark that "at festivals the young girls dress picturesquely in gaudy colours, pale blue jackets, and paneled skirts of every hue interwoven with gold thread."[9] This description seems to refer to the festive dresses of the T'ai Mao.

Scott and Hardiman also mention another type of cloth produced by the Shan of Hsen Wi State. They describe these as "curious sleeping-mats or cloths" which are "of zig-zag or diamond shaped pattern, woven usually in black or red on a white ground, and carried out with the nicest exactness and regularity of detail."[10] Such cloths commonly are given as gifts to monks and today are associated with the Buddhist traditions of T'ai Mao culture.

Leslie Milne provides a description of the best known Shan ceremonial textiles, their ceremonial banners known as *tung*. These are produced by the Shan and neighboring T'ai groups for *thawt kathin,* lasting from mid-October to mid-November, which celebrates the ending of Buddhist lent (*phansaa*). New monastic robes are also offered to monks during thawt kathin and new clothes are prepared for all members of the family. She describes these tung as follows:

> Women...prepare great streamers, which, when attached to bamboo, are raised in remembrance of dead relatives or friends. These streamers are from one to three feet wide, and are often many yards in length. They may be of plain cloth, but some are ornamented with geometrical designs cut out of gold paper; others are of thin white cotton cloth, covering many small hoops of bamboo...Sometimes the streamers are not white, but are embroidered with elaborate designs. Pagodas and birds are represented; there is generally a boat, in which a passenger is being rowed across a river by one or more boatmen, and the water is full of fish.[11]

The same authors also provides descriptions of T'ai Nüa clothing. Leslie Milne describes their dress thus:

> The men wear garments cut in the usual Shan fashion, but always dark blue in colour...Their women dress as British Shan, with the exception of the turban, which is made of a very long piece

> of thin black cloth, wound round and round the head in a tall cylindrical shape. They also wear coloured gaiters. The young girls among them have paneled skirts of bright hues, but they lay aside their gay clothes when little more than children, dressing themselves in sober colours at an earlier age than their sisters in British territory.[12]

Davies observes that the turban of T'ai Nüa women varies according to locality: "west of the Salween, the women are conspicuous by the size of their turbans, which appear to be nearly a foot high and get broader at the top," while east of the Salween the turban "is about the same size as that worn west of the river, but is put on in a different way, in a low oval shape, with ends of the oval sticking out at each side."[13]

Contemporary T'ai Mao Textiles and Dress

The political conditions of the T'ai Mao have affected their society in many ways and this is reflected in their production and use of textiles. By and large, the T'ai Mao in Burma have adopted the Burmese styles of dress in recent years. (*Plate 5.3*) However, many T'ai Mao continue to wear their characteristic red sash around their waist over their Burmese clothing as a subtle means of ethnic identification. (*Plate 5.4*) In addition, some T'ai Mao living distant from Muang Mou Luang have preserved their traditional dress and on occasion even T'ai Mao of Muang Mou Luang may be seen wearing traditional costumes. (*Plates 5.5, 5.6, 5.7, 5.8*)

Women continue to weave in Muang Nam Khung. In fact, the community has emerged as something of a center to supply textiles to other T'ai Mao in the vicinity—in both Burma and China. Among the more popular items that they produce are shoulder bags that can be distinguished as T'ai Mao. (*Plate 5.9*)

For the most part, traditional T'ai Mao styles of weaving, including patterns and colors, have been forgotten in China. Also, although many

T'ai Mao in China now wear Chinese-style clothing, some continue to wear distinctive T'ai Mao dress. (*Plate 5.10*) Recently, as the Chinese have allowed more freedom in expressing religion and culture, some weaving has starting again. In particular, textiles are now being woven for use in rituals, primarily to be given to monks. However, the majority of the textiles used in rituals today are older ones that were hidden and preserved rather than new ones. The tung produced for the *dumkorn* ritual now often use a piece of Chinese commercial cloth decorated with pieces of T'ai Mao textiles. (*Plate 5.11*)

Conclusion

Although direct coercion as well as more subtle acculturative pressures have resulted in the loss of much of their distinctive textile and dress traditions, the T'ai Mao of Burma and China have not succumbed completely to these outside influences. Some T'ai Mao, primarily those in more remote localities, continue to dress in a distinctive style. Even those who are more integrated into the dominant Chinese and Burmese societies, however, often have retained at least small elements in their dress that indicate their distinct ethnic identity.

Textiles have also played an important role in efforts by the T'ai Mao to keep their religious traditions alive. Even during the Cultural Revolution in China, they were able to hide some textiles associated with their Buddhist practices. Today, once again, these textiles as well as new textiles are widely used in religious ceremonies as tungs and as gifts to monks. Both in terms of dress and within the context of religious beliefs and practices, therefore, we can see how the T'ai Mao have viewed their textiles as important parts of the ethnic identity.

Notes

1. I wish to thank the Office of the National Cultural Commission for financial support for my research and Dr. Graham Fordham, Coordinator of Thai Studies at Griffith University, for assistance in translation of some of the material from Thai to English.

2. Historical background and information on traditional dress of the T'ai Yai and T'ai Nüa is taken from Michael C. Howard, *Textiles of the Hill Tribes of Burma* (Bangkok: White Lotus, forthcoming).

3. Erik Seidenfaden, *The Thai Peoples: Book I: The Origins and Habitats of the Thai Peoples with a Sketch of their Material and Spiritual Culture* (Bangkok: The Siam Society, 1967), p. 21.

4. E.R. Leach, *Political Systems of Highland Burma* (Cambridge, MA: Harvard University Press, 1954), p. 32.

5. Seidenfaden, *The Thai Peoples,* p. 24.

6. James George Scott and J.P. Hardiman, *Gazetteer of Upper Burma and the Shan States* (Rangoon: Superintendent of Government Printing and Stationery, 1900), vols. I/II, p. 319.

7. Scott and Hardiman, *Gazetteer of Upper Burma and the Shan States,* vols. I/II, p. 319.

8. Seidenfaden, *The Thai Peoples,* p. 32.

9. Seidenfaden, *The Thai Peoples,* p. 32.

10. Scott and Hardiman, *Gazetteer of Upper Burma and the Shan States,* vols. I/II, p. 371.

11. Leslie Milne, *Shans at Home* (London: John Murray, 1910), pp. 121-123.

12. Milne, *Shans at Home,* pp. 135-136. Also see Seidenfaden, *The Thai Peoples,* p. 24.

13. H.R. Davies, *Yünnan: The Link Between India and the Yangtze* (Cambridge: Cambridge University Press, 1909), p. 381.

6

From Buddha Images to Mickey Mouse Figures: The Transformation of Ban Thawai Carvings

Erik Cohen

The village of Ban Thawai is a major center for carvings and other craft products in northern Thailand.[1] In this chapter the dynamics of change in the production and marketing of crafts in the village will be presented and analyzed as a process of continuous disassociation between components which at an earlier stage tended to be closely associated. It will be argued that this process is a consequence of the growing integration of the village into wider regional, national, and international frameworks. While this integration helped the expansion and diversification of craft production and marketing in the village, some contemporary developments may transform the character of the village.

The Model

In order to create a point of reference, in relation to which the process of disassociation can be described, a somewhat schematic model of craft production in rural areas of the Third World, including Thailand, in the period preceding commercialization is here proposed. The model comprises six principal components:

1. *Materials*: The materials for craft production are typically locally available; they may be either collected or grown by the artisans themselves or bartered or bought from local or regional markets.
2. *Knowledge, skills, and technologies:* Craft production is typically based on informally acquired and transmitted native knowledge, skills, and technologies that are passed on within households or from master artisans to apprentices. Though knowledge, skills, and technologies are not necessarily locally invented, and may have been borrowed from other localities or cultural groups, they are typically well integrated into local tradition.
3. *Designs and decorations:* The designs of objects and their decorations will typically reflect wider ethnic or regional styles, though they may also feature some distinctive local traits.
4. *Workforce:* Artisans are typically local, while employees and apprentices are either local or come from the near surroundings of the locality.
5. *Production process:* All or most stages of the production process are performed locally by the artisans themselves, or with the assistance of employees and apprentices.
6. *Distribution and consumption:* Most ordinary craft products are intended either for self-use or for barter or sale to households or shops in the locality itself or in the surrounding region; fine crafts have in the past been sent as tribute to rulers or traded in remote urban centers, but even in such cases, the members of the élite who acquire them still constitute an "internal audience,"[2] sharing the basic cultural premises of the producers.

Folk crafts in the era preceding commercialization are not static and unchanging. However, the process of change is slow and innovations, whether independently invented or borrowed from the outside, tend to be integrated into the prevailing style so that no acute gradients appear dividing one stylistic period from another, and no marked difference between the style of one artisan and another can usually be noted.

In this chapter, the above model is used as a point of reference to which the process of disassociation between the components of the model can be referred. Such a process can be found to some extent in most craft producing villages in northern Thailand. In this chapter it will be illustrated through an extended case study of Ban Thawai, where it is particularly pronounced.

Ban Thawai

Ban Thawai is located fifteen kilometers west of Chiang Mai, the major urban center of northern Thailand. Its traditional economy was based on irrigated sticky-rice cultivation. Contrary to the popular image,[3] Ban Thawai was not one of the traditional craft villages,[4] since the villagers began to engage in wood carving only in the 1960s. However, the village is now a major center for the production, finishing, and marketing of carvings and other craft products of northern Thailand. The village is popular with Thai and foreign visitors and business people and has acquired a reputation as a tourist destination.[5] Great quantities of carvings are exported abroad from the village.

The village at the time of writing consists of about 200 households, around 150 of which are in some way engaged in craft production. Although most villagers continue to cultivate rice, mainly for their own consumption, crafts are the principal source of employment and income for the local population.

The ecology of craft production and marketing in Ban Thawai has been described, on the basis of data for 1991, in an earlier publication.[6] Since then, some important changes have taken place in the ecological structure of marketing, especially the emergence of two markets in the area of the village, which will be discussed below.

When the production of carvings was initiated in the village in the past prior to commercialization, it approximated in most respects the model presented above, although it did not reflect it completely. During the subsequent period of commercialization and up to the present, a continuous process of disassociation between the components of the model has occurred, transforming the nature of craft production and marketing in the village.

In the following section, this process will be described in some detail on the basis of information collected in the village in the course of repeated visits and surveys between the years 1991 and 1996.

The Process of Disassociation in Ban Thawai

In the promotional materials, Ban Thawai carvings are often presented as deeply rooted in local and northern Thai traditions. Thus, an article on the village in a tourist publication claims that "the skills of these humble craftsmen, women and children are not learned from specialist schools…The skills they picked up and developed are from their fathers, who, in turn, drew from their fathers. This has gone on for generations…"[7] Unlike some traditional Thai craft villages, such as the nearby pottery village of Muang Koog or the basket-weaving village of Ban Pha Bong in the district of Saraphi in Chiang Mai province, the villagers of Ban Thawai did not in the past engage in carving as a local specialization, although some of them may have known how to carve such items as temple gables and similar ornaments, as did the villagers in many other northern Thai localities. In fact, the origins of figurative carving in Ban Thawai are extraneous to the village, and rooted in the trade of Buddha images along the Thai-Burmese border.

In the late 1960s, some Ban Thawai villagers were employed by an antiques shop in Chiang Mai in the restoration of such images, which often reached the city in a state of considerable disrepair. As they acquired the necessary skills, the villagers began to produce copies of Burmese Buddha images and other religious statuary in that shop.[8] However, they soon left the urban workshop and relocated into the village, producing there the same objects on their own account in simple workshops, located mostly within their household compounds. According to informants, all members of the first generation of carvers in the village learned their trade in that Chiang Mai antiques shop; they later transmitted their skills to their offspring and to other villagers. This is sometimes recognized even by writers of promotional material: seeking to compromise the historical recency of Ban Thawai carving with the desired image of a traditional craft village. One of them states that "…the present Thawai people are the descendants of master sculptors which made their mark 20 years ago."[9]

The base-line from which my analysis departs will be the late 1960s or early 1970s, when the production of figurative carvings in Burmese style started in the village. I shall examine in detail the transformation of craft production and marketing in terms of the components of the model outlined above during the following three decades, and especially during the five years of my study of the village.

Raw Materials

Burmese Buddha images were carved of teak wood. The early Ban Thawai carvings were similarly made of teak. At the time teak was found in the surrounding forests. However, the intensive exploitation of teak forests made the material increasingly scarce and more expensive. Eventually, the authorities prohibited the cutting of teak trees and the use of teak for carvings. Consequently, Ban Thawai carvers turned to other, cheaper but also coarser, less finely grained kinds of wood, especially the raintree (*ton chamcha*), popularly known as monkeypod, which abounded in the surrounding region. The vast majority of Ban Thawai carvings are presently made of raintree wood. As the production of carvings expanded, however, raintrees also began to disappear from the area. Raintree wood, and in particular big tree trunks needed for the carving of large objects such as elephants, subsequently had to be brought in from ever more distant areas: at first from provinces adjoining Chiang Mai province, later from more remote northern provinces (such as Tak), and eventually from far-away regions, particularly from the northeast, at distance of up to one thousand kilometers from Ban Thawai.

The origin of the raw materials for the carvings was thus gradually disassociated from the resource base of the village and its surroundings. With increasing scarcity of the wood and distance of its origin from the village, its price increased progressively. This led to an intensification of its use, which, in turn, influenced the size and kinds of carvings. Since a tree consists of a voluminous trunk and branches of ever-smaller size, intensification of the use of the wood is reflected in the production of even larger numbers of increasingly smaller objects, so that virtually all the wood is utilized. An extreme example of this process is the recent appearance of pencils made of small finger-thick branches of the tree.

Another consequence was the employment of other kinds of wood. Included here were softer and less valuable types of wood that were more readily available locally. Such woods, however, can generally be used only for the carving of relatively simple, small objects. Also used were pieces of recycled old teak wood, especially from old agricultural implements, such as mortars, animal feeding troughs, boats, and carts, which villagers have discarded as they have modernized their technology and lifestyle. Such old teak wood has been used, often with considerable effect, for the carving of large, chiseled objects, including religious statuary and reliefs with mythological themes. (*Plate 6.1*) Since trading in old teak wood is permitted by law, some dealers and workshop owners have openly accumulated large amounts of this material, probably in anticipation of its exhaustion in the future.

The huge expansion in the mass production of carvings in Ban Thawai and other northern Thai carving villages has, perhaps unexpectedly, contributed to an emergent ecological problem: the gradual disappearance of trees near settlements and the overall deforestation of northern Thailand. While perhaps a minor factor in view of the large-scale destruction of Thai forests, destruction caused by the use of wood for carving may have increased in relative importance after the ban on logging in 1989, since raintrees and other low-quality woods were not protected by the ban.[10]

To ameliorate the situation of the growing scarcity of wood, some carving villages have begun to plant raintree saplings, in order to assure themselves of a supply of raw materials in the future: the trees will be ready for cutting in about a decade. No such initiative has been undertaken in Ban Thawai, as the villagers tend to acquire raw carvings from other localities and specialize in the finishing and marketing of the products. Moreover, since land is becoming ever scarcer and more expensive owing to the penetration of urban land use into the area of the village, it also became increasingly hard to find the necessary land for a substantial plantation of raintrees.

Knowledge, Skills, and Techniques

Contrary to the assumptions of the model, the knowledge, skills, and techniques for the production of carvings did not emerge locally, nor were they slowly absorbed from others in the past. Rather, they were acquired relatively recently through the employment of villagers in a shop in Chiang Mai. However, the knowledge, skills, and techniques so acquired were part of an artisanal tradition, although a Burmese one. This is not exceptional, but rather a specific instance of a historical process of cultural exchange between northern Thailand and Burma.

In Chiang Mai the villagers learned how to carve Buddha images and other religious statuary from teak and to lacquer, gild, and ornament them in a specific style, consisting of patterns of curved, embossed lines, often inlaid with pieces of glass. (*Plate 6.2*) This was, from my perspective, the base-line from which the process of disassociation in the domain of knowledge, skills, and techniques started, as Ban Thawai carvers subsequently opened up to new influences and ideas and experienced pressures to adapt to new market demands. On the one hand, new skills were acquired as carvers learned to produce an extraordinary variety of objects and developed a facility to reproduce items from a sample or even a photograph. Also, new finishing styles were added to the Burmese style used at the base-line. On the other hand, however, several simplifications were introduced into the production process. These reduced the level of skill needed for making some products. Machinery was introduced into some stages of production. In particular, electric saws are now frequently used to cut the wood into approximate forms before carving, and roughly carved objects are also frequently polished by machine rather than rubbed down by hand as before. Moreover, some finishing styles, such as the painting of carvings with industrial paints rather than with *lac* (a natural paint), are cheaper and simpler, and demand less skill than the older elaborate lacquering, gilding, and ornamentation of the Burmese style. Such simplifications made it possible to employ growing numbers of laborers, many of them young girls, on low wages, in the mass production and decoration of carvings.

Some of the more elaborate techniques of decoration may thus fall into disuse and eventually be forgotten. However, most carving skills are still well preserved, and loss of skills, as has occurred in some more traditional craft villages, has not yet become a problem. Skills are transmitted informally between generations or from master carvers to apprentices. No formal training of local carvers takes place within the village or in handicraft training centers, such as those belonging to the Queen's SUPPORT Foundation.[11]

Designs and Decorations

Ban Thawai carvings, which at the base-line consisted of Buddha images and religious statuary decorated in Burmese style, underwent a rapid process of "heterogeneization".[12] In the early 1970s the Thai authorities prohibited the export of Buddha images, thereby disposing carvers to look for other lines of production. The owner of the antiques shop in Chiang Mai had already at this early stage asked a local artist to devise new designs for carvings, such as various animals and fishes. These were later adopted by Ban Thawai carvers and produced in the village. Some of the new designs were related to northern Thai cultural heritage: one of the most popular products in the 1970s and 1980s were sets of musicians playing different Thai instruments. These came in several sizes and were at first decorated in Burmese style. (*Plate 6.3*) Later they were painted in a variety of colors and hues. (*Plate 6.4*)

The expansion of the export market spurred on the process of heterogeneziation. As Ban Thawai acquired a reputation as a source of relatively cheap carvings of good quality, orders were received for new products, samples or drawings of which were supplied by intermediaries or exporters. Most of these new products were utterly unrelated to Thai cultural traditions.

The variety of local products was already considerable when I started my study of Ban Thawai. It accelerated in the next five years and presently defies exhaustive classification. I shall, therefore, only briefly outline a typology of the principal carving styles observed in the village in the course of my study. These will be presented in accordance with their relative affinity to Thai, Burmese, or other regional traditions (i.e., their "orthogeneity"),[13] as against their lack of connection to these traditions and origination in other, especially Western, models and influences (i.e., their "heterogeneity").[14] Five main styles can be distinguished along this spectrum:

1. *Classicist:* This style draws on the ancient traditions of Thai, Burmese, Khmer, Chinese, and Indian art. Products in this style are mostly copies of old religious or mythical images, made mostly from teak wood. (*Plate 6.1*) New compositions in this style, predominantly large teak reliefs, are also common. (*Plate 6.4*) A neo-classicist variation of this style consists of precise copies, from photographs, of portraits of popular contemporary Buddhist monks, such as Luang Pho Koon. (*Plate 6.6*)
2. *Traditionalist:* This is a style that continues the artistic tradition preva-

lent at the base-line. It consists of the production of Burmese-type Buddha figures and other Buddhist images, such as dancers or worshippers (*Plate 6.7*), as well as some related objects, such as sets of lotus flowers, leaves, and pods for Buddhist altars.

3. *Neo-traditionalist:* A style which is based on local, mostly northern Thai or Chinese popular culture. Carved in this style are animals figuring in popular religious customs, such as elephants or tigers (*Plate 6.8*), sets of musicians, reliefs (*Plate 6.9*), mirror frames in flowery designs, and a variety of artificial flowers (which probably evolved from the lotus set mentioned above).
4. *Local-innovative:* A new style which depicts the local life and environment, without being intrinsically related to local cultural traditions. In this style are produced images of Thai, Chinese, or hill tribe men, women, and children, mostly in simplified ethnic attire, in different pursuits or postures, such as carrying baskets or *wai*- ing (a posture of respectful salutation), and a variety of figurines of house animals, such as pigs and chickens, birds, and various kinds of fish.
5. *Extraneous-innovative:* A new style (or family of styles) that is unrelated to any past religious traditions or local culture, life, or environment. This style, or styles, has been adopted from outside sources and is primarily expressed in copies of various objects from Western or Asian models, such as dogs, ducks, frogs with umbrellas, masks, golf players (*Plate 6.10*), and characters from Disney films (*Plate 6.11, 6.12*). In the 1990s, the production of statuary associated with the American West became widespread: cowboy busts and heads and busts or full-sized native Americans proliferated. One of the more extreme instances is the figure of a bare-chested Apache, with a shield and spear, wearing jeans and shoes. (*Plate 6.13*)

Probably not all Ban Thawai carvings could be subsumed under one or another of these styles. Also, the typology does not include other local products, such as decorated basketware and furniture. Even with these limitations, it reflects well the staggering variety of Ban Thawai carving styles.

It should be noted that even as new innovative stylistic types have emerged, the older ones have not been given up. Thus, Buddha images in Burmese style are still produced, besides native American busts and Mickey Mouse figurines. However, in recent years a trend away from the older traditionalist and neo-traditionalist styles towards the innovative styles, especially that based on extraneous models and influences, has taken place. Ban Thawai carvings have thus become increasingly heterogenetic, unrelated to either the local or the wider regional cultures. This trend is not unique to Ban Thawai; it can be found in many other Thai craft villages and has been documented by myself for Ban Kwien pottery.[15] However, a contrary secondary trend is also observable: the increased production of carvings in the classicist style, harking back to ancient stylistic models, which, unlike work in the traditionalist style, are unrelated to any continuously vital regional style.

Such a duality of opposing trends, one harking back, the other looking ahead, can be observed elsewhere in Thailand (e.g., in contemporary "Sukhothai" pottery). It is also found in the tourist art of other Third World countries.[16]

The expansion of the production of Ban Thawai carvings was accompanied by constant innovations of designs. This is partly a consequence of changing demand in the world market, but it is probably also due to competition between producers. At least for a short time, innovators have an edge on the market. However, they quickly lose that advantage as others copy their innovative designs.[17]

Changes also took place over time in the decoration and ornamentation of Ban Thawai products. The curved embossed pattern with glass inlays, dominant at the early stages of production, is still used— sometimes, indeed, incongruously, on objects unrelated to local traditions, such as on a pair of kangaroos. (*Plate 6.14*) Another early technique of decoration is purposely produced cracked paint, which endows the object with the appearance of antiquity. However, as mass production expanded, objects were increasingly more simply decorated. At present, most are only painted in a variety of hues, or partly painted and partly merely varnished. (*Plate 6.15*) The fact that the same objects are made in different sizes, and often decorated in a variety of styles, increases considerably the heterogeneity of Ban Thawai carvings.

Labor Force

The extent of disassociation in the domain of the labor force has been relatively minor in Ban Thawai. The bulk of the labor force employed is still local. The great majority of the owners of carving enterprises are locals, or individuals who married into local families. Only in a few cases have outsiders settled in the village expressly in order to establish a woodcarving workshop—even though one of the finest craftsmen in the village is an outsider from another northern Thai district. Employees of local enterprises—mostly girls and young women engaged in the decoration of carvings—are either of local origin or inhabitants of adjoining villages. There has been no significant influx of an outside labor force into local craft production. In contrast to some other craft-producing villages in the Chiang Mai area, such as the basket-weaving village in the Saraphi district, inter-generational continuity in Ban Thawai workshops is relatively high, sons continuing in the steps of their fathers. This continuity is due to the relatively high profitability of Ban Thawai crafts in comparison with the earning potential of alternative employment opportunities.

This relatively high profitability, however, is due to an increasing division of labor between Ban Thawai and other craft-producing villages. Owing to the advantageous location of the village, the villagers have succeeded in retaining the more profitable stages of production, while externalizing the less profitable ones to other localities. The continuity in the local labor force has, therefore, been a consequence of the externalization. Instead of bringing in workers from the outside, work has been delegated to outside producers. The stages of the productive process have thus been disassociated from one another.

Production Process

At the base-line, Ban Thawai carvers executed all the main stages of the production process by themselves. They cut the wood blocks, carved the objects, decorated, and marketed them. Though Ban Thawai is still known as a carving village, the part of the locals in the production process has, in fact, gradually contracted over the years. Though some villagers still engage in carving, at the time of writing most workshops specialize in the finishing process, while acquiring the raw, semi-finished carvings from elsewhere—particularly from several localities in the district of Mae Tha in the adjoining province of Lamphun, and from the more remote village of Ban Lùk in Lampang province. Workshop owners in Ban Thawai usually order large quantities of such raw carvings from individual carvers or from carving enterprises in these localities, and paint and decorate them in their own village.

The favorable location of Ban Thawai and the growing demand for its products made this specialization possible. Being located in the vicinity of the city of Chiang Mai, Ban Thawai is easily accessible to visitors and buyers from both Thailand and abroad. As ever larger quantities of their products were ordered by local distributors and exporters, Ban Thawai producers gradually delegated the less profitable stages of production to carvers in more remote, less accessible villages, which had few direct outlets to the market and in which wages were lower. Meanwhile, the Ban Thawai producers concentrated on the later, more profitable finishing and marketing stages. By buying semi-finished products from elsewhere, they also rid themselves of the need to tie up their capital in large stores of raw materials, particularly raintree wood. Rather, they enjoyed a high turn-over of capital by ordering and purchasing semi-finished carvings according to market demand and finishing them quickly for sale. The carvers in the more remote villages until recently lacked some of the skills and, particularly, the necessary market contacts to finish the products according to clients' demands and market them directly. This state of affairs is changing, and will change even more in the future as a hard-surface road which is about to be completed will make the carving villages of Mae Tha district more easily accessible to outsiders.

Distribution and Consumption

Ban Thawai carvings were from the outset not intended for a local audience, but were oriented exclusively to an external audience. Villagers of the region do not tend to purchase Ban Thawai carvings for their own use. Ban Thawai differs in this respect from traditional craft villages, such as the potters' villages of Dan Kwien in northeast Thailand or Tung Luang in Sukhothai province, where products for local use still constitute a significant part of production.

Ban Thawai, and the road leading to the village from Chiang Mai, constitute the principal marketing area for carvings in northern Thailand, and increasingly also for other kinds of craft products. The marketing establishments in that area range from simple shacks and shops to huge production-cum-marketing compounds and modern touristic craft centers. The clientele is equally varied and ranges from local and foreign tourists buying a few souvenirs to distributors and shopkeepers from major Thai cities and exporters who buy or order great quantities of woodcarvings at wholesale prices.

The extent and importance of Ban Thawai as a crafts-marketing center grew considerably in the early-1980s. In the course of my study I undertook several surveys of the business establishments in Ban Thawai itself and along the routes to the village.[18] The results of these surveys are summarized in Table 6.1. The data in the table are divided according to the principal areas in which craft products are marketed: the village of Ban Thawai and the access road leading from the district town of Hang Dong to the village.

Type of Product	Ban Thawai			HD-BT Access Road			Total		
	1991	1994	1996	1991	1994*	1996	1991	1994*	1996
woodcarvings only	75	118	92	41		22	116		114
w/c & other crafts	1	9	64	2		19	3		83
total woodcarvings	76	127	156	43		41	119		197
furniture	0	0	25	1		5	1		30
antiques	0	0	1	1		11	1		12
textiles & clothing	0	4	11	0		0	0		11
pottery & ceramics	0	2	11	1		2	1		13
carved flowers	1	1	4	1		1	2		5
basketry	0	4	9	0		0	0		9
various crafts	0	3	7	1		2	1		9
total other crafts	1	14	68	5		21	6		89
total crafts	77	141	224	48		62	125		286
services & non-craft shops	0	5	28	2		5	2		33
grand total	77	146	252	50		67	127		319

*no data

Table 6.1: Development of Craft and Other Business Establishments in Ban Thawai and its Access Roads, 1991-1996

In 1991, virtually all craft-trading establishments in the area of the village of Ban Thawai were located in a ribbon pattern either along a track just before the entrance to the village proper or along the main street of the village itself. In the period between 1991 and 1994 this pattern changed: the establishments came to be concentrated in two markets, rather than strung out along a ribbon. The main market was established in front of the village and is now composed of several rows of shops, grouped on both sides of the track leading into the village; the track itself was upgraded into a hard-surface road in 1995. This market was constructed on land owned partly by the owners of two of the major craft enterprises in Ban Thawai. A second, smaller market, however, emerged along a *klong* (canal) in the village itself. It had originally been put up temporarily in 1994 for a village fair, but was left in place after the fair and has become a permanent—and expanding—feature of the village.

These ecological changes also had some structural consequences. With the concentration of marketing in the markets, the ribbon of shops along the main street of the village virtually disappeared. Only the big compounds of two of the largest craft-producing and marketing enterprises remained in their previous locations on the street, in the immediate vicinity of the market at the entrance to the village. In the majority of cases, however, a separation took place between the location of the production and marketing activities.

Up to the early-1990s both production and marketing was concentrated in household compounds along the main street of the village. In 1991 there was in most cases no clear separation between the two kinds of activities. The finished products were mostly put on shelves or merely assembled on the floor in front of the working area. There existed only a few shops in the sense of a spatially demarcated area in which products are intentionally displayed in order to attract the attention of potential customers. With the emergence of the two markets, marketing was separated from the households in which production takes place. Some minor finishing activities, however, are conducted in the stalls and shops in the new markets. Most workshops along the main street ceased to serve as outlets for sale, although many owners maintain their own shops in the new markets.

The sphere of marketing has been increasingly penetrated by outsiders. With the opening of the market at the entrance of the village, many shops were established by people from other localities. Some are from nearby villages and towns, but others hail from Chiang Mai, from other provinces, and even from Bangkok. They sell both Ban Thawai products and craft products from other areas. At the time of writing outsiders are found only in the market at the entrance of the village. They have not yet penetrated the smaller market along the klong in the village itself.

The craft-selling establishments along the access road from Hang Dong to Ban Thawai have from the outset differed from those in the village proper in several respects. Many of them are relatively large, export-oriented enterprises owned by people from outside the village. They display large quantities of carved products in simple, elongated huts which serve as storage-cum-showrooms. These enterprises cater primarily to middlemen and business people, rather than to tourists and other individual customers. While some of them employ their own carvers, most purchase raw carvings from other localities and engage primarily in finishing the products on the premises.

In 1991 the craft establishments within the area of the village as well as on the access roads to it were homogeneous in character: the great majority engaged exclusively in the sale of wood carvings. During the five years between 1991 and 1996 the crafts business in both areas underwent considerable expansion and heterogeneization. In the area of the village, the number of craft-selling establishments tripled, from seventy-seven to 224. The increase was much smaller along the access road, only about half as many again, mainly because some of the smaller establishments moved from the road to the big new market at the entrance to the village. The expansion in the number of establishments was accompanied by a rapid diversification of the products sold in them. Whereas in 1991 woodcarvings were virtually the only merchandise sold, in 1996 the majority of the establishments carried some other crafts, either exclusively or in addition to carvings.

As a consequence, the number of enterprises selling only carvings declined and in 1996 constitutes a minority in both marketing areas. In the village area their number peaked in 1994 at 118 and to ninety-two in 1996. On the access road their number fell almost halves between 1991 and 1996: from forty-one to twenty-two. The total number of establishments selling carvings, including those which also sell some other products, however, increased in the village area substantially, from seventy-six to 156. Meanwhile, on the access road their number declined slightly, from forty-three to forty-one. Indeed, several large enterprises on the road closed shop up to 1996. This decline may well indicate the increased importance of the new craft markets as the magnet attracting customers, at the expense of the establishments along the ribbons.

The greatest increase in both areas during the 1991-1996 period occurred in the number of establishments selling other kinds of crafts, such as furniture, antiques, textiles, clothing, and pottery. From virtually none in 1991 their number increased to sixty-eight in 1996 in the village area and from five to twenty-one on the access road. There were also in 1996 nine establishments in the village area selling basketware only. It should be noted, however, that the finishing of basketry is an important side-line of many wood carving establishments in Ban Thawai. While the raw baskets are made elsewhere, they are painted and decorated in the village in the same styles as the woodcarvings.

Finally, there was also a considerable increase in the number of service establishments in the village. From none in 1991, their number reached twenty-eight in 1996. Some of these are auxiliary services, such as paint stores and packing and transporting enterprises, others are personal services, especially small restaurants and drink stalls, serving locals, employees of the market, and visitors.

The retail and wholesale sectors of the crafts market are not segregated in Ban Thawai, even though some specialization exists. Larger establishments generally focus upon the wholesale and export business, but also sell single pieces to individual buyers. However, in a more abstract sense the dynamics of the two sectors has been different. The ongoing diversification of products is characteristic primarily of the retail sector. As Ban Thawai acquired a reputation as the carvers' village and growing numbers of Thai and foreign tourists came to shop there, locals who previously dealt only in carvings found it profitable to diversify their wares. Others, particularly outsiders, added further diversity by opening shops selling other kinds of crafts. As in the case of the pottery village of Dan Kwien, the growing reputation for a specific type of craft has, somewhat ironically, created a growing market for other kinds of crafts as well.

The wholesale sector, however, evolved differently. It remained on the whole homogeneous, specializing in selling carvings to an expanding national and international market. Indeed, Ban Thawai is probably the main center of the national wood carving market. Its products can be encountered in souvenir and tourist shops in many remote corners of the world. But no other craft products, except locally ornamented basketware, are marketed wholesale either in the village area or on the access road. Ban Thawai as a distribution center thus developed in two directions: it attracted to itself crafts from other localities to be marketed to visitors in small quantities, while its own principal products, wood carvings, are distributed on an expanding world market to a growing number of far-away clients.

Conclusion

Despite appearances, Ban Thawai became a carvers' village only in the recent past. Wood carving was not a traditional occupation of the villagers and the carvers never catered to a local audience. Their products were from the outset commercialized and destined for an external audience. In this respect, the initial stage of the dynamics of wood carving in the village failed to reflect the model proposed at the beginning of this chapter. In other respects, however, the initial stage reflected the model fairly closely.

In the body of this chapter, the process of gradual disassociation between the components of the model, relative to that stage, was described in some detail. In 1996 little was left of the integrated production and marketing of carvings in a traditional Burmese style, characteristic of the beginnings of wood carving in the village. The various stages of the production process have been divided between different localities, the kinds of objects and their styles have changed enormously, and the local crafts market has become increasingly diversified, in terms both of products as well as the origins of the shop-owners.

While a similar process of disassociation is found in other crafts villages in Thailand (e.g., the pottery village of Dan Kwien), it appears to be more pronounced in Ban Thawai than in most other craft villages. I shall attempt in this concluding section to clarify the factors which intensified this process.

The location of Ban Thawai within the metropolitan catchment area of Chiang Mai appears to be the key for the explanation of the difference. Chiang Mai is the principal tourist destination of northern Thailand and the regional crafts center. Its Night Bazaar, in which a wide variety of crafts and other products are displayed, is itself a major tourist attraction.

Ban Thai is close enough to the city to be easily accessible, but has, at least until recently, been remote enough not to be swallowed by its metropolitan expansion. Unlike some villages nearer the city, it has therefore preserved its identity. Local carvers, who in fact initially learned their trade in the city, have been able easily to keep abreast of trends and fashions in the urban crafts market. Much of the production of the village at the early stages was marketed through enterprises located in Chiang Mai. Later on, however, business people and intermediaries began to approach the producers of Ban Thawai directly, and some eventually located their own businesses along the access road to the village, as did some of the packing and transporting agencies. In the area of marketing and dispatch of products, Ban Thawai thus gradually achieved some degree of autonomy from Chiang Mai.

The combination of accessibility and autonomy engendered developments in two directions, both of which accelerated the process of disassociation: expansion of marketing in the locality on the one hand and integration of its products into ever wider local and international markets on the other hand.

The growing reputation of Ban Thawai as a carving village brought growing numbers of customers—tourists, intermediaries, agents, and shopkeepers—to the village. The increased demand at the local level led to structural changes: production was separated from marketing; the earlier ribbon-pattern of small workshops along the main street of the village, in which carvings were both produced and sold, disappeared; and in its place, two markets emerged in the area of the village. The markets, in turn, engendered further developments: local shopkeepers diversified the scope of products offered by introducing crafts produced in other localities. The disassociation between production and marketing culminated in the penetration of one of the markets by outsiders, who opened shops selling a variety of merchandise completely extraneous to the locality. In 1995 the village became more easily accessible with the improvement of the access road from the town of Hang Dong, occasioned by the hosting of the SEA Games by the city of Chiang Mai. Easier access has brought even more visitors to the village in turn giving impetus to further market diversification.

The contrary process of the growing penetration of Ban Thawai carvings into expanding markets has encouraged the process of disassociation in a different direction: it has led to a loss of markedness of local products. Individual visitors, especially ethnic or cultural tourists,[19] tend to seek products which are "marked"—that is, even if not necessarily authentic, they have to bear some recognizable marks relating them to the local ambiance. As the market expands and reaches new increasingly remote audiences, however, such as mass tourists and, through exports, customers in further-off locations—as it did in the case of Ban Thawai—the importance of the ethnic and cultural marks of the products declines, since potential clients are less knowledgeable and/or less interested in them. Instead, they tend to seek attractive, well-made decorative or functional objects at comparatively low prices. The feedback from the market to the producers induces them to adapt products, styles, materials, and production methods and organization to the changed circumstances, thus engendering or intensifying the process of disassociation. Mass production of unmarked, relatively cheap products, in a variety of styles—iconically embodied in the Mickey Mouse figures—is the ultimate outcome of the process of market expansion.

This transition to mass production has been facilitated by the background of Ban Thawai woodcarving and by the governmental policy towards it. The fact that the village is not a traditional craft village may have facilitated the process of disassociation and the adaptation of Ban Thawai producers to the expanding crafts market. Although, in a broad sense, the local carvers engaged at the outset in a traditional craft activity (carving of Buddha images and other religious statuary), they did not work within an ingrained local tradition and had no local clientele. They were, therefore, probably more prepared to adopt innovations than artisans in crafts villages who grew up within a strong, established local tradition.

The initiation, expansion, and heterogeneization of Ban Thawai craft production proceeded spontaneously and did not receive governmental encouragement or support. The village has not been included in the Queen's project, SUPPORT, nor in any other government craft promotion project. Nonetheless, governmental decisions and policies have had some impact upon the direction in which craft production developed in Ban Thawai and upon the process of disassociation described above. The government's prohibition of the export of Buddha images gave an early impetus to the diversification of products. The prohibition of the cutting of teak trees and of the use of teak for carvings induced the carvers to use cheaper and more abundant varieties of wood, especially the raintree. This change in the basic raw material was a crucial step towards the mass production of cheaper carvings. Finally, the decision of the authorities to construct a cultural center in front of the village encouraged the establishment of the big new market there—which prospered though the cultural center remained closed.

As we have seen, Ban Thawai is at the time of writing a major craft center of northern Thailand and may well eventually become the western counterpart of the well-known "umbrella village" of Bo Sang, a major tourist attraction on the so-called Handicraft Road to the east of Chiang Mai.[20] Ban Thawai's very success, however, is gradually changing its character.

Perhaps the most paradoxical outcome of the growing reputation of Ban Thawai as the carving village is that fewer and fewer locals actually engage in carving. Rather, as the market for Ban Thawai products has increased, locals have concentrated to an ever larger extent on the more profitable finishing and marketing stages of production, while relegating the earlier stages to other localities. Ban Thawai has thus come to occupy the top position in a regional hierarchy of craft villages. However, mass wood carving in the region as a whole is threatened by the growing scarcity of its basic raw material.

Ban Thawai and the villages which supply it with rough carvings are major consumers of wood and the mass production of carvings is one of the factors contributing to the gradual denudation of northern and north-eastern Thailand. Wood is now imported from remote sources. As the once abundant kinds of wood, especially raintree, become generally ever scarcer and more expensive, the mass production of carvings, particularly the large ones, such as elephants, may become seriously affected.

As pointed out above, Ban Thawai, though easily accessible from the city of Chiang Mai, has preserved its distinctiveness. But there are signs that the village is becoming ever more integrated into the metropolitan region of Chiang Mai. The wave of urban expansion is currently hitting the immediate surroundings of Ban Thawai. Along the access road to the village from the district town of Hang Dong, three housing estates were under construction in early 1996, on what used to be rice fields. Ban Thawai may thus gradually lose its distinctive rural character, and its inhabitants become ever more drawn into the urban economy. The younger generation will probably be increasingly attracted to employment in the encroaching urban area, as are the inhabitants of other villages within the metropolitan area of Chiang Mai. Local owners of craft workshops will, therefore, have to compete with urban wages. Such an increase in wages, combined with the growing costs of raw materials, will make Ban Thawai carvings more expensive and hence less competitive on the world crafts market.

Locals might therefore tend gradually to give up the production of carvings, including the finishing stages. Indeed, in the more peripheral carving villages there is a growing tendency for producers to finish their carvings themselves, rather than sell them in a raw state to Ban Thawai workshops. Ban Thawai craft persons can be expected to concentrate ever more on the marketing of crafts and other products imported to the local markets from elsewhere, rather than engage in the production themselves. The reality of Ban Thawai will then become ever more remote from its image as the carvers' village. Ironically, this growing discrepancy between image and reality would be largely a consequence of the very success of Ban Thawai as a woodcarving center. For it is its reputation which attracts visitors and other potential customers to the village in the first place—and which thus helps to make the transition to a marketing center in which diverse crafts and other wares are taking up an increasing part of the market.

The transition which Ban Thawai faces is not exceptional. Other northern Thai craft villages, such as San Khampaeng, are at a more advanced stage of the same transition and have already lost much of their distinctive character. Bo Sang, the umbrella village,[21] is also undergoing a similar rapid change, as the production of umbrellas is being displaced by the marketing of a wide variety of other wares.[22] The process of disassociation thus seems to lead to an eventual transformation of the character of successful craft-producing villages, in the course of which the very traits on which their distinctive identity has been established gradually vanish. This appears to be an instance of a broader process found in other touristic localities. Many resorts, for example, have built their reputation on the basis of certain local amenities which are subsequently badly damaged by the very success of the resorts. Their continued success then depends on their ability to offer a variety of contrived attractions, unrelated to their initial function.[23] Such similarities between apparently very different localities should be given more systematic attention in the comparative study of the dynamics of tourist destinations.

Notes

1. This chapter is based on material collected within the framework of a broader project on the commercialization of Thai crafts funded, in part, by a grant from the Netherlands-Israel Research Project, whose support is hereby gratefully acknowledged.

2. Nelson H.H. Graburn, "Introduction: Arts of the Fourth World," in N.H.H. Graburn (ed.), *Ethnic and Tourist Arts* (Berkeley: University of California Press, 1976), p. 8.

3. See K. Yee, "Banh Tawai, handicraft village," in *Smile-a-While,* January-March, 1992, pp. 20-25.

4. B.M. Gallagher, "Craft villages of northern Thailand," in *Arts of Asia,* vol. 3, no. 3, 1973, pp. 48-55.

5. R. Emmons, "The carvers of Tawai," in *Thailand Traveler,* June, 1992, pp. 18-24.

6. Erik Cohen, "Touristic craft ribbon development in Thailand," in *Tourism Management,* vol. 16, no. 3, 1995, pp. 230-232.

7. Yee, "Banh Tawai, handicraft village," p. 20.

8. Also see Emmons, "The carvers of Tawai."

9. "This shop sells quality," in *Exports from Thailand,* vol. 1, no. 6, 1990, p. 40.

10. P. Charasdamrong, "Where have all the trees gone?," in *Bangkok Post,* 20 October 1991, p. 8.

11. *SUPPORT: The Royal Project of Thai Folk Arts and Crafts for Farmers* (Bangkok: Office of Her Majesty's Private Secretary, 1985); B. Davis, "SUPPORT: A Queen's foundation for Her people," in *Sawasdee,* August, 1987, pp. 10-15.

12. Erik Cohen, "The heterogeneization of a tourist art," in *Annals of Tourism Research,* vol. 20, no. 1, 1993, pp. 138-163.

13. See A. Shiloah and Erik Cohen, "The dynamics of change in Jewish Oriental ethnic music in Israel," in *Ethnomusicology,* vol. 27, no. 2, 1983, pp. 227-252.

14. Shiloah and Cohen, "The dynamics of change in Jewish Oriental ethnic music in Israel."

15. Cohen, "The heterogeneization of a tourist art."

16. See Erik Cohen, "Tourist arts," in *Progress in Tourism, Recreation and Hospitality Management,* vol. 20, no. 1, 1992, pp. 20-21.

17. See Cohen, "The heterogeneization of a tourist art."

18. Cohen, "Touristic craft ribbon development in Thailand," pp. 230-232. In this article I dealt with the development of "craft ribbons" along the roads of Thailand. I dealt with the pattern of craft marketing in Ban Thawai, and along the roads leading to it from the city of Chiang Mai, in terms of a "ramified" ribbon, composed of four sections: (1) the main road from the city of Chiang Mai to the district town of Hang Dong; (2) the access road from Hang Dong to the track leading into the village of Ban Thawai; (3) the track leading from the access road to Ban Thawai; and (4) the main street of Ban Thawai itself. The first section is not dealt with here since it is not directly relevant for present purposes. The last two sections are combined in Table 6.1 under "Ban Thawai" owing to changes (to be discussed below) in the ecology of craft marketing in the area of the village.

19. See Charles F. Keyes and P.L. van den Berghe (eds.), *Tourism and Ethnicity,* special issue of *Annals of Tourism Research,* vol. 11, no. 3, 1984, pp. 343-501.

20. 'Amethyst', "Chiang Mai's colorful Bo Sarng umbrellas: Setting a handicraft route in motion," in *Kinnaree,* vol. 8, no. 5, 1991, pp. 42-51.

21. P. Suvapiromchote, "Bringing the umbrella village back to life," in *Bangkok Post,* 3 May 1988, p. 30; "Umbrella making," in *Sawaddi,* vol. 39, no. 1, 1993, pp. 34-37.

22. Cohen, "Touristic craft ribbon development in Thailand," p. 233.

23. Erik Cohen, "Contemporary tourism—Trends and challenges," in R. Butler and D. Pearce (eds.), *Change in Tourism* (London: Routledge, 1995), pp. 23-24.

7

Women in Thai Society as Depicted in Mural Paintings

Alec Gordon[1]

The Thai phrase *pharb kark* or "the dregs" is the technical term in Thai art criticism for the ordinary people who appear in vivid fashion in the sense of everyday life in murals. These form a part of Thai murals from about the seventeenth century AD onwards that are distinct from portrayals of deities, heavenly beings, or princes either as part of a larger painting occupying a whole panel or even on their own. Although the term dregs is used in modern art criticism merely to identify a section of the murals in a supposedly neutral fashion, it should not be overlooked that the original phrase itself is derogatory. It suggests the insignificance of the subject. While in terms of historical status this is true enough, I cannot accept the veiled suggestion, the connotation that this part of the painting is insignificant. Socially, the term is appropriate for these people occupied the lower rungs of society, like real dregs. And in terms of their location in the painting the real-life scenes are most often found at the bottom. Ironically, in terms of condition and deterioration of the paintings, Fate has not forgotten the social status of the dregs. Being at the lowest part of the painting on the wall, these scenes are the most susceptible to destruction by moisture or vandalism, while deities and princes in the upper parts are more likely to survive.

Curiously, the term pharb kark does not figure prominently, if at all, in the better known writings of foreign writers (e.g., Boisselier, Wenk, Wyatt, or Ringis). Possibly this is because, for the most part, they were little interested in this portion of the painting.

The question arises whether it is legitimate to concentrate on this one part, that some would call a subsidiary part, of a painting or group of paintings. My procedure may be considered dubious by some for whom the religious message or the overall aesthetic value of the mural are the sole objects of interest. However, these are not the province of the present study, which is to use the pictures as evidence for social history. Nor is there any reason to agree that religious or political messages or aesthetic values constitute the only objects of these paintings.

Precedents for my stand exist. The paintings have been widely used to identify styles of Thai architecture in certain periods of the past according to the buildings shown. Past styles of clothing are commonly ascertained by reference to murals. Courtly and common ceremonies are studied from mural illustrations. And even today, professional dancers are taught correct postures for classical dancing by reference to the many historical portrayals. Consequently, my endeavor though new in itself follows a well-established path.

Nevertheless, further discussion is necessary. A common viewpoint is that all the murals and everything in them express immanently religious meaning and instruction. In considering this statement, we must still note that it is open to different interpretations. For example, some writers, in insisting that even scenes of daily life must have a religious meaning, take what is an extreme functionalist position. For them, by definition, everything in the painting equally serves religion. This definition denies the possibility of autonomy of the parts of the picture or that they may differ from each other in intent or may even contradict each other. According to this view, representations of daily life can have no function or meaning other than to display some, usually unspecified, aspect of religious teaching. Now if this were true, my attempt to use the pictures of daily life as direct evidence would fail because they could not display independently real-life at all since they are utterly controlled by and subservient to the painting's overall ideological message of religious morality. Thus, a picture of, say, a couple making love ought to have a deeper significance according to this approach and its real meaning transcends what the eye can see.

The last example is by no means impossible in specific cases, but in general the approach has to be rejected. In the first place, it is based solely on assumptions then develops merely through assertions derived from those assumptions. There is no room for argument or reasoning. Everything depends on the functionalist assumption that every part of the whole, in this case a painting, must serve to benefit and positively support the functioning of the whole. Second, this type of approach can be advanced without even seeing the painting! It exists with superior status outside the painting. (Or even before the picture was painted.) According to this approach we actually can know the meaning of a painting before we see it since we know in advance what must be in it. This has to be considered a wrong and indeed ridiculous approach.

However, it still seems reasonable to suppose that such paintings will convey the ideological messages of their time to a greater or lesser extent. And if the portrayals of women were heavily ideological—that is, they portray women as they were supposed to be according to then current male-dominated social prescriptions rather than as they were—then they may not form a basis for real direct evidence. The weight of ideology cannot easily be avoided once the teaching, moralizing intent of murals is accepted. Moreover, since precepts about proper behavior involve social conduct there is inevitably a strong infusion of ruling class ideology. In many cases the figures in the celestial and princely scenes are meant to be associated with the actual rulers.

And, of course, the dregs are portrayed as their betters think fit. The main characters are of royalty or the nobility and are shown in incidents of appropriate behavior to each other in the princely sphere as well as receiving the respect, deference, adoration, services, and tribute from their followers and from the common people. Social and political hierarchy is well displayed and supported. In this respect the princely scenes are idealistic. They seek to show what is proper and what the ruling ideology asserts ought to be rather than what might actually have been the case. This does not, however, render them completely invalid as evidence. But it does introduce a substantial layer of mediation which, if present in the daily-life scenes, would create serious problems for the present project to use them as direct evidence. This is one reason why I refer to the princely scenes as rarely as possible.

What I argue is that the daily-life scenes lie mainly outside the ideological spheres of the celestial and princely portions. I remain reasonably confident that the scenes which we are dealing with, such as two farmers courting a woman drawing water or a peasant smoking, do not form part of the panoply of power. It might be argued that they form the sugar coating to the pill of élite ideology to help ordinary people swallow the claims of the power holders made in other parts of the murals. Even so, they remain distinct and separate in their identity. The function as well as the actual personnel of the daily-life scenes reduces their ideological content. There is no ideological reason for their being there at all. Their presence is explained by the argument that they were meant to entertain rather than to instruct or moralize. They do not perform a role in relation to the message as a whole. The daily-life scenes provide a relief from the serious, solemn, dignified, sometimes terrifying, and possibly occasionally boring scenes elsewhere in the mural. After all, many of the real-life scenes are very funny indeed. This induced relaxation on the part of the viewer may help the eye more easily to return to the serious parts. However, the process it permits actually requires that the high ideal norms be relaxed or neglected in the sphere of the real-life parts. In other words, not only can they be separated from the other parts of the painting for consideration, they may have to be considered separately. This is what Boisselier appears to have concluded when he remarks that the artistic rules "require that no divine being, no prince should conduct himself/herself like the ordinary beings...In the last analysis, for everyone a clear class distinction holds. Some obey a whole ensemble of very strict rules of conduct, the others [ordinary people] show themselves according to their true nature."[2]

Reference to the paintings themselves, the obvious but too often neglected procedure, should clarify matters. If we consider a bay in Wat Chong Nonsi (twenty-third century BE, seventeenth century AD) that illustrates an episode from the Vidhurapandita Jataka where the virtuous sage Vidhura is bidding farewell to his family as the ogre Punnaka dismounts to drag him off, the emphasis is not on the supposed theme at all. Not merely do we have a rice pounding. Crude courting scene with dregs prominent in the left lower foreground, we see in the upper foreground what might well be described as a small sex orgy. Bare legs, buttocks, and vital parts of several people are depicted with great verve by the artist. Other inhabitants of the palace are staring with avid interest at the scene or even performing participant observation. The bay will be discussed in detail below, but it is already clear that these two activities constitute the real theme of the picture and it has nothing to do with the supposed moral lesson whatsoever.

Furthermore, while we may accept that the overall intent of the individual mural or series around the temple walls is religious, we must be aware that paintings ostensibly about religious subjects or in religious places are not necessarily religious paintings. Here it may not strain comparison too much if we remind ourselves that in Western Europe the supposedly religious art of the Book of Hours, originally designed to enable pious Christians to say the correct prayer at the same hour as monks and priests were saying theirs, strayed from the path of worship. The manuscript illustrations commissioned by the Duke of Berry are widely considered to be the most outstanding of their genre, but a head curator of the

Bibliotheque Nationale in Paris has this to say of them:

> ...they relegate the pious original of the Book of Hours to a very secondary role...even further removed from the spiritual tranquillity which they are supposed to inspire. One is moved deeply and intensely but not with religious emotion as such. The sentiment aroused by this work is essentially one of aesthetic enjoyment...Here, despite the nature of the subject-matter the reader can scarcely escape the conclusion that God was the last thing the artists were thinking about.[3]

Too direct a link with Thai murals should not be established. The Book of Hours manuscript in question was meant for private, personal consumption whereas the murals were and are public statements. Nevertheless, the idea should be borne in mind that the content of the murals is not determined exclusively by Buddhist teachings.

Even scenes dealing with palace members who are by no means of the pharb kark illustrate this point. Mural renderings of the popular and solemn episode of the Great Departure (for ordination) regularly depict amorous and affectionate activities taking place meantime among the women of the orchestra. Referring to one such scene from the Ayutthaya period Wat Sangkrachai,[4] Niyada Laosunthorn remarks:

> At the time of the departure for ordination, the palace scene is portrayed as if it were a scene from a palace of the Ayutthaya era. As a result one often finds a eunuch illustrated with the female court members. Actually the *Samuthakhol* text demands that there be only female members. In this case artistic tradition was more powerful than literary tradition.[5]

In a similar vein and discussing a *samut khoi* illustrated manuscript ordered by King Taksin, Wenk noted that while the text relating the birth of Buddha refers to it as a supernatural event, the picture shows a normal birth in the presence of many midwives.[6]

Unnecessary argument and confusion may be avoided if we summarize as follows. Parts of the painting are indeed generally conceived of as a whole by the artists and basically this is designed to present instruction concerning morality according to certain conventions. However, this does not exclude the possibility that parts of the painting may make different or even contradictory contributions to the whole. In other words, the artistic rules of composition of the parts (celestial, princely, and daily life) are different from and autonomous from each other.

This perspective permits us to consider one part of the whole on its own. Even more, if we actually observe the paintings, instead of talking or philosophizing about their possibilities in the abstract, we see that often the daily life scenes are portrayed with such verve, loving care, and experience of the events that it is difficult to avoid concluding that this is what the painter was most interested in. This need not distract from the overall message of a particular painting, but it does seem in many cases that the rendering is so compelling as to divert attention away from the painting's ostensible object. The paintings used to decorate the walls of Wat Thong Noppakhum provide an extreme case that illustrates this point:

> ...there were seven female angels with peculiar manners as follows: one was sitting down urinating with her skirt pulled up to her hips;...one was changing her clothes; one was falling down dropping her garment. The drawings of these seven women were finely done...They were not meant to be trivial. Besides that section was right in front of the main Buddha and the royal seat. When the monks gathered to perform religious rites in the chapel, they would have to view these drawings till the end of their stay.[7]

These aberrations it may be noted were actually in the celestial part of the painting and not among the dregs. It is clearly an example of where the particular painting contributes nothing at all to the religious message and is actually contradicting it.

Finally, it is worth observing that Thai writers are more sensitive than foreign experts to the notion that the paintings have meanings and uses beyond the religious. Consider the following from one such commentator in his discussion of an Ayutthaya period wat:

> Art is a mirror of culture…Even though Thai painting is a symbolic or conceptual art with no desire to illustrate in any direct manner the culture of the Thai people, such illustrations can be found tucked away in the corners so to speak…However, it is just in these subordinate portions of a painting that the cultural aspects are most apparent.[8]

And I conclude this section with a judgment on the matter by the famous naturalized Thai artist and teacher, Silpa Birasri: "Thai art, therefore, has two distinct styles: one corresponding to the aesthetic inspired by religion and the other style corresponds to the inward feelings of the people."[9]

The Time Period

It appears probable that real-life scenes were not painted much before the early 1600s. Although Jataka stories (in which later the ordinary people usually appear) do figure in the pre-1600 murals inside the *prangs* of Ratchaburi's Wat Mahathat and Ayudhaya's Wat Ratchaburana, they are of a formal nature and do not contain real-life representations. Precisely because they did appear on walls in the confined interior (crypt) of the prangs there is little or no space to expand into popular renderings of the holy texts. Moreover, in these instances there would be no need for a popular exposition. The cramped space within the crypts of the prangs implies that the few people who could view them would be initiates, either priests or royals. There was little call for exposition of texts and none at all for popularization. Moreover, it seems that at least some of the crypts were in fact closed and hence visible to no one. According to Sonthiwan Intralib,[10] the crypts of Wat Ratchaburana were closed soon after construction.

It is only in the late Ayutthaya period that temple buildings such as the *bot* (or *ubosot*) and *viharn* had sufficient wall space to support popular propagandizing with illustrations of the texts. The very early brick or stone bots and viharns had lateral walls with narrow slit windows separated by very narrow wall spaces that provided scant room for narrative paintings. Temples also featured partially open *sala* which were partially covered by wooden boards, many of which have subsequently rotted away (although happily one late-sixteenth-century AD painting in Lampang survives).

These latter buildings evolved with increasingly long lateral walls with varying numbers of sizable windows separated by relatively wide wall spaces or even with windowless walls that could be illuminated by opening the doors and/or by interior lamps. Such buildings were suited for narrative real-life types of pictures and it would seem that the appearance of such buildings coincided with the advent of Thai murals being viewed by the public. Murals now became a means of popular teaching in a style far removed from prior traditions. The more formal style of painting was retained in many instances, however, often alongside or rather above the popular illustrations of the Jataka tales.

The earliest real-life scenes featured in my research date from 1660-1670 AD. My cut-off point in the present study is around 1900 AD.

The Illustrations

The photos that I have selected illustrate various expected and unexpected activities involving women and scenes related to the social position of women in Thai society.

There are three photos illustrating expected tasks and activities. The first of these photos is from Phetchaburi's Wat Ko Kauw (1660/1670 AD). (*Plate 7.1*) This scene is of earth and water bound sellers in a busy setting that is not entirely different from activities carried out today. The second photo in this group is from Nan's Wat Phumin and is of a woman weaving (around 1890 AD). (*Plate 7.2*) Women playing musical instruments are also well represented in murals. I have selected a representative photo of court musicians from Wat Khongkharam in Ratchaburi province (c. 1780 AD). (*Plate 7.3*) Such tasks are expected and would seem to require no further comment.

While most of the representations of women in murals have them engaged in activities that one would expect, there are also some illustrations of women engaged in activities that one would usually expect of males or of men doing things commonly associated with women.

Among the initial surprises are the women shown as *mahouts,* elephant drivers. This is a task generally regarded as an exclusive male task and nowadays is such. One may think, of course, that the retinue of queens or princesses at times had to be composed of females and, consequently, female mahouts here should not be entirely unexpected. On the other hand, in other pictures men are also shown as mahouts to princesses.

Unfortunately, the early murals showing women mahouts are in poor condition. The most clearly visible evidence of women working as mahouts is to be found in the *samut khoi* manuscript paintings. One volume has no fewer than six reproductions of paintings with female mahouts, included one dating to the reign of King Prasat Thong (1629-1656 AD).[11] Other samut khoi examples of female mahouts are illustrated in the standard work on Ayutthaya period paintings by Wannipa Na Songkhla.[12]

I have included photos of female mahouts from two wats. Study of the reproduction from Wat Chong Nonsi in Bangkok (1660/1670 AD) reveals at least one woman mahout. (*Plate 7.4*) The king's elephant in the front has two male drivers. The second photo of a female mahout is from Wat Ko Kauw, Phetchaburi.

Men too occasionally appear in murals performing what normally would be considered female tasks. A particularly interesting example of this is a painting of a male pounding rice from the ubosot of Wat Chong Nonsi in Bangkok (1660/1670 AD). (*Plate 7.5*) The task of rice pounding in this picture, however, is being carried out by a man and a woman together. Joint male-female activities are common themes in real-life mural paintings and tend to relate to questions concerning courtship and sexuality. It is to this theme that I now turn.

Affection need not always be displayed by love-making. And sexual intercourse may or may not be a sign of affection. However, such associations can be distinguished and there are murals where affection is clearly depicted. An example of this from Wat Khongkaram in Ratchaburi (*c.* 1780 AD) in particular is striking. (*Plate 7.6*) The couple depicted, who apparently are members of the evil Mara's hosts being swept away by the flood that engulfs them all, are seen clinging to one another and helping each other to stay afloat. Among the other figures of terror, ferocity, and despair they are strikingly human in their tenderness. Another mural in the same wat (not illustrated) shows a couple at home affectionately caressing. Another illustration of affection is provided by a scene from Wat Phumin, Nan province.

An interesting article by Bhasit Chitrabasa entitled "Sex—the lifeblood of art and culture" does not refer specifically to murals, but to song, dance, poetry, and drama.[13] Still, its message would seem to apply to murals too for there, as in real-life, sexual relations are often presented as natural and recurrent events. A scene from Wat Koh Bangphut in Bangkok (mid-nineteenth century AD) is a fine example. Many similar portrayals appear in scenes of everyday life in other murals. Most often, though not always, these are humorous portrayals of erotic scenes. Such sexual scenes are not always in accordance with the solemn episode that is the ostensible theme of the picture. They harmonize unaffectedly as a fitting part of the real-life scene, usually in the pharb kark parts, but not exclusively so. They appear in some princely scenes as well and even in the Defeat of Mara. As in the paintings of many other countries, sexual relations appear as so fitting a part of the overall scene in which they appear that we might expect to discuss the theme without excessive emphasis and without further ado just as if it were, say, cooking.

Yet some leading authorities on these murals have prevented this simple treatment by their distortion of the issue. One might even suspect that there was a tacit conspiracy by some to ignore or even deny the existence of sexual relations in the murals. The massive and magnificent tome by Wenk, despite the general detail of its discussion of the scenes depicted in the murals, barely mentions sex.[14] Ringis concentrates on the exclusively theoretical religious aspects.[15] Boisselier, in his otherwise fine book, practically dismisses their presence when he claims that a prominent erotic scene in one Rattanakosin painting at Wat Na Phra That (Pak Thong Chai) is a notable exception in the tradition of Thai mural painting. He comments that "Thai art and literature do not bring up problems dealing with sexuality except in a most discreet manner" and considers this example "remarkable" for this reason.[16]

A few of the standard texts on murals of the Ayutthaya period, such as those by Santi Lesukhum and Kamol Chayawatana and Wannipa Na Songkhla, fortunately do not distort in this fashion.[17] They show sexual scenes in their illustrations in a straightforward manner, but do so without comment. This lack of commentary unfortunately does not help to correct the misrepresentations of others. One paper by Sone Simatrang does discuss the erotic as such, but it is far too short and appears in a non-scholarly publication (meaning that scholars who want to can ignore it).[18] Besides, he makes a remark that is somewhat misleading: "The location of the scene would not be in such a way as to distract the viewer from the main theme."[19] While in many cases this is correct, there are sufficient examples where this is not true to prevent his statement from being a valid generalization.

The distorted representation of the role of the erotic or sex in mural paintings is important for not merely does it obscure different types of sexual relations depicted (such as flirting, courting, having sex, prostitution, and rape), but it prevents related analysis of the social context of sexual behavior such as the stigma applied to certain forms of sex that entail negative discriminatory attitudes towards women and punishment of women.

While many scenes of sexual activity are tucked in corners, others are quite conspicuous. I have already noted Rama V's indignation over the presence of prominent erotic distractions at one royal wat. Another outstanding example is the (now faded) large pictures of women in the residence of the then supreme patriarch at Wat Buddhaisawan in Ayutthaya. Although still visible to the careful eye, they are too distorted to make comprehensible photographs now.

Let us then consider the most prominent example in the Ayutthaya era murals at Wat Chong Nonsi that I referred to earlier. (*Plate 7.7*) Although the ostensible main theme is of Vidurapandita being taken away by the ogre Punnaka, at least equal prominence is given to two sexual themes. The lower one is a very funny scene where rice pounding is combined with preliminary courting. (*Plate 7.5*) The humor is earthy, but it shows the budding sexual relationship as joyful and affectionate even though outside forces in the shape of children playing a trick are about to disrupt it in humorous fashion. The scene above is different in tone. (*Plate 7.8*) It appears to be showing the tail end of a small sex orgy. Assorted couples seem to be still at it, resting, or spectating, while one woman, looking exhausted and downcast, staggers partly clad and disheveled out of doors from another room. Two neatly dressed women are pointing their fingers at her presumably in disapproval of her conduct.

The main and richly illustrated publication on Wat Chong Nonsi discusses this scene largely as a contribution to our understanding of Ayutthaya architecture.[20] Only minimally and reluctantly does it concede the existence of erotic scenes in a rather shamefaced fashion (the enlargement on the front cover of the book excludes both erotic scenes and the other enlargement on page 75 of the book cuts off part of the upper scene.) It then hastens to say that other countries do it too, and that it is so common as to need no further comment. Well indeed, it would not have required much further comment if so much effort had not been devoted to diverting our attention away from it in the first place. In general on such matters, it would seem that many writers are confused and restricted by their personal attitudes, by prudery, or just by sheer embarrassment, and it is this attitude or prejudice of theirs, rather than the criteria of scholarly aesthetics or historical judgment, that determines their analyses. Understandable as it may be in people of their generation, it must nevertheless be rejected as bad and misleading scholarship. How misleading it may be is demonstrated in the discussion below where socially important scenes from a prominent mural cannot be discussed unless one openly concedes the (fairly obvious) sexual nature of some of the proceedings.

Discrimination against women in Thai society in terms of disparity of punishment of sexual misdemeanors is well established as a fact. The extent to which such facts penetrate the general level of awareness is less well established. Hence a curious painting at Wat Khongkharam (partly painted over later) merits close attention. Ostensibly the scene is part of the Mahosadha Jataka, and if so it would flow on from the famous episode of the attack on the city by King Culani. The foreground, though much has deteriorated or been removed, probably does follow on as it seems to be the remains of the scene where the family of Culani is escaping in the tunnel. By far the greater part of the scene, however, appears to have no connection with this.

We see a narrative of two (or possibly more) court ladies, but not princesses, who are eventually hoisted up in the air in a basket. I cannot accept the interpretation in No Na Paknam's brief commentary in the large and well illustrated volume on the wat which finds that "two soldiers are teasing court ladies" and that they are "drawing some ladies out of the palace."[21] Instead, the sequence depicted in four stages in the painting appears clearly to be:

1. Ladies are unwillingly being carried off from the palace by four soldiers. (*Plate 7.9*)
2. In a quiet corner by the city wall, the abduction is being followed up by sexual intercourse (or should it be rape?) involving two ladies and four soldiers. This scene is quite explicit. Although it has escaped the attention of No Na Paknam, other visitors to or inmates of the wat have marked it carefully by trying to scrape off parts of this particular scene where offending sexual organs were painted. (*Plate 7.10*)
3. Next two ladies are led off by armed soldiers.

4. Finally the two ladies are hoisted in the air in a basket (or *chak sarag*) attached to the roof of the palace. (*Plate 7.11*)

The final scene would seem to be an example of *chak sarag*, an old punishment and disgrace of women found to be offending against sexual mores. It is a punishment that applies to women and not to their male partners in what are deemed sexual crimes. The phrase chak sarag forms part of an old saying that lingered until recently in the vocabulary of abuse of some court ladies.[22] Its latter-day connotation is a refined insult to a lazy woman who acts (or rather fails to do anything) as if she were hoisted up in a basket well out of the way of the world of work below. This may be traced back to the earlier function of the actual hoisting in a basket for shameful public display. Similar shameful displays existed in some European countries, although the male sometimes was also publicly disgraced in the same way. Pointedly, in the scene in the mural, it is the male partners who are actually carrying out the punishment on the women.

The monk who was the author's guide explained that this was a scene showing the punishment awaiting those who had transgressed sexually. This seems an obvious comment. Such a scene of punishment might even be considered to be necessary by some people in order to restore a tone of propriety and (male) morality that might otherwise be undermined by the fact that the wat's murals are particularly rich in sexual innuendoes. These are too numerous to illustrate here, but the reader will find some of them displayed (without comment) in the aforementioned publication by No Na Paknam.[23]

There is no disguising the fact that some writers' squeamishness results in avoiding implications of the erotic in the murals. In instances such as the one just discussed this creates an inability to realize and analyze a discriminatory social stigma against women resulting in reproach and disgrace.

One feature that strikes me as being peculiar in murals is the absence of portrayals of scenes showing the main occupation of most Thai families—namely the cultivation of rice. To western eyes this seems rather strange. In works like The Book of Hours of the Duke of Berry so many of the normal and necessary tasks of the French peasants are shown. In Europe, art patrons liked work. Seemingly they could look at pictures of it for hours. Indian Moghul and some Chinese historical paintings also show work scenes. But this is not the case in Thailand. Work scenes do appear, but the main portrayals are of preparation for feasts or simply meals. Why this great omission?

One explanation may be that the scenes of the Jataka stories are set in the city or in the jungle—neither permitting the portrayal of rice cultivation. Yet there is one incident in the historical life of Buddha, namely his father ploughing the rice field at Buddha's birth, and another in royal ploughing ceremonies that offer opportunities. Several portrayals of royal ploughing ceremonies exist in murals, but they are formally presented. The only depiction of a natural rice cultivation scene found (so far) is a northern one from Wat Pa Daet in Chiang Mai province dating from around the turn of the century. (*Plate 7.12*) This shows beautifully the division of labor between the male ploughing the field and women transplanting the rice seedlings. Two questions arise that have yet to be solved. Why the ignoring of such an important and, in many ways, aesthetically satisfying aspect of Thai life in general? And why is it portrayed in this temple and not elsewhere?

Conclusions

The preliminary nature of the studies so far undertaken must be acknowledged. My study has followed a chronological sequence starting with the earliest paintings. Effectively, this means that the material presented here draws primarily on works from the Ayutthaya period—from which, fortunately, there are hundreds of relevant surviving murals to study. Further study of murals from the Rattanakosin period lies ahead and will, undoubtedly, provide a rich source of data.

From my analyses to date already it can be concluded that certain modern suppositions about women's traditional tasks may be mistaken, or at least overly generalized. In addition, it is clear that certain inhibitions in investigating scenes of sexuality in murals have resulted, to a large extent, in a failure to fully utilize a valuable source of information about women's roles as well as giving a somewhat distorted vision of the position of women in Thai society.

Notes

1. Most of the illustrations in this chapter are from copies of slides in the archives of the Department of Fine Arts and appear by permission. The advice of Napat Sirisambhand, collaborator in earlier work on this topic, is warmly appreciated.

2. Jean Boisselier, *La Peinture en Thailand* (Fribourg: Office du Livre, 1976), p. 74.

3. Edmond Pognon, "Texts" to *Les Trés Riches Heures du Duc de Berry* (Geneva: Liber, 1987), p. 10.

4. These murals are now totally destroyed. However, a drawing of the one inquisition is illustrated in Niyada Laosunthorn, *Illustrations from Thai Literature* (Bangkok: Volume for the Cremation of Somdet Phra Buddhacarya, 2526/1983), p. 37.

5. Niyada Laosunthorn, *Illustrations from Thai Literature,* p. 36.

6. Klaus Wenk, *Mural Paintings in Thailand* (Zurich: Von Oppersdorff Verlag, 1976), p. 22.

7. Rama V as translated in Plainoi Sompat, *Mural Painting* (Bangkok: Office of the National Culture Commission, 1985), p. 8.

8. Silpachai Chinprasert, *Wat Yai Intharam* (Bangkok: Muang Boran, 1982).

9. Silpa Birasri, "Notes on a library of the Ayudhya period," in *Lacquer Pavilion at Suan Pakkad* (Bangkok: Siva Phorn, 1960), p. 13.

10. Sonthiwan Intralib, *Thai Traditional Paintings* (Bangkok, published privately, 1994), p. 11.

11. Sompat, *Mural Painting.*

12. Wannipa Na Songkhla, *Paintings in the Ayutthaya Period* [in Thai] (Bangkok: Section of Mural Conservation, Department of Fine Arts, 2535/1993), p. 4.

13. Bhasit Chitabasa, "Sex—the lifeblood of art and poetry" [in Thai], in *Art and Culture,* August, 2533 BE (1991), p. 96.

14. Wenk, *Mural Paintings in Thailand.*

15. Rita Ringis, *Thai Temples and Temple Murals* (Singapore: Oxford University Press, 1990).

16. Boisselier, *La Peinture en Thailand,* p. 114.

17. Santi Lesukhum and Kamol Chayawatana, *Mural Painting of the Ayutthaya Period* (Bangkok: Charoenwit Press, 1981); Wannipa Na Songkhla, *Paintings in the Ayutthaya Period.*

18. Sone Simatrang, "Erotic art in Thai mural paintings," in *Thailand's Profile,* August-September, 1971, pp. 40-41.

19. Sone Simatrang, "Erotic art in Thai mural paintings, pp. 40-41.

20. *Wat Chong Nonsi* (Bangkok: Muang Boran Publishing House, 1982), pp. 30, 73, 74.

21. No Na Paknam, *Wat Khongkharam* (Bangkok: Muang Boran Publishing House, 1994), p. 3.

22. Oral information from Khun Sawing Pradithsamai.

23. No Na Paknam, *Wat Khongkharam,* pp. 47, 75, 83, 87.

8

The Use of Traditional T'ai Images in Contemporary Thai Painting

Wattana Wattanapun

Thailand is a country where two worlds meet: the world of traditional Thai culture and the world of modern global culture.[1] Many aspects of the traditional Thai culture, however, have been heavily influenced by interaction with the global culture. For example, imported technology, trade, and foreign values have radically altered the traditional way of life. Despite such influences, there is still a distinctive Thai stamp to much of the country's culture. This is especially true of Thailand's art. This chapter will examine both change and persistence in the artistic style that is evident in contemporary Thai painting. It will examine two influences: the *external* and the *internal*. Each of these influences has had an impact on the identity and nature of Thai painting. This analysis will focus on the materials used, the techniques of the artists, and their use of images, as well as on how the people of Thailand have responded to the different kinds of Thai painting.

Artistic exchange among cultures is a normal occurrence and often reflects the dominance of particular cultures within the world community at a given time. Throughout the twentieth century the Western and international art worlds have spread new "isms" and innovations far and wide. Thailand has not escaped these powerful external influences which have been so readily accepted world-wide. Partially because of these influences, Thailand's art has changed and developed in ways that are markedly different from the ways in which it evolved during its earlier history.

Previous Influences on Thai Art

It is worth examining the history of Southeast Asian art as a unit to demonstrate how influences have been exchanged between neighboring and outside cultures in the past. Southeast Asian art for centuries was greatly influenced by the cultures of China and India. Thus, Southeast Asian artists adopted modes and rules of artistic expression from Hindu and Buddhist concepts, although their inspiration and expression usually retained local characteristics. Although influenced by Indian and Chinese culture, such works should not be viewed as inferior. Early Southeast Asian artists created works that are clearly masterpieces even when compared with the best of Chinese or Indian art.

Early Southeast Asian art was not only influenced by China and India, but also often influenced from within Southeast Asia itself. In the case of Thailand, while India and China provided general influences, nearby regions usually had the most significant specific influence on local artistic developments. Thus, Lan Na and Sukhothai had important influences on one another's art, as did Sukhothai and Ayutthaya. Also of considerable importance was the influence of Khmer art on Ayutthaya, and their art in turn on Bangkok's art. The specific characteristics of the art of these regions were more influenced by one another than they were by the art of India and China.

Past Materials and Techniques in Thai Art

A knowledge of the materials and techniques used by Thai artists in the past is essential for understanding the preferences of contemporary Thai artists in terms of what materials they use and how they use them.

Traditionally, Thai artists preferred simple materials, such as clay or wood, for creating sculpture and earth pigments (tempera) for painting. Soft and yielding materials were especially popular among early Thai artists. Mon artists carved stone in their earliest works, but later changed to clay which was readily available and more pliable in their hands. This change of materials resulted in the superb Dvaravati terracottas. Sukhothai sculpture achieved its fluidity of line and form through the use of clay or wax in bronze casting. In the case of both Mon and Sukhothai sculpture, both materials and techniques were local adaptations that evolved as a result of internal exchanges within what is today Thailand.

Traditional Thai paintings were done in tempera, both as murals on temple walls and on cloth or paper. This is not to say that Thai artists only used tempera. It seems, for instance, that fresco was introduced in the seventeenth century AD, but it never became widely used. Thai artists found fresco too restrictive, for example, in not allowing them to pause in their work whenever they wished. Therefore, they discontinued its use. Watercolor and ink were also used a little, but they required a certain modus operandi and formulas that made them unpopular with Thai artists, despite their common use among Chinese artists.

Chinese and British artists were able to demonstrate a powerful transparency through the use of fine textured pigments ground in water-color and ink. To create different transparent effects, Thai artists used gold leaf (which also represented the divinity of the images). By and large, however, Thai artists preferred the simplicity and opaqueness of tempera. Tempera also allowed them to work more easily than watercolor on the delicate, fine details which Thai artists have favored since ancient times.

Techniques involving working in negative space to result in a positive image also became popular in early Thai art. Such techniques necessitated image reversal in the artist's conception. This use of negative space is especially noticeable on lacquer ware and batik cloth in Southeast Asia.

Traditional Local Influences on Contemporary Thai Artists

It can be argued that contemporary Thai art continues to respond to internal influences in its selection of materials used, techniques employed, motifs, and themes. To illustrate this I will examine the work of two prominent contemporary Thai artists who can be said to epitomize contemporary Thai painters: Angkarn Kalayanapong and Thawan Duchanee.[2]

Angkarn, who is famous among Thais for his paintings and drawings, is also considered Thailand's greatest living poet. His works are evocative of classical Thai murals and largely concerned with Thai Buddhist iconography and themes. (*Plate 8.1*) In short, Angkarn's work is strongly traditional in its posture. Contemporary Thai art that is heavily influenced by traditional art is often contrived and uninteresting and most audiences view it as a conventional preservative art. This is not the case with Angkarn's art. His works of art are among the most prestigious in the rapidly changing society of modern Thailand. Many offices and banks have his paintings on their walls amidst modern technology and office workers. Such traditionally styled works could be seen as misplaced in an ultra-modern setting. However, Angkarn is not striving to preserve traditional Thai painting. Despite his use of classical Thai design elements and themes, his work is innovative. In addition to creating a sense of the cultural uniqueness of Thai heritage, he manipulates symbols and concepts with a sophisticated hand and offers enough of a modern flair to capture the interest, both aesthetically and didactically, of contemporary Thai people. He extends the traditional into a modern context.

Thawan's art is more controversial. (*Plate 8.2*) Where Angkarn's work has arrived at a particular type of maturity and become somewhat static, Thawan is evidently still seeking and searching for his artistic equation. His work can be viewed as evocative of Leonardo Da Vinci and

Schongauer as well as Hieronymus Bosch. Nevertheless, despite the many different interpretations he has expressed in his art and how profound or bizarre-looking his painting is, his works all are derived from internal sources of inspiration, such as Thai Buddhist concepts and Thai motifs. In terms of techniques and materials, Thawan's oil paintings are perhaps the least successful of his works, being somewhat bold in the use of color. As was discussed above, Thai artists traditionally preferred simple techniques and media. In contrast to his oil paintings, Thawan's work is probably most successful when using techniques that are more simple. Thawan excels in this simplicity of technique, for example, by masterfully using a ball-point pen on paper in some of his works. He is perhaps the world master in the artistic use of the ball-point pen. (*Plate 8.3*)

Both Thawan and Angkarn have achieved enormous fame in Thailand and yet they are vastly different individuals. Thawan has educated others, both in Thailand and in The Netherlands, has traveled widely, speaks several languages, and has received international recognition. In contrast, Angkarn speaks only Thai, has never traveled to the West, and receives his support and patronage only from within Thailand. Both artists, however, consider themselves profoundly Thai.

There are a number of younger Thai painters whose works also rely heavily on traditional sources of inspiration. These include Chalermchai Kositpipat (*Plates 8.4, 8.5*), Preecha Thowthong, and Panya Vijinthanasan. These painters have used traditional Thai images and Buddhist themes in their work as well as traditional techniques such as tempera on *sa* paper and gold leaf. These artists sometimes use commercial acrylic and metallic pigments, but it is water-based paints that are the most suitable for their work when they paint in considerable detail. These artists have received both fame and patronage from their Thai audience. One of Preecha's paintings, for instance, has been reproduced on the ATM bank machine cards for the Thai Farmers' Bank.

Contemporary Thai Art in Global Context

For over twenty years, Silpakorn University in Bangkok, the Faculty of Fine Arts at Chiang Mai University, as well as other art schools in Thailand, have been training art students with expensive equipment used for media such as print-making, lithography, etching, silk-screen, iron bars, and sheet welding. A number of quality works have been produced with these media and many of these works have been given awards, but these works have not proven popular with the Thai populace at large. Such a lack of popularity is also evident in the public response to the conceptual art, happening art, and installation art movements which are at the time of writing attracting the attention of young Thai artists. Perhaps the reason for this lack of popularity is that these art styles are clearly derived from external sources and this may make most Thais feel alienated from them. For many Thais, such forms of art compare unfavorably with the more traditional Thai forms of happening or installation art, such as a funeral ceremony with all of its elaborate ritual and artistic labor used to produce a beautiful *prasat* for the cremation. Most Thais see greater artistic merit in the burning of the prasat than burning a few rags in a contemporary work of happening art. (*Plate 8.6*)

I am not against any of these new art movements. However, for such external influences to have a meaningful impact on Thai art and culture the works that they inspire must still be grounded and presented in a way that is firmly based on Thai values and traditions. As an example, consider the influence brought to Thai art by Professor Silpa Bhirasri, the foreign-born father of contemporary Thai art. He not only taught about Western art; he also urged his students to examine their cultural roots for inspiration and instituted a program in the history of Thai art and the restoration of temple paintings. In addition, he designed and constructed numerous public monuments to glorify aspects and figures of Thai history—in an Italian Neo-classic style.

Mention should also be made of those contemporary Thai artists who have been living abroad. These include Parawat Laucharoen (*Plate 8.8*), Thana Laohakaikul, and Kamol Tasnanchalee. Even though they live and work amidst Western culture and may have been influenced by contemporary Western art, their works remain decidedly Thai. Illustrations of this can be seen in Kamol's "Nang Yai" series which comes from indigenous Thai images, although he lives and works in Los Angeles. (*Plate 8.7*) Thana, who lives in Austin, Texas, has created installation art related to the Chao Phraya River. Prawat is a master print-maker who has lived in New York for over twenty years, yet his art always reflects something deep about his Thai roots. I, too, am an artist living in two cultures. Half of my time is spent in North America and half in Chiang Mai. Despite this, my work has been mostly inspired by Thai political, social, and cultural issues.[3] (*Plates 8.9, 8.10*)

Conclusion

Modern art in Thailand is dynamic and, while some of today's art in Thailand is derivative of Western art, this is not universally true, and there are many contemporary painters whose work is distinctly Thai and reflects internal cultural roots. These roots have grown deep both in Thai artists and among the Thai people and remain a powerful force despite outside influences and modern globalization. No matter where Thai people live, they carry their roots with them and many Thai artists look to their own culture for inspiration. Those artists who use traditional Thai images, use them powerfully, vitally, and creatively, and not in a static, preservative way.

Perhaps one of the reasons for this dynamic traditionalism is Thailand's success in having remained free from foreign colonial rule. This has allowed Thailand to enjoy and develop its own culture without interruption and to be far more selective in regard to foreign influences. From the standpoint of art, Thailand is a good example to the world of how different it is when a country remains free from external political control.

Notes

1. Photos 8.1, 8.3, and 8.6 are by the author; 8.2, 8.9 and 8.10 are by Michael Howard; the remaining photos are provided by the respective artists.

2. See Apinan Poshyananda, *Modern Art in Thailand: Nineteenth and Twentieth Centuries* (Singapore: Oxford University Press, 1992), pp. 141-155.

3. See Michael C. Howard, "An Artist of Two Worlds," in *Asian Art News*, Vol. 4, No. 2, 1994, pp. 64-66.

9

Traditional T'ai Dance in Vietnam under *Doi Moi*

Michael Howard and Be Kim Nhung

Policies of economic liberalization in communist and formerly communist countries have had a profound impact on the arts as state support and state control have given way to the market forces and globalization. International media attention has focused on the economic problems faced by ballet, symphonic music, and other arts in the former Soviet Union since the advent of perestroika. Less attention has been paid to the impact of such reforms on the arts in other communist and former communist countries.

The *doi moi* reforms that have been initiated in Vietnam since 1986 have also influenced the arts in that country. A recent article in the *Financial Times,* on a visit by the composer Rostropovich to Hanoi, commented that Vietnam's "musical infrastructure is in tatters" and noted that "the conservatoire has not been able to buy sheet music in years."[1] In contrast, the demand for new imported forms of music grew rapidly after 1986 and karaoke lounges seemed to be springing up everywhere—prompting the government recently to try to put a brake on this development.

In this chapter we focuse on ethnic dance of the T'ai-speaking peoples of northern Vietnam and examine the impact of doi moi reforms on such dance. Particular attention is given to the impact of a reduction of state support and greater reliance on market forces and changing public tastes in dance in Vietnamese society. Recent developments in T'ai dance are viewed as reflecting not only economic and cultural changes within Vietnam, but also the nature of ethnic relations and ethnic identity.

The T'ai Peoples of Vietnam and their Traditional Dances

There are over one million speakers of various T'ai languages in Vietnam. The various T'ai speaking groups of Vietnam are to be found primarily in the provinces of Lai Châu and Son La, as well as in the western portions of Thanh Hóa and Nghê An in northern Vietnam along the border with Laos. The T'ai Khao or White T'ai are found mainly in Lai Châu province and the T'ai Dam or Black T'ai in Son La province. A southern group of T'ai Khao (known as T'ai Dón) lives in western Hòa Binh and Thanh Hóa provinces. T'ai Thanh and T'ai Muoi live in Nghê An province. T'ai Lü and Lao are found scattered in Lai Châu province. Within this region, the T'ai live primarily in upland valleys in villages and small towns with subsistence activities centered around growing paddy rice. A small number of T'ai also live in Hanoi.

Within Vietnam the T'ai are recognized as having a rich tradition of folk dances.[2] Among these dances are the following (*xòe* is the term usually used for dance by the T'ai Dam, while *muá* is the term usually used by the T'ai Khao):

1. the *xòe vòng*
2. the *múa sap* (bamboo dance) (*Plate 9.1*)
3. the *xòe nôc dung* (peacock dance)
4. the *muá com khau* (dance of the rice baskets)
5. the *chei thuyen* (boat rowing dance)
6. the shield dance

7. a xòe dance around the wine bowl in a circle with question and answer singing
8. the *xòe khan pieu* or *muá khan* (scarf dance)
9. the *muá non Thai* (T'ai hat dance) (*Plate 9.2*)
10. the *muá nhac* (the bell dance)
11. the *muá nang ua* (a dance with a plot concerning a woman)
12. the *muá quat* (fan dance) (*Plate 9.3*)
13. the *muá dan tinh* (a dance performed by four men with stringed instruments)
14. the *muá chai* (dance of invitation with a scarf)
15. the *muá moi lâu* (dance of invitation to drink) (*Plate 9.5*)

Traditionally, dances were performed for almost every special occasion—for example, when greeting guests, at New Year, or when a baby is born. Some of the above dances may be performed at a variety of times. Thus, the xòe vòng is performed by young people on festival nights. Others are performed only at restricted times. The peacock dance, for instance, traditionally was performed by one or two dancers in the praying house only every three years at the time called *xên cha.* During this period no one may enter or leave the village. In addition, while some dances, such as the xòe vòng, might be performed by a relatively wide range of people and required limited training, others, like the peacock dance, were performed by only a limited number of people who were expected to demonstrate more skill as a performer.

Dancing in the past was largely community-based, but on occasion dancers from one community would travel to dance in other communities. Moreover, traveling dance troupes were not always from the T'ai ethnic group. Robert, for example, in his pre-Second World War study of the so-called T'ai Daeng (they are T'ai Dón) of Lang Chanh, Thanh Hóa province, describes a dance performed at T'ai Daeng funerals by a troupe of Muòng dancers.[3] Thus, there is some basis in tradition for seeing dances not only on the basis of ethnicity, but also as having a regional dimension.

The T'ai Khao king, Deo Van Long, who lived near the present town of Lai Châu at Ban Châu (now known as Ban Deo Van Long, after the name of the last king), actively promoted T'ai musical and dance performances. (*Plate 9.4*) He choreographed and composed songs himself for performances at his court. The dance group at the palace was comprised of eight to twelve dancers and two musicians. They would perform between sixteen and eighteen dance items most evenings at the palace. The musicians would themselves also sometimes perform dances.

Public Support for Traditional T'ai Dances

The Vietnamese state has sought to support ethnic dance in a variety of means since the early post-Second World War period. After independence from the French, the military played a role in promoting traditional dance. There were regional cultural groups in the various military zones that included dancers. Within the army, the singers and dancers were considered professionals and held ranks. Largely non-professional dance groups were also provided some support at the provincial and national level. These groups trained young dancers and performed in a variety of settings. Folk dancers toured the country to perform before soldiers, visiting dignitaries, and for many special occasions. There were also tours abroad to countries which had relations with Vietnam. With the advent of television, state-supported folk dance became a common feature of government-supported programming.

T'ai folk dances were taught in Hanoi to those studying to perform with national dance troupes. Within the T'ai region itself, the most important dance group is the Son La dance group or Doan ca Mu, which was founded in 1952 and based in the provincial town of Son La. The Son La dance group recruits promising young people from throughout Son La province and trains them as dancers and musicians. There were fifteen dancers and thirteen musicians and singers with the group in 1996. The group performs mainly within Son La province, including in relatively remote villages. While the group has an office and facilities for practicing in Son La town, it does not have a permanent venue in which to perform.

The Son La dance group is a provincial and not ethnic dance group and it attempts to represent all of the ethnic groups within the province. Therefore, although most of the dances performed by the group and its membership are T'ai, the dance group also performs dances from other ethnic groups. Among those represented in the dance group are Muòng, Hmông, Dao (Zao or Mien), Hà Nhì, Công, Si La, Xinh-munh, Kháng, and various Kho-mú groups.

At the village level within Son La, Lai Châu, and the other provinces occupied by T'ai-speakers, the national government also supported village cultural promotion teams. These do not appear to have been very effective or widely supported by local populations and did not play much of a role in promoting traditional dance.

The folk dances performed by national and provincial dance troupes generally were not replicas of T'ai dances as they were performed in villages. Rather, they were dances that were based on these more traditional dances, but choreographed in keeping with changes in venue and taste. During the decades following the Second World War there were also changes in T'ai dance at the village level. T'ai dance was not taught in village schools. Many youths were still taught the dances, but the level of informality in the instruction and performance often increased. Acculturation in some instances led to the cessation of dance performances or to a reduction in the range and frequency of dance performances. In addition, while the more secular forms of dance often survived, albeit in modified form, those dances more closely associated with traditional religion or esoteric beliefs and practices, such as the peacock dance, generally did not.

The Impact of Doi Moi Policies on Traditional T'ai Dance

Vietnam has undergone profound economic and cultural changes since the advent of the doi moi reforms in 1986. These changes have had an important impact on T'ai and other forms of traditional dance in Vietnam.

One general development influencing all traditional dance forms in Vietnam is a marked change in the type of dance that interests the Vietnamese public. Access to outside influences through television, recorded music, cinema, and the like is still relatively limited in Vietnam when compared with more open societies in the region. Nevertheless, major changes are already taking place, especially in urban areas, as public taste for more traditional forms of entertainment declines in favor of a greater desire for dance and other entertainment forms associated with global culture as evidenced by the karaoke plague that has spread through Vietnam and discos in urban centers. Even on television, while most Vietnamese are still restricted to watching local television programs (that continue to feature traditional dance), those with access to satellite broadcasting are faced with a steady diet of pop music from India-based Star's Channel V.

At the same time that general public interest in traditional dance has declined, those who had performed such dances faced a drastic loss in the level of state financial support. Such state support has not vanished, but it is clearly inadequate and it leaves state-supported dancers feeling impoverished in comparison with those earning money in the emerging private sector. An increasing number of dancers have, since the late 1980s, found it difficult to earn a decent living in the new economy solely by performing folk dances. For many, such dancing is no longer possible as a full-time career. Private sector support for traditional dance has been very limited and has yet to provide adequate career opportunities either.

Both the cultural and economic impact of liberalization and openness on traditional dance can be seen in the provinces inhabited by T'ai-speakers. During a visit to several less isolated White T'ai villages in Lai Châu province in early 1996 it was learned that traditional dances were no longer performed. In one village, Ban Phuong Danh, disco dancing had replaced traditional dances at the spring festival. The Son La dance group suffered a sharp reduction in funding during 1988-89 and the activities of the group had to be sharply reduced. Visits by the group to remote villages became especially difficult since the government was willing only to cover the cost of travel and nothing extra. Adapting to a partial market economy also proved difficult since the dance group usually must perform in the open air and therefore only rarely is able to arrange a show where tickets can be sold. In a recent interview, the group's director emphasized the need for a theater in which the group could perform and sell tickets.

There is increasing evidence, however, that the initial adverse impact of the doi moi reforms on traditional T'ai dance may represent a period of difficult adjustment and not the advent of terminal decline. In the same interview, the director of the Son La dance group commented that, although things had been very rough for a couple of years after 1988, in 1993 funds began to flow again and the group's financial situation had improved and he was relatively optimistic about the future. At the time of writing the group has over one hundred performances and programs a year—which its members consider a good number.

On the day of the interview with the director of the Son La Dance group, the group was busy preparing a tape of music to be sent to Hanoi for a New Year dance performance for the T'ai community in Hanoi. (*Plate 9.6*) This event is indicative an especially important development—something of a cultural renaissance among the T'ai. It appears as if the cultural teams in T'ai villages are now much more autonomous under the doi moi reforms and as a result have come to enjoy greater community support and have become more active. This is despite a sharp decline in government financial support. One interviewee commented that in the past these cultural support groups had to conform to government plans, whereas now they could more readily respond to local demands.

A new financial base of support for traditional T'ai dance is also emerging with the growth of the tourist industry. In the T'ai-speaking area, this tourist industry is centered around Diên Biên in southern Lai Châu province. Tourists are primarily attracted to Diên Biên because of the famous battle fought there between the Vietnamese and French, but once there they also often take an interest in the local T'ai culture. In response to the perceived opportunity offered by the growing number of tourists, the Diên Biên museum and one local hotel started arranging dances for tourists in 1993. The dances are performed mainly in September and October, during the peak tourist season. The dances are most often performed by people from Ban Long Nhai, located on the outskirts of Diên Biên. The villagers say that they performed between ten and twelve dances for tourists in 1995. About ten dancers take part in each performance and they are paid VD3,000 (US $0.25) each (there is also a catering charge). Thus, the dancers of Ban Long Nhai are far from being able to support themselves solely on the proceeds from their dancing, but the money earned is a much appreciated addition to their income and there is the promise of more to come as the number of tourist arrivals continues to increase. Undoubtedly, as infrastructural improvements allow more tourists to visit northwestern Vietnam there will be more opportunities for other communities to earn money from dance performances as well.

In T'ai Khao communities in Lai Châu province, where performance of T'ai Khao traditional dances has remained largely on a non-professional basis, the impact of the doi moi reforms has been negligible, although, as noted above, the general forces of modernization facing all of Vietnam have served to undermine interest in dance in some communities. There are exceptions to this trend, however, and not just in the most isolated villages. The village of Ban Dan, located on the outskirts of Lai Châu town, continues to have a very active T'ai Khao dance tradition. Especially noteworthy in this regard have been the activities of one family. The father, Dieu Van Sam, has played traditional music since the time of the T'ai Khao king. (*Plate 9.7*) More recently, he has been active in promoting the teaching of traditional T'ai Khao music in the local school curriculum. His wife was a dancer in the army shortly after independence in the 1950s. After leaving the army she returned to her home, but continued to dance non-professionally with the local Culture House. This musical tradition has been carried on by their daughter, Dieu Thi Chuyên, who actively works with the provincial Culture House (Nhà Van Hoá Tinh Lai Châu). In 1996 she won a gold medal for her performance in a dance competition involving three of the northern provinces (Hòa Binh, Son La, and Lai Châu) while wearing one of her mother's dresses that was made in the 1950s. (*Plate 9.8*) The dances performed today in Ban Dan at various festivals are similar to those performed in the days of the T'ai king, Deo Van Long, although some innovation has taken place.

Conclusions

The doi moi reforms have created two contradictory cultural tendencies in Vietnam. On the one hand, liberalization has introduced global forces that undermine traditional dance in favor of karaoke, disco music, and the like. On the other hand, liberalization has also led to a cultural revival among T'ai speakers and greater interest among them in their cultural traditions.

Recent government efforts to crack down on foreign cultural influences are seeking to confront the tidal wave of global pop culture that is washing over Vietnam. While this initiative may only slow down the engulfing waters of global pop culture, evidence from neighboring countries with more open cultural policies indicates that local culture is unlikely to vanish beneath the waves. In fact, evidence from Thailand, where there has been a resurgence of interest in traditional art forms among the country's growing middle class, gives some room for optimism in the case of Vietnam that traditional forms of culture, albeit in modified form, can survive in the face of a massive influence from globalized culture. In the case of Thailand, this is due to a combination of factors, including government initiatives aimed at promoting traditional practices and prolonged economic prosperity.

The situation is somewhat different in Vietnam, however, from that in Thailand. In Thailand, the interest in traditional dance and other cultural practices is focused on the culture of the T'ai-speaking majority, while there is far less interest in the cultures of non-T'ai minorities. In Vietnam, the T'ai-speakers are a minority and it is unlikely that a revival of interest in traditional culture among the Vietnamese majority would include an interest in the cultures of ethnic minorities. Attitudes towards ethnic minorities in Vietnam are largely acculturative, as they are among most T'ais in Thailand in regard to that country's minorities.

Nevertheless, there are factors that are likely to lead to a revival of T'ai ethnic dance in Vietnam. These factors include market-driven and identity-related interests among the T'ai themselves. While there is no denying that many younger ethnic T'ai in Vietnam have adopted many aspects of national and global cultures and will do so even more in the future, there is also evidence even among younger T'ais of interest in their own cultural traditions. There are many examples from around the world of so-called folk dances surviving as an important element of maintaining ethnic identity, even where many other distinctive cultural features have vanished. It seems likely that traditional dance will be a significant part of the current cultural revival among Vietnam's T'ai minority.

The market-related factors are primarily a result of the growth of tourism in the T'ai area. European and North American tourists are coming to Vietnam in increasing numbers and more of them are going into T'ai areas. There are also tourists from Thailand with a keen interest in ethnic T'ai who want to learn more about their own roots. Both of these groups of tourists have created a market for traditional T'ai dance that will likely grow considerably in the near future.

Thus, while there are many forces at work that are undermining interest in traditional forms of T'ai dance, there are also important forces at work that are promoting such interest. It is likely that, although the T'ai of Vietnam will adopt more aspects of non-T'ai culture, traditional dance will survive as an element of T'ai ethnic identity and economic adaptation.

Notes

1. Jeremy Grant, "Comrades in culture," in *Weekend Financial Times,* 8/9 June 1996, p. XV.

2. Dang Nghiêm Van, Chu Thái Son, and Luu Hùng, *Ethnic Minorities in Vietnam* (Hanoi: The GIOI Publishers, 1993), p. 118.

3. R. Robert, *Notes sur les Tay Dèng de Lang Chánh (Thanh-hoá-Annam)* (Hanoi: Institut Indochinois pour l'Étude de l'Homme, 1941), pp. 53-54.

10

The Martial Art of *Muay Thai* in Thai Society

Michael Mackenzie

Thailand's history has been so plagued with warfare that the history of Thai martial arts is, in a sense, also the history of the Thai people. The martial arts of Thailand are an essential part of Thai culture. They combine the combative prowess and warriorship of the Thai people with the integrity of the Buddhist religion which serves to define Thailand. *Muay Thai* represents a large portion of this martial heritage and is a vibrant cultural example of the beauty and simplicity of Thai artistic expression.

Muay Thai has been referred to as the science of the eight limbs as it combines the use of the hands, feet, elbows, and knees. Thai boxers or *nak muay* are well known throughout the world for their amazing level of physical conditioning and for the seemingly brutal effectiveness of their art. One must not be misled though, as the supreme goal of traditional muay Thai is for the boxer to "behave with integrity according to Dharma, namely, to be honest, to speak only the truth, to be reliable, to behave in a moderate way by refraining from committing sins or vices."[1] For the practitioner, muay Thai is a profession, a way of life, and a spiritual encounter.

Muay Thai is Thailand's national sport. (*Plates 10.1, 10.2*) It is loved by Thai people of every social status from the very poorest of the Thai citizenry to the nobility and royalty. Many Thai kings were either experts in the art of muay Thai or great patrons of the art. In present-day Thailand several hours a week are devoted to televised bouts and there are numerous newspapers and magazines devoted entirely to the art of muay Thai. One finds the chiseled features of the nak muay on everything from postage stamps to matchbox covers and telephone calling cards. However, today in many ways muay Thai also has been degraded to no more than a sport to be wagered upon. At present only the poorest of Thai people enter the ring in the hope of escaping poverty and creating a better life for their families.

Since the Second World War muay Thai has grown in fame internationally and is now practiced in many countries. As a result of this popularity around the world there has been a resurgence of interest in the art of muay Thai by the Thai government, which has begun to take notice of how well recognized and profitable muay Thai has become in other countries. This has led to the formation of both amateur and professional sanctioning bodies by the Thai government in the hope of generating even more foreign interest in the sport.

In contemporary Thailand muay Thai is viewed as an element of Thai art and culture as well as a sport and business. In recent years individuals have found themselves in one of two camps, either promoting the sport of muay Thai at the expense of its cultural and historical context or as staunch traditionalists abhorring any innovation in the art. The task that muay Thai faces in the coming years is to find a balance between these two perspectives.

The Art of Muay Thai

Muay Thai is a martial art that is similar in some ways to dance and drama. Each muay Thai match is in itself a story, a unique and highly condensed drama without words. The beginning motions of the *ram muay* ceremony (described below), accompanied by the ethereal music of the *pi muay,* sets the stage for the struggle between two boxers. The spectacle surrounding the combative prowess of muay Thai boxers has attracted large audiences among the Thai for centuries. Such boxers combine the drama of combat with the grace and beauty of dance, displaying their martial skills so, as one ancient Thai classic suggests, "that one may enjoy the sight." Each muay Thai match is a microcosm of the past, present, and future of the art.

The art of muay Thai combines important spiritual elements of Buddhism, Hinduism, and animism. This blend of religion is most evident in the pre-fight ram muay ceremony as well as in the names of many of the techniques of muay Thai. The Indian epic the Ramayana, known as the Ramakien in Thailand, also provides strong imagery and symbolism in muay Thai. The Ramakien is a battle epic deeply concerned with struggle, defeat, and victory and is a constant source of inspiration for all aspects of Thai art and culture that have been adapted and integrated into the practice of muay Thai.

Muay Thai has many variants and is practiced quite differently throughout the kingdom. The art is divided into different styles by many different criteria. Muay Thai can be stylistically associated with a geographical place, such as muay Chaiya or muay Isan, or with a figure from Thai history, such as muay Nai Khanom Thom or Phra Ya Phichai muay Thai. In the present era styles are often known by the training camp they come from, such as Muangsurin, Pontawee, or Fairtex, and each camp exhibits its own techniques, ceremonies, and beliefs.

The individual nak muay is an extension of his camp's combative heritage and does not enter the ring as a mere individual. A boxer enters the ring with the teachings of his martial ancestors as his protection and potential means of victory. If the boxer fails to grasp the teachings of his ancestors and does not fully embody the art as it has been passed on to him it is believed that he will suffer and face defeat until he has mastered the skills that those before him have sought to perfect over the centuries.

Moreover, it is through the practice of muay Thai that the teachings of the nak muay's ancestors live on. In this sense, the art of muay Thai is a dance that has carried on uninterrupted throughout the centuries with many variations and many performers.

History

Since ancient times Thai rulers have attached great importance to the training of their soldiers and lay people in the martial arts. Muay Thai originated on the battlefield as part of the Thai weapons art of *krabi krabong* and became the fighting art of the Thai nobility and military. On the battlefield muay Thai was used in conjunction with an individual's weapons to keep the opponent off balance and in isolation as a means to fight off-opponents after one's own weapons had been lost. These traditions date back to the days when skills in hand-to-hand combat were a necessity for survival.

When Ayutthaya was ransacked in 1767 most of the archives of Thai history were lost. As a result, much of the information on the early history of muay Thai was destroyed. A great deal of what is known about the early history of muay Thai comes from Burmese and Cambodian accounts of warfare, early European journals, and accounts in the La Na chronicles of Chiang Mai. This historical gap has left a great deal of muay Thai's past open to speculation and conjecture as well as to fable and myth.

Muay Thai historian Thawat Watthana relates that during the Sukhothai era (1238-1376) a piece of ground in front of the royal palace was used for practicing the martial arts by the king himself.[2] This space was also used as an area where boxing contests were held to select proficient boxers as palace guards. In those days, in order to become king, a prince had to be well versed in the arts of sword play, muay Thai, and military strategy.

Muay Thai began really to take shape during the Ayutthaya era. Ayutthaya was founded in 1351 by Prince U Thong, later known as King

Ramathibodi, who reigned until 1369. The king was a great warrior and his contribution to the Thai martial arts is recognized to this day. In the reign of King Ramathibodi II (1491-1529) the military was reorganized and strengthened and the *Chuppasart,* a military manual, was compiled. This volume outlined, among other things, the practice of Thai martial arts. The *Chuppasart* described methods of armed and unarmed combat and was written as a means of teaching fighting skills to the Thai people. This book had an important influence on the development of muay Thai.

Training at this time focused primarily on weapons. Muay Thai was the result of applying the principles of weapons training to unarmed combat. For example, the movement of the leg for attack and defense was akin to the movements of blocking and striking with a staff. The offensive use of the arms and elbows were compared to the slashing motion of twin swords. The use of the fists, feet, and knees to jab at an opponent were considered similar to the thrusting motion of the spear. Muay Thai and weapons training became inseparable and soldiers were well versed in both aspects of fighting.

King Naresuan the Great, who ruled Ayutthaya from 1590 to 1605, was said to have been an excellent boxer who made muay Thai a required part of military training for all Thai soldiers. During his reign there began to be some separation between weapons training and training in unarmed combat.

When Naresuan was a boy of nine he was taken hostage by the Burmeses, who had captured Ayutthaya in 1569 and installed Naresuan's father, Maha Thammaraja, as ruler. Naresuan was allowed to return to Ayutthaya six years later after defeating a Burmese boxer in 1574. Naresuan sought to guarantee the autonomy of Thailand in 1592 by issuing a challenge to the Burmese crown prince to meet him in combat on elephant back. The crown prince was killed and the Burmese forces driven off by Naresuan's army. The story of this historic battle has been retold since then in order to "glorify the heroic deeds of King Naresuan who liberated the country from the Burmese."[3] After returning to Ayutthaya , Naresuan devoted the rest of his life to "teaching the skills of warfare and spiritual combat to his people."[4]

Another king who believed heartily in the art of muay Thai and was well known for his expertise in the art was Phra Sanpetch VIII, Phra Chao Sua (the Tiger King), who reigned from 1703 to 1709. Historian David Wyatt comments that the title Tiger King "reflects the ruthlessness, even bloodthirstiness, with which he pursued power."[5] Phra Chao Sua promoted the art of muay Thai as a national sport by encouraging prize fights and the development of muay Thai training camps for soldiers.

Phra Chao Sua was a formidable boxer himself and participated in many matches in disguise, as the penalty for touching royalty at the time was death. Unfortunately, Phra Chao Sua did not use his skills constructively. Thai historian Manich Jumsai remarks that he "lived more a life of dissipation, drunkenness, and lavishness."[6]

The story of Nai Kanom Thom figures as one of the greatest events in the history of muay Thai. Nai Khanom Thom was a commoner who was taken prisoner by the Burmeses at the time of their conquest of Ayutthaya in 1767. At a temple festival held in Rangoon in 1770 he gained his freedom by defeating ten Burmese boxers in a row before the Burmese court. An astonished King Mangra exclaimed that "every part of the Thai is blessed with venom, even with his bare hands he can fell nine or ten opponents."[7] Nai Khanom Thom fought the Burmese boxers in order to uphold the reputation of the Thais, who badly needed a morale booster at this time. To this day, every March seventeenth is dedicated to Nai Khanom Thom, and is known as "boxer's night" in every stadium in Thailand.

King Taksin, who ruled from Thon Buri from 1767 to 1782, was also an active proponent of martial arts. During Taksin's reign a fighter known as Phraya Phichai of the Broken Sword led the Thais in repelling the Burmeses in Uttaradit. Phraya Phichai had been a famous boxer in his youth and had received his appellation by once breaking a sword in fierce combat with the enemy. After his sword broke he fought on using his muay Thai skills in conjunction with the broken sword. As a result of these heroic efforts he was made governor of Phichai and his statue still stands outside the provincial office in Uttaradit. The Phraya Phichai school of muay Thai lives on under the supervision of Somporn Sangchai of Bangkok.

Phra Phutthaya Yotfa, or Rama the First (1782-1809), who founded the Chakri dynasty, was a great supporter of muay Thai. The grounds in front of his palace in Bangkok was used as an arena where boxing matches were held in order to select guardsmen.

In 1788, during the reign of Rama I, a famous contest took place between a Thai boxer named Muen Phlan and two French boxers. The Frenchmen were brothers who had come to Thailand looking for a high stakes boxing match after having fought a series of successful matches in Indochina. Rama I accepted their challenge and offered a purse of 4,000 baht on the advice of his brother, who argued that:

> Since the foreigners have made a challenge, it would be considered an insult if we did not come up with Thai boxers to compete against them. It would be said that no Thais in all the capital could fight. Our reputation would suffer. The dishonor would spread abroad.[8]

The king's brother assigned the task of defeating the French brothers to his foremost boxer, Muen Phlan, a member of the royal guard. The bout took place on the grounds near the royal palace and Muen Phlan defeated the brothers, one after the other.

King Chulalongkorn, Rama V (1868-1910), frequently watched muay Thai matches and awarded winners with rank and money. His enthusiasm for muay Thai probably stemmed from his own practice of the Thai weapons art of krabi krabong, of which he is said to have been quite an expert. During Rama V's reign the towns of Chaiya, Korat, and Lopburi were especially well known for muay Thai. Muay Thai was one of the traditional Thai arts that Rama V promoted to help instill a sense of national pride in his people.

King Vajiravudh, Rama VI (1910-1925), sought to promote patriotism and military preparedness in a variety of ways that often included promotion of martial arts. He founded the Boy Scouts of Thailand as well as its adult counterpart, the Wild Tigers, a nationwide paramilitary corps. The aim of the Wild Tigers was to defend the nation, religion, and king against all domestic and foreign enemies and to promote the unity of the nation. Both the Wild Tigers and the Boy Scouts of Thailand were involved extensively in the promotion of muay Thai.

Until the 1920s there were no rings or rounds in muay Thai matches, and essentially no referee. Two opponents, regardless of size, would square off against one another and the last one standing would be declared the victor. Such boxers relied more on skill than strength and demonstrated great respect for one another. One did not take undue advantage of an opponent. To do so would result in a loss of face. In traditional muay Thai the referee played a very small part in the match. The referee would sit cross-legged and dictate the beginning, any subsequent instructions, and the end of the fight. The rules of the fight were largely left up to the morals of each boxer and notions of fair play. Rather than in a ring, boxers would fight on the ground. They would fight either bare-fisted or with hands bound with starched rope that created a highly abrasive surface. Fighting with bound hands was known as *muay kad cheung*.

Thailand's first boxing stadium, Sanam Muay Suan Kularb, was built in 1921 under the auspices of King Rama VI. Two other stadiums, Sanam Muay Lak Muang and Sanam Muay Ta Chang, were built between 1923 and 1929. The use of bound fists was disallowed and gloves were introduced in 1929 after a ring death at Sanam Muay Lak Muang. Sanam Muay Suan Sanuk, at Lumpini Park, was opened in 1929, featuring a boxing stadium along with amusement park attractions such as a ferris wheel and merry-go-round. Between 1935 and 1942 muay Thai competitions took place at Sanam Muay Chai Chet, where muay Thai became entrenched as one of Thailand's most popular sports. Muay Thai found a more permanent home in 1945 with the opening of Sanam Muay Rajadamnoen, where fights are still held at present. A second stadium, Sanam Muay Lumpini, was opened in 1953.

Muay Thai began to change in significant ways during the late 1920s and early 1930s. A set of modern regulations were introduced at this time that were based on the international Marquess of Queensberry rules. This was in part the result of the decision by Thai sporting authorities to "standardize the rules of Muay Thai, to make it acceptable world-wide and to establish recognized standards."[9] Muay Thai matches from this time on have taken place in a modern ring. Competitors have been required to wear six-ounce gloves and have been divided into sixteen weight divisions. Each muay Thai match now consists of five rounds of three minutes with two-minute breaks between them.

One of the more interesting stories in the modern history of muay Thai is that of Tokyo promoter Osamu Noguchi. Muay Thai historian Hardy Stockman relates that Noguchi established the Noguchi Boxing Gym in Thailand in response to frequent visits by Japanese kickboxers to Thailand for special training by Thai teachers.[10] This was the first foreign-owned boxing gym in Thailand. The business, actually a combination gym and coffee shop, was initially successful until Noguchi declared in public that he was the originator of kickboxing. Noguchi failed to make it clear that he was referring to the Japanese version of kickboxing, which is largely a modified version of karate, and not muay Thai. The Thais were furious and in October 1972, less than a month after the gym had opened, Noguchi began receiving death threats, shots were fired into the gym, and demonstrators threw rocks through the windows. Noguchi closed the gym and fled back to Tokyo. To this day if a Thai hears you mention kickboxing in reference to muay Thai you will be promptly and firmly corrected.

Muay Thai has slowly developed from a battle-tested survival skill into a combative sport in which Thais have fought each other as well as individuals from other countries. Throughout Thai history there are frequent references to Thai boxers beating the best fighters of other countries. In the past, the best Thai boxers would be given prestigious positions as élite guards of the nobility. Muay Thai exemplified Thai nationalism and the potential for the Thai people as a whole. The art of muay Thai reflected the Thai's image of themselves as an unconquerable nation. Muay Thai was seen to enrich one's physical and moral well-being and as an important aspect of Thai culture in general. The importance assigned to muay Thai in Thai culture resulted in a great deal of respect being given to boxers.

In recent years muay Thai has been transformed into a ring sport. Thai boxers have quickly adopted anything that might give them an edge in the ring, including various Western boxing techniques, training methods, and strategies. The modern-day boxer primarily uses his feet, knees, and fists as weapons. Pushing by foot and elbow is hardly applied in the ring now. Kionshak Ngammeesri has analyzed the use of different skills in contemporary muay Thai. Dividing these skills into five categories, he has found them used in the following percentages: kicking 45.51%, knee hitting 24.41%, boxing 22.13%, push boxing 7.49%, elbows 0.46%.[11]

The modern evolution of muay Thai as a ring sport has resulted in the loss of many traditional skills. Many of the old masters believe that muay Thai has been diluted since the inter-war years when modern rules and regulations were introduced. They believe that modern muay Thai boxers are handicapped by the restrictions of these new rules and the introduction of weight divisions. Modern muay Thai practitioners lack the mental aptitude and many of the techniques of previous fighters. The late Chaiya muay Thai master, Achaan Kyet Sriyapai, remarked that boxers nowadays "look like two dogs biting at each other," with little discipline and forethought in the techniques they are delivering. Chaiya muay Thai instructor Achaan Panya Kraitus believes that "now Muay Thai is for gambling. Not for sport, not for culture."[12]

Philosophy

The art of muay Thai has developed as an element of enhancing personal capability. The boxer's occupation is viewed as noble when practiced with the intention of conducting oneself in accordance with *dhamma,* as the

Buddhist sees the essence of civilization not in the multiplication of wants, but in the purification of the human character. Codes of conduct were established in the art of muay Thai not only to prepare boxers for success in a fight, but also to integrate the boxer into the broader framework of Thai society. The training a boxer received is intended to make him perform in what is deemed a correct manner in society at large.

The boxer's disposition is exemplified in the idiomatic phrases of *jai yen* and *jai ron,* or cool heart and hot heart. The boxer with the cool heart is revered in Thai boxing circles. He is one who performs his duty with equanimity and who enters the ring not out of ulterior motives, but simply to perform a task. The boxer with the hot heart is often reviled as it is his emotion that has fueled his desire to enter the ring. In muay Thai the spiritual component of Buddhism allows a boxer to keep his heart cool, giving the boxer courage and enabling him to concentrate on the fight at hand.

Muay Thai is based on the principle of "doing no more than to teach a lesson." The properly trained muay Thai practitioner develops a cool heart and loses the urge to fight. The boxer is said to behave like a sharp sword in its sheath. On the outside he shows nothing of his capabilities, yet he is always ready, his skills honed to perfection. Muay Thai is about control of the opponent and the exhibition of skill. In the past, nak muay would not destroy their opponent in combat even if they knew that they could. Rather, they would teach their opponent what pain was and to have respect for it. The idea was to stop the opponent's attack, control him, and control oneself.[13] As a result, there are fewer knockouts in muay Thai matches than in Western boxing.

Ceremonies

To be accepted as a student of a muay Thai teacher, each boxer goes through a small ceremony, known as the *khun khruu,* whereby the potential muay Thai student asks for permission to learn the art of muay Thai and offers himself for submission to the teacher's command. This ceremony is extremely important as the knowledge of muay Thai is transferred primarily through direct teaching from master to student.

The ceremony takes place on a Thursday, as this is deemed teachers' day in Thailand, and is performed in front of a Buddha image. The potential student makes offerings of flowers, incense sticks, and candles so that the teacher may pray for his entrance into the camp and for his protection in training.

The potential student also must accept an oath given to him by his prospective teacher that outlines proper conduct. If a student does not follow these oaths he will be seen as offending his ancestors and believes he will be destined to receive bad luck.[14] Master Kimseng Taveesith, a Chaiya muay Thai exponent who was boxing master during the reign of King Rama VI, states the four oaths as follows:

1. I will take care of myself to keep clean and strong and will live my life with honesty and truth;
2. I will not harm the weak and will love and unite and help others whenever possible;
3. I will sacrifice for others and love dearly my nation; and
4. I will avoid any kind of unpeaceful events.

The *khun khruu* ceremony is intended to ensure a feeling of unity in the camps between boxer and trainer. This bond ensures that the boxer is respectful of his instructor and conducts himself ethically. It is important to note, however, that this ceremony has become less prevalent in modern times.

The *yok khruu* is a similar ceremony to the *khun khruu* except that it is more elaborate and all of the teacher's students participate. In the *yok khruu* ceremony, pupils present offerings of incense, candles, and flowers to their teacher. Money and other objects may also be given. This ceremony gives pupils an opportunity to show respect for and complete faith in their teacher and to thank him for the lessons that he has taught them.

Usually a large feast is held afterwards.[15] The *yok khruu* ceremony usually takes place once a year and is also performed on a Thursday.

Training

Most young Thai boxers learn to fight in a camp. Thais may enter these camps as young as the age of eleven, often to relieve their poor parents of the burden of an extra mouth to feed. The camp provides the boxers with the basic necessities of food, clothing, and shelter, as well as training them.

Training in the camp environment is grueling for young Thais and is all-consuming. Most boxers train twice a day, six days a week, leaving the camp only in the morning to run or on nights when they are required to fight. The relationship between the young boxer and his trainer is paramount. In fact, a boxer loses his previous identity upon entering the camp as he takes on the name of the camp as his surname. The boxers are, for all intents and purposes, owned by their camp and fight for it as well as their family's and their own continued survival.

After being accepted into a muay Thai training camp, the young boxer is first schooled in the *ram muay* ceremony so that he may pay proper respect to his teachers and cultivate a proper attitude in his training from the outset. The young boxer is then taught the *yang sam khum* or "three strides movement." The *yang sam khum* is the most important of all the skills the boxer must learn as it is the basis of all footwork in muay Thai. A boxer who has perfected the *yang sam khum* is able to defend and simultaneously counter all attacking movements of an opponent in an efficient and subtle manner. It is believed that the yang sam khum movement reached its peak under the Buddhist monk Luang Phor Ma, a Chaiya boxing master and abbot of Wat Thung Jab Chang.

The student is then taught the *nawa-attawut* or use of the nine principal weapons of muay Thai. These include the use of the head, two fists, two elbows, two feet, and two knees (although in modern muay Thai the use of the head is not allowed).

The trainee is now ready to begin practicing *mae mai muay Thai.* The *mae mai* are the master tricks of muay Thai. A thorough knowledge of these techniques allows a boxer to more effectively counter the attacks of an opponent. The *mae mai* are usually divided into fifteen *mai* or techniques. After acquiring proficiency in *mae mai* the student is ready to proceed to the *luk mai,* the complementary tricks of muay Thai. *Luk mai* are more detailed and sophisticated tricks than *mae mai* and in some cases are designed to counter *mae mai* techniques. *Luk mai* are usually divided into fifteen *mai.* The names of the *mae mai* and *luk mai* techniques come from occurrences in the Ramakien, Thai folk literature, and everyday life. These names serve as mnemonic devices for the boxer.

The boxer's daily training routine is a simple one. (*Plate 10.3*) The *nak muay* awakes in the early morning hours to run. His morning run is followed by several rounds of shadow boxing to warm the body, several rounds of work on the heavy bag, and several rounds on the Thai pads. The young *nak muay* may then work on fighting techniques, clenching, and do some light sparring. Most workouts are followed by conditioning exercises such as squats, push-ups, sit-ups, pull-ups, and weight lifting. In the afternoon a boxer goes through much the same routine except that he may skip the warm-up if it is too hot. Surprisingly, although muay Thai is known for its explosive high round kicks, very little time is spent stretching. Formal training varies, but a proficient fighter can qualify in about six months.

In conformity with the Buddhist tenets which figure prominently in the life of almost every Thai, the young *nak muay* is aware that life is *dukkha* or suffering and imperfect. The boxer, if he is to remain successful, believes that he must remove *tanha* or craving from his heart and focus on training to express his devotion to the art of muay Thai. The boxer is transformed by his training, taking what is deemed by the non-participant as an inordinate amount of physical punishment. Yet somehow the boxer makes sense of it, learning to utilize his suffering in a constructive way. The boxer comes to know suffering intimately and the lessons that lie therein. With each thrust of his hand, foot, knee, and elbow the boxer sees room for improvement and strives to perfect his combative repertoire so that he may be victorious in the ring.

Through the *nak muay*'s training and discipline ego-centered motivation disappears. The boxer becomes less focused on the circumstances that have brought him to the ring and the consequences of a win or loss and focuses entirely on the subject matter at hand, which is the perfection of his body and mind through relentless hours of practice. The boxer knows well the Buddha's lesson of the middle way, as each activity is practiced at a sincere and steady rate. The boxer ultimately fights purely for the fight itself. He becomes fully aware of the transitory nature of life and knows that each victory and loss are only temporary moments in the passage of time and that his training is the true test of his merit.

Muay Thai is the result of diligence, perseverance, trial and error, and endless practice sessions, mastering those techniques that transform a beginner into an expert. Experience becomes the boxer's primary teacher in muay Thai. The boxer knows that his training is a continual process aiming towards perfection, marked by public displays demonstrating the progress that he has made along the path. As a line from an old muay Thai manuscript says, "top boxers are as rare as diamonds. Their edges are cut by years of training, their techniques are polished to perfection as the surface of the glittering diamond; magnificent in its beauty and unique in its strength."[16]

Kruang Ruang

Muay Thai boxers are prone to believe in magic, spells, and the occult. In the past, a muay Thai instructor not only taught his students how to fight, but also gave them lessons in magic and protective charms to help ensure their success. *Kruang ruang* are the charms a boxer wears before and during a match. These charms can be seen as spiritual armor and the *kruang*

ruang are believed not only to ensure protection from injury, but to encourage victory as well by providing power and strength. There are two types of *kruang ruang*: the *mongkhon,* which a boxer wears before entering the ring and during the *ram muay* ceremony, and the *praciat,* which a boxer wears during the fight. In the past, a boxer could be identified by his *mongkhon* or *praciat.*

The *mongkhon* consists of a narrow strip of cloth that contains magical letters or symbols that has been rolled into a cord and then tied with a protective thread known as a *sai sin.* This cord is then wrapped with a second strip of cloth that has been blessed by a master of the magic arts. This is finally twisted into a coil and tied at the ends to form a tail.[17] The *mongkhon* reminds the boxer to be, polite and forever respectful of his teacher as well as having protective and auspicious qualities.

The *praciat* is a protective charm worn round the biceps. It also contains numbers or symbols infused with magical powers by a teacher of the magical arts. Many *praciat* contain cloth portraits of Hanuman, the monkey king of the Ramakien, or contain small Buddha images. *Praciat* are worn in the belief that they bestow courage, endurance, and the will power to triumph, and offer protection against pain. It is thought that the praciat can ward off or protect the boxer from danger.

Music

Music is an indispensable part of any muay Thai match. (*Plate 10.4*) As Bowers notes:

> The Thais believe that music came from the hunter beating on sticks of wood in order to rouse game (these are the drums and clappers of the orchestra), twanging his bow string to release an arrow (this inspired all string instruments), and blowing his horn to announce the quarry and killing, and to call other hunters (all reed instruments). This emphasis on the hunt-killing, and warfare by extension, and by still further extension, strategy, figures prominently in Siamese dancing.[18]

Muay Thai incorporates a number of instruments into its performance as a meditative tool and as a device to rouse courage in each boxer.

The musical instruments which accompany a muay Thai match are the *pi Java* or Javanese pipe, two *glawng kaek* or Indian drums (one of high pitch and one of low pitch), and the *ching* or cymbals. The music is intended to soften the brutality of the battle and give the boxers rhythm and encouragement. The music matches the progress of the fight. It starts slowly, cautiously, and quietly during the ram muay ceremony. This helps the boxers to focus and creates a meditative atmosphere. A faster song is played with the beginning of the match and as the intensity of the fight increases there is a corresponding increase in the tempo of the music. The pace of the fight is often dictated by the music played at the side of the ring and the boxer who best understands its rhythms is often the victor.

Ram Muay

There has always been a strong connection between combat and dance in Thailand. Thai dance evolved from the Brahman conviction that Hindu gods taught humans how to dance, specifically to be able to pay homage to the deities. In this regard, the *ram muay,* literally the boxing dance, can be considered to be divinely inspired. The ram muay is also intended to encourage humility and a sense of gratitude and indebtedness to elders and teachers.

The ram muay ceremony has been performed by each boxer before the muay Thai match since time immemorial. (*Plate 10.5*) Before entering the ring, nak muay kneel and offer homage to the ring's guardian spirit. Once in the ring the boxer begins the ram muay ceremony. The boxer first pays respect to his mother and father, who gave him life and continue to take care of him. Next a boxer pays respect to the teacher who gave him the skills he needs as a boxer. Then he pays his respects to the Buddha and to the Buddhist community for their teachings, as these teachings reflect the boxer's role in the community. This part of the ceremony is known as the *wai khruu.* The boxer then reminds himself of the four Buddhist virtues of *metta, karuna, mudita,* and *upekkha* (loving-kindness, compassion, sympathetic joy, and equanimity). This part of the ceremony is known as the *prom sii naa.* Finally, the boxer asks for protection and a safe victory.

The *ram muay* ceremony is a process of centering, emphasizing body awareness and control of movement. It builds confidence and also serves as a warm-up before each match. The *ram muay* is intended to "steady the nerves and warm the blood." A great deal of significance is placed on the *ram muay* since it displays the spirit and heart of the boxer. A boxer's abilities may be accurately judged by his ram muay performance.

The style of dance differs from region to region. Boxers from northern Thailand usually have especially strong legs and are larger. Therefore, their dancing is firm, stiff, and heavy. Boxers from the south dance smoothly and softly as their style of boxing is more for protection and evasion. In the past one could tell which camp boxers were from by their ram muay and if it was discovered that they were from the same camp they would not be allowed to fight each other.

The Fight

In Thailand's rural areas boxers fight just about anywhere, including makeshift arenas, at Buddhist temple fairs, on military bases, and in backwater provincial rings. Individual boxers usually fight every two to four weeks, with champions defending their titles every six weeks. A camp only profits when its fighters win and profits from a match are usually split fifty-fifty between the camp and the boxer. The amount won is meager until boxers become proficient enough to fight in the large stadiums of Lumpini and Rajadamnoen in Bangkok.

Muay Thai matches in Bangkok are staged three days a week at Lumpinee stadium and four days a week at Rajadamnoen stadium. There are usually eight fights on each card, with the main event usually being the fifth fight. Each fight consists of five three-minute rounds, with a two minute rest period. In addition to the referee, there are two judges, a time keeper, and an attending physician, who has earlier checked both contestants. The boxers wear either blue or red shorts over a groin protector and corners are designated blue or red for the benefit of the announcer, the public, and the judges. The combatants are barefoot, with only ankle straps for support. In addition, the boxers wear a praciat during the bout and a mongkhon during the ram muay ceremony.

Despite the perceived violence, muay Thai is above all a celebration of skill. When two boxers of equal skill and pure heart meet in the ring one is amazed by the near-joyful quality of their match. They look more like old comrades embraced in the throes of some combative dance than mortal enemies. It is at these times that the ring seems like a veritable refuge from the chaos of the world. The music of the pi muay drives the match as the boxers become more and more invigorated with each round. As most muay Thai matches do not result in a knock-out, judges' decisions are based on the skill and proficiency exhibited by each boxer.

For the audience, the experience of a muay Thai match is quite voyeuristic. Audience members sit apart from the boxer's world, unable to relate directly to what takes place in the ring, yet fascinated by it. The audience is aware of the hard work and skill invested in the match by the nak muay, yet they are unable to fathom the boxers' motivations. At such times the most violence in the stadium flows from the audience, which is largely focused on the outcome of the fight rather than the process itself. The head of Bangkok's celebrated Muangsurin camp, Khru Ratkae Muangsurin, has stated that modern muay Thai has changed "from a good sport to a form of entertainment that only is used to please the audience. It appears more and more that both the boxers and the audience do not consider the 'sport' an important aspect."[19] Fights are now more for business than for the art itself and rumors of fighters taking pay-offs to decide the outcomes of fights are widespread.

Contemporary *Muay Thai*

At the time of writing there are approximately 66,000 boxers in Thailand in over 6,000 camps.[20] Most of these boxers come from the northeastern provinces, traditionally the poorest region of Thailand. Many of these boxers are the sons of farmers whose land is so poor that it can barely sustain even the meager needs of such an Isan family. These boxers enter the ring out of economic necessity. The camp offers them and their families a chance to escape poverty. Boxers fight in order to win so that they may send a percentage of the money they make to their families.

In the past muay Thai was a matter of pride for the Thai, but contemporary muay Thai is more a matter of economics. Fights now are more for business than for the art of muay Thai itself. The current emphasis placed on the business aspect of muay Thai has almost completely overshadowed the cultural aspects, especially in international competition.

These changes can be partially attributed to the Thai's love of gambling. "Gambling is a part of Thai culture. Two raindrops slipping down a window-pane are fair game for a bet."[21] This penchant for gambling on muay Thai matches by the audience ensures that everyone in attendance has a piece of advice for their boxer. Many camps now also gamble on their boxers in order to make ends meet. Such betting on the part of camps has resulted in the expectation that boxers fight more and lose considerable weight on a regular basis before each match to help even the odds between fighters for betting purposes. The effects of such rapid weight loss are potentially very harmful since it leaves the young boxer physically drained and unable to perform to full capacity. This stress on the body also leaves the fighter more susceptible to injury.

Despite the hardships faced by young boxers, in many cases the camp offers them a more secure life than they would have known at home. Boxers are given a sense of recognition and may even attain a degree of fame that would never have been possible had they remained toiling in the fields at home. Fame for a boxer in Thailand, however, usually is rather fleeting as titles change hands rapidly and a fighter is only considered as good as his last match. Those who do succeed in the ring may also attain some level of financial security. The greatest accomplishment for any boxer is to have been able to bring his family out of poverty.

Ultimately, these rewards are only for the few who achieve success in the stadiums of Bangkok. The rest are doomed to spend years in a training camp, fighting for small cash purses in rural areas until they grow too old to fight and are ejected into Thai society at large. Benny Urquidez, a noted kickboxing champion in North America, who had the opportunity to fight muay Thai, explains the situation thus: "there is no life for them after the ring. That is all they do for a living. They walk and talk and sleep and dream fighting day in and day out. They don't go outside the camp.'[22]

Muay Thai in Thailand has changed considerably since the early part of this century. It is no longer the sport of kings, a cultural heritage to be respected and admired. It is perhaps more appropriate now to view muay Thai as serving poor young Thai males as a means of economic survival in a rapidly changing society. Moreover, muay Thai no longer brings Thai people together, but divides them into spectator and boxer, rich and poor.

Muay Thai Internationally

Muay Thai has become popular internationally and has spread rapidly to many other nations. Competition between nations in the art of muay Thai has become of great importance to the Thai and they go to great lengths to uphold their status in the sport at home and abroad. They have been able especially to dominate the sport in the lower weight divisions. This is due to a number of factors, such as the young age at which Thais start training as well as the single-minded focus on muay Thai resulting from life in the camp environment.

In the mid-1990s, muay Thai has been recognized by the Thai government as an international activity. The Thai government has sought to standardize muay Thai for an international audience. Public and private organizations now actively promote muay Thai at home and abroad. This support has led to the formation of two major Thailand-based international sanctioning bodies, the International Amateur Muay Thai Federation (IAMTF) and the World Muay Thai Council (WMTC).

The IAMTF was established in 1995 with the full support of the Ministry of Education. Its headquarters is within the Department of Physical Education and it has an international office in Manchester, United Kingdom. The IAMTF was set up by the Thai government to develop cooperation between all countries currently practicing muay Thai in order to maintain a competitive standard and to facilitate activities with international coaches, judges, and referees, as well as to propagate muay Thai at the international level. At the time of writing, fifty-four countries are registered members of the IAMTF.

The IAMTF organized the first World Amateur Muay Thai Championships in Bangkok in 1995. The second championships were held in 1996. These were supported by the Thai government as well as private interests. Among the government bodies helping to support these events were the National Culture Commission, the Department of Physical Education, the Sports Authority of Thailand, the Tourism Authority of Thailand, and Thai Airways International. The IAMTF is working to get the International Olympic Committee to recognize muay Thai as a sport for Olympic competition. Muay Thai has already been included in the Southeast Asian Games and the Thais are working diligently to have muay Thai included in other Asian games as well.

The inaugural meeting of the WMTC was held in September 1996. The WMTC is headquartered at the Royal Thai Army Officers' Club in Bangkok. The objectives of the WMTC are to maintain and promote excellence in muay Thai and to foster and preserve Thai culture in muay Thai as an art form and as a form of self-defense and a popular ring sport. The WMTC hopes to bring all international muay Thai organizations under one regulatory council in order to promote muay Thai on the world stage under the banner of "One World—One Muay Thai." At the time of writing, the WMTC is involved in establishing a top-ten ranking for all weight divisions, setting up courses for judges, referees, trainers, and fighters from other countries, and clarifying the rules and fault scoring for international competition.

Another organization of note is the Amateur Muay Thai Association of Thailand (AMTAT). This is the only muay Thai organization in Thailand that receives the full support of Thai royalty. The AMTAT has been promoting matches since the 1960s and only recently has opened these to competitors from other countries.

Conclusion

Muay Thai has gone through many changes since its inception. From fighting on the battlefield for survival to fighting in the ring for money, muay Thai has always functioned in the broader context of Thai society and has thus changed along with it. Despite the many changes that it has undergone, muay Thai retains much of its artistic and cultural heritage and continues to be an important element of Thai culture.

Opinions about contemporary muay Thai are sharply divided. Some find muay Thai today as a thoroughly modern invention that has developed at the expense of a true understanding of authentic cultural traditions. Others see more continuity and believe that contemporary muay Thai preserves the spirit of traditional arts and is an important tool for interesting a broad audience in Thailand's cultural heritage.

That muay Thai today does serve, at least in part, as a cultural marker that is infused with traditional aspects that serve to remind a contemporary population of its past. One may argue that such modern manifestations of traditional culture distort the past and do little to provide a positive link with Thai heritage. I disagree with such negative sentiments. Instead, I see muay Thai as a highly adaptive art form that is growing in popularity and serves as a highly visible component of contemporary Thai culture as well as being an important element of Thailand's cultural heritage.

Notes

1. Panya Kraitus, *Textbook of Pahuyuth Muay Thai: The Most Distinguished Art of Fighting,* third edition (Bangkok: Asia Books, 1992), p. c.
2. Thawat Watthana, *A Brief History of Thai Boxing* (http://www.ctrl-c.liu.se/other/lifak/muaydef.html, December 1996).
3. Manich Jumsai, *History of Thai Literature,* second edition (Bangkok: Chalermnit, 1992), p. 219.
4."Monkhon crown and amulet charms," in Patrick Cusick (ed.), *Muay Thai: Champions of the Ring* (Bangkok: Artasia Press, 1992), p. 34.
5. David K. Wyatt, *Thailand: A Short History* (New Haven, CT: Yale University Press, 1984), p. 126.
6. Jumsai, *History of Thai Literature,* p. 169.
7. "The story of Thailand's greatest fighting legend," in Cusick (ed.,) *Muay Thai,* p. 37.
8. Quoted in Kraitus, *Textbook of Pahuyuth Muay Thai,* p. 23.
9. "Rules and philosophy of muay Thai," in Cusick (ed.), *Muay Thai,* p. 41.
10. Hardy Stockman, *Kick Boxing: Muay Thai: The Siamese Art of Unarmed Combat* (Burbank, CA: Ohara Publications, 1976), pp. 12-13.
11. Presentation by Kionshak Ngammeesri, International Seminar on the Preservation and Promotion of the Art of Muay Thai, sponsored by the International Amateur Muay Thai Federation, Bangkok, Thailand, 1-4 April 1996.
12. Michael Mackenzie, "The man and muay Thai's future: An interview with Acharn Panya Kraitus," in *Round One North American and World Kickboxing News,* vol. 2, no. 1, 1995, p. 40.
13. Mike Miles, "Chaiya Thai boxing—the southern style muay that," *Round One North American and World Kickboxing News,* vol. 2, no. 3, 1995, p. 27.
14. Kraitus, *Textbook of Pahuyuth Muay Thai,* pp. 27-29.
15. Kraitus, *Textbook of Pahuyuth Muay Thai,* pp. 27-28.
16. Zoran Rebac, *Thai Boxing Dynamite: The Explosive Art of Muay Thai* (Boulder, CO: Paladin Press, 1987), p. 113.
17. Kraitus, *Textbook of Pahuyuth Muay Thai,* p. 55.
18. Faubion Bowers, *Theatre in the East* (New York: Grove Press, 1960), p. 150.

19. Mike Miles, "The jet is still flying high," in *Round One North American and World Kickboxing News,* vol. 1, no. 2, 1994, p. 16.
20. Garry Ohmert, "The camp where champs are made," in *Muay Thai: Thai Championship Boxing,* volume 1 (Bangkok: Artasia Press, 1990), p. 77
21. Gerry Ohmert, "Lumpinee fight night," in *Muay Thai: Thai Championship Boxing,* volume 1 (Bangkok: Artasia Press, 1990), p. 37.
22. Miles, "The jet is still flying high," p. 13.

Bibliography

Apinan Poshyananda, *Modern Art in Thailand: Nineteenth and Twentieth Centuries* (Singapore: Oxford University Press, 1992).

Bhasit Chitabasa, "Sex—the lifeblood of art and poetry" [in Thai], in *Art and Culture*, August, 2533 BE (1991).

Boisselier, Jean, *La Peinture en Thailand* (Fribourg: Office du Livre, 1976).

Bowers, Faubion, *Theatre in the East* (New York: Grove Press, 1960).

Chand Chirayu Rajani, M.C. *Thai Imageries of Suwanbhumi* (Bangkok: Amerin Printing Group Co., 1987).

Cheesman, Patricia, *Lao Textiles: Ancient Symbols, Living Art* (Bangkok: White Lotus, 1988).

Chira Chongkol, "Textiles and costumes in Thailand," in *Arts of Asia,* vol. 12, no. 6, 1982, pp. 121-131.

Chu Thái Son and Dào Hùng, *Vietnam: A Multicultural Mosaic* (Hanoi: Vietnam Foreign Languages Publishing House, 1991).

Chuda Jitpoituck, "Hand-made cloth in Koh Yor," in *Journal of the National Research Council of Thailand,* vol. 16, no. 2, 1984, pp. 1-18.

Cohen, Erik, "From tribal costume to pop fashion: The 'boutiquisation' of the textiles of the hilltribes of northern Thailand," in *Studies in Popular Culture,* vol. 11, no. 2, 1988, pp. 49-59.

______ "Tourist arts," in *Progress in Tourism, Recreation and Hospitality Management,* vol. 20, no. 1, 1992, pp. 3-32.

______ "The heterogeneization of a tourist art," in *Annals of Tourism Research,* vol. 20, no. 1, 1993, pp. 138-163.

______ "Touristic craft ribbon development in Thailand," in *Tourism Management,* vol. 16, no. 3, 1995, pp. 225-235.

______ "Contemporary tourism—Trends and challenges," in R. Butler and D. Pearce (eds.), *Change in Tourism* (London: Routledge, 1995), pp. 12-29.

Cusick, Patrick (ed.), *Muay Thai: Champions of the Ring* (Bangkok: Artasia Press, 1992).

Dang Nghiêm Van, Chu Thái Son and Luu Hùng, *Ethnic Minorities in Vietnam* (Hanoi: GIOI Publishers, 1993).

Davies, H.R., *Yünnan: The Link Between India and the Yangtze* (Cambridge: Cambridge University Press, 1909).

Davis, Bonnie, "SUPPORT: A Queen's foundation for Her people," in *Sawasdee,* August, 1987, pp. 10-15.

______ "Thai dress through the ages," in *Living in Thailand,* vol. 20, no. 9, 1991, pp. 14-18.

Gallagher, B.M., "Craft villages of northern Thailand," in *Arts of Asia,* vol. 3, no. 3, 1973, pp. 48-55.

Gittinger, Mattiebelle and H. Leedom Lefferts, Jr., *Textiles and the Tai Experience in Southeast Asia* (Washington, DC: The Textile Museum, 1992).

Hoskin, John, *Ten Contemporary Thai Artists* (Bangkok: Graphics Company Inc., 1984).

Howard, Michael C., *Textiles of Southeast Asia: An Annotated & Illustrated Bibliography* (Bangkok: White Lotus, 1994).

______ "An artist of two worlds," in *Asian Art News,* vol. 4, no. 2, 1994, pp. 64-66.

______ *Textiles of the Hill Tribes of Burma* (Bangkok: White Lotus, forthcoming)

Leach, E.R., *Political Systems of Highland Burma* (Cambridge, MA: Harvard University Press, 1954).

Mackenzie, Michael, "The man and muay Thai's future: An interview with Acharn Panya Kraitus," in *Round One North American and World Kickboxing News,* vol. 2, no. 1, Spring 1995 (Calgary), pp. 39-41, 58.

Manich Jumsai *History of Thai Literature,* second edition (Bangkok: Chalermnit, 1992).

Miles, Mike, "The jet is still flying high," in *Round One North American and World Kickboxing News,* vol. 1, no. 2, 1994, pp. 11-16, 65.

______ "Chaiya Thai boxing—the southern style muay Thai," in *Round One North American and World Kickboxing News,* vol. 2, no. 3, 1995, pp. 26-28, 71.

Milne, Leslie, *Shans at Home* (London: John Murray, 1910).

Muang Boran Publishing House, *Wat Chong Nonsi* (Bangkok: Muang Boran Publishing House, 1982).

Naenna, Patricia, "Isan textiles," in *Thai Textiles: Threads of a Cultural Heritage* (Bangkok: The National Identity Board, Office of the Prime Minister, 1994), pp. 77-95.

Niyada Laosunthorn, *Illustrations from Thai Literature* (Bangkok: Volume for the Cremation of Somdet Phra Buddhacarya, 2526/1983).

No Na Paknam, *Wat Khongkharam* (Bangkok: Muang Boran Publishing House, 1994).

Office of Her Majesty's Private Secretary, *SUPPORT: The Royal Project of Thai Folk Arts and Crafts for Farmers* (Bangkok: Office of Her Majesty's Private Secretary, 1985).

Office of the National Culture Commission, *The Art of Muay Thai* (Bangkok: Kurusapha Press, 1997).

Ohmert, Garry, "Lumpinee fight night," in *Muay Thai: Thai Championship Boxing,* volume 1 (Bangkok: Artasia Press, 1990), p. 37.

______ "The camp where champs are made," in *Muay Thai: Thai Championship Boxing,* volume 1 (Bangkok: Artasia Press, 1990), pp. 74-77.

Orathai Phondi, "The Tai Yuan Jok fabric designs of Ratchaburi," *in Silk Magazine,* vol. 2, no. 13, 1993, pp. 91-97.

Panya Kraitus and Pitisuk Kraitua, *Textbook of Pahuyuth Muay Thai: The Most Distinguished Art of Fighting,* third edition (Bangkok: Asia Books, 1992).

Phillips, Herbert, *The Integrative Art of Modern Thailand* (Berkeley, CA: Lowie Museum of Anthropology, University of California, 1992).

Plainoi Sompat, *Mural Painting* (Bangkok: Office of the National Culture Commission, 1985).

Rebac, Zoran, *Thai Boxing Dynamite: The Explosive Art of Muay Thai* (Boulder, CO: Paladin Press, 1987).

Ringis, Rita, *Thai Temples and Temple Murals* (Singapore: Oxford University Press, 1990).

Robert, R., *Notes sur les Tay Dèng de Lang Chánh (Thanh-hoá - Annam)* (Hanoi: Institut Indochinois pour l'Étude de l'Homme, 1941).

Sams, Bert F., *Tradition and Modernity in a Lao Song Dam Village of Central Thailand* (Ph.D. dissertation, University of California, Los Angeles, 1987).

Santi Lesukhum and Kamol Chayawatana, *Mural Painting of the Ayudhaya Period* (Bangkok: Charoenwit Press, 1981).

Sanunya Suriyarattanakorn, "Evolution of Thai uniform," in *Muang Boran,* vol. 18, no. 1, 1992, pp. 120-126.

Scott, James George, and J.P. Hardiman, *Gazetteer of Upper Burma and the Shan States* (Rangoon: Superintendent of Government Printing and Stationery, 1900).

Seidenfaden, Erik, *The Thai Peoples: Book I: The Origins and Habitats of the Thai Peoples with a Sketch of their Material and Spiritual Culture* (Bangkok: The Siam Society, 1967).

Sharp, Ruth B., "Tribal arts and crafts in northern Thailand," in Lucien Hanks, *et al., A Report on the Tribal Peoples in Chiangrai Province North of the Mae Kok River* (Bangkok: The Siam Society, Bennington-Cornell Anthropological Survey of Hill Tribes in Thailand, 1964), Appendix I.

Silpa Bhirasri, *Contemporary Art in Thailand* (Bangkok: The Fine Arts Department, 1959).

______ "Notes on a library of the Ayudhaya period," in *Lacquer Pavilion at Suan Pakkad* (Bangkok: Siva Phorn, 1960).

Silpachai Chinprasert, *Wat Yai Intharam* (Bangkok: Muang Boran, 1982).

Sone Simatrang, "Erotic art in Thai mural paintings," in *Thailand's Profile,* August-September, 1971.

Songsak Prangwatthanakun and Patricia Cheesman, *Lan Na Textiles: Yuan, Lue, Lao* (Chiang Mai: Center for the Promotion of Arts and Crafts, 1987).

______ and Patricia Naenna, *Chiang Mai's Textile Heritage* (Chiang Mai: Studio Naenna, 1990).

Sonthiwan Intralib, *Thai Traditional Paintings* (Bangkok, published privately, 1994).

Stockman, Hardy, *Thai Boxing/Muay Thai: The Art of Siamese Un-armed Combat* (Burbank, CA: Ohara Publications, 1976).

Suddan Wisudthiluck, "Changes in fabric design and meaning at Ban Had Siew," in *Muang Boran,* vol. 18, nos. 3/4, 1992, pp. 63-74.

Suddaen Visuthilak, *Changes in the Production of Traditional Cloth: Ban Haad Sieo, Amphoe Srisatchanaalai, Changwat Sukhothai* (M.A. thesis, Thammasat University, 1991).

Suraphong Kanchananaga, *Muay Thai: Thai Culture, Social Customs, and Manners* (Bangkok: Suraphong Kanchananaga, 1979).

Thawat Watthana, *A Brief History of Thai Boxing* (http://www.ctrl-c.liu.se/other/lifak/muaydef.html, December 1996).

Uab Sanasen, "Notes on a weaving village," in *Muang Boran,* vol. 6, no. 1, 1979, pp. 5-7, 13-14.

Vilawan Virunuwat (ed.), *Catalogue of the Queen's Mudmee Collection* (Bangkok: SUPPORT, 1991).

Vithida Srivichai, "Vidhi Panichphan: A conservator of Lanna heritage," in *Silk Magazine*, vol. 1, no. 8, 1993, pp. 36-40.

Wannipa Na Songkhla, *Paintings in the Ayudhaya Period* [in Thai] (Bangkok: Section of Mural Conservation, Department of Fine Arts, 2535/1993).

Warren, William, *Legendary American: The Remarkable Career and Strange Disappearance of Jim Thompson* (Boston: Houghton Mifflin, 1970).

Wenk, Klaus, *Mural Paintings in Thailand* (Zurich: Von Oppersdorff Verlag, 1976).

Wyatt, David, *Thailand: A Short History* (Bangkok: Trasvin Publications/ New Haven, CT: Yale University Press, 1984).

Contributors

Michael C. Howard, Department of Sociology and Anthropology, Simon Fraser University, Burnaby, BC, V5A 1V6, Canada

Patricia Cheesman Naenna, Studio Naenna, 138/8 Soi Chiangkien, Tambon Chang Puek, Chiang Mai 50300, Thailand

Songsak Prangwattanakun, Faculty of Fine Arts, Chiang Mai University, Chiang Mai 50200, Thailand

Raynou Athamasar, Rajabhat Institute Chiangmai, Chotana Road, Chiang Mai 50300, Thailand

Erik Cohen, Department of Sociology and Anthropology, The Hebrew University of Jerusalem, Mount Scopus, Jerusalem 91905, Israel

Alec Gordon, Chulalongkorn University Social Research Institute (CUSRI), Chulalongkorn University, Phayathai Road, Bangkok 10330, Thailand

Wattana Wattanapun, Faculty of Fine Arts, Chiang Mai University, Chiang Mai 50200, Thailand

Be Kim Nhung, Vietnam Theatre of Song, Dance, and Music, Ministry of Culture and Information, 200 Son Tay Street, Kim Ma, Ba Dinh, Hanoi, Vietnam

Michael Mackenzie, Udomsuksa School, Bangkok, Thailand